D1067880

# Shadow of a Revolution

## Indonesia and the Generals

### Roland Challis

SUTTON PUBLISHING

First published in 2001 by
Sutton Publishing Limited · Phoenix Mill
Thrupp · Stroud · Gloucestershire · GL5 2BU

Reprinted in 2001

British Library Cataloguing in Publication Data
A catalogue record for this book is available from the British Library.

ISBN 0-7509-2453-5

*Dedicated with respect to the memory of more than one million
Indonesians who died and are still dying because of the greed,
brutality and ruthless indifference of the military, politicians, global
corporations and 'statesmen' of all nations.*

Typeset in 11/14.5pt Sabon.
Typesetting and origination by
Sutton Publishing Limited.
Printed and bound in England by
J.H. Haynes & Co. Ltd, Sparkford.

# Contents

# Acknowledgements

Many have helped me, both on the record and off, in preparing *Shadow of a Revolution*, and I am beholden to them for their time, their thoughtfulness and in several cases for delving so deep into the past. Since I have presented some matters in a way with which they might not all concur, it is important to make clear that my interpretations are my own. As for the facts, many are still hotly contested – and often intentionally concealed. If I am found to have erred, the fault must be attributed either to me or to the current state of knowledge.

I have relied heavily on archives, notably the Public Record Office, the Mass Observation Archive at the University of Sussex, the Churchill Archive in Cambridge and the BBC Written Archives Centre. Personal assistance beyond the call of duty was extended by all the members of the staff in the library of the Royal Institute of International Affairs, by John Claro, the Royal Naval historian at the Admiralty Library and by Carmel Budiardjo whose Indonesia Human Rights Campaign TAPOL is a resource beyond price. My special thanks are due to Joyce Challis for having helped to conserve the important elements in my own collection of papers during the 1960s. As for the on-going story in Indonesia, apart from the chaos of the Worldwide Web I know of no source to compare remotely with the daily documentation provided by BBC Monitoring at Caversham Park.

Whilst it has been necessary to preserve the anonymity of some contributors, at the head of any list is the late Norman Reddaway who got me started on the book and whose critical scrutiny of the final product I would so much have valued. Working with him at a critical time in 1965–6 were Alec Adams and E.F. 'Jock' Given who allowed me to ransack their memories. Invaluable insights, historical and contemporary, were offered to me by Tan Sri Mohammed Ghazali Shafie, Malaysia's former Foreign Minister, and HE Nana Sutresna, the Indonesian Ambassador in London. I am also indebted to Sir Roger Carrick, Sir James Murray, Admiral of the Fleet Lord Peter Hill-Norton, Marshal of the Royal Air Force Sir John Grandy, Captain A.M. Jones RN, Michael Tene, Andrew Roadnight,

Gordon Etherington-Smith, Laurence O'Keeffe and James Rayner – plus a good many more. If there are any whose useful researches I have quoted, from whom I have not been able to obtain the necessary permissions, my apologies. No breach of copyright is intended and I should be grateful to hear from them if offence has been taken.

Not the least of the problems of trying to write accessibly and simply about Indonesia are the complexities of language and nomenclature. Places change their names, names change their spellings, inconsistencies reflect cultural, geographical, even political variations in this scattered and diverse country. The dj that used to stand at the beginning of Jakarta became j and finally y as in modern Yogyakarta. The oe in the name of the youthful Soekarno became a u, although confusingly Suharto clung to the oe. It is not for the rank outsider to attempt consistency where a culture-conscious people have failed.

Another disconcerting Indonesian characteristic is their love of Orwellian acronyms. I have avoided as many as possible; specialists will note, for instance, that I have not employed the initials TNI, once used to denote the army but now, more recently, the whole of the armed forces. I have avoided the reader having to resort frequently to a list of abbreviations by giving the meaning as often as possible in the text. I pray that the confusion thus generated is less than might otherwise have occurred.

Final thanks are owed to my editors at Sutton's, Jonathan Falconer and Paul Ingrams; while special mention must be made of Survival, the London-based, non-aligned charity that speaks up for the civil and human rights of the dispossessed tribal peoples of the world, and who have kindly supplied some of the photographic content. They can be contacted at www.survival-international.org or telephone +44(0)207 687 8700.

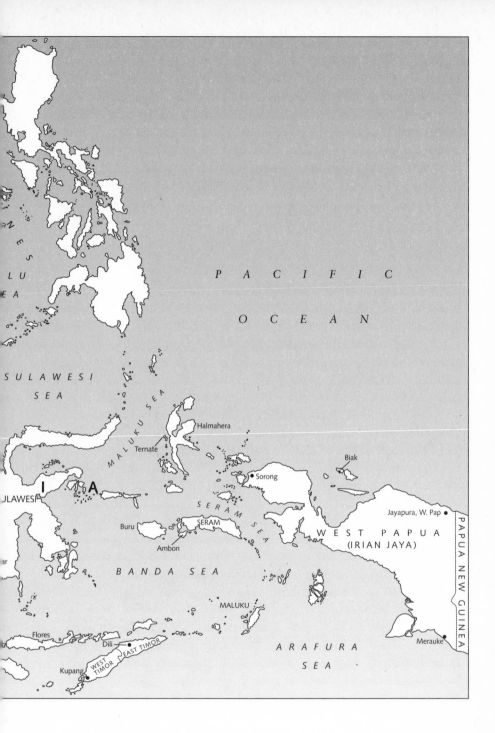

# List of Illustrations

# Introduction

Thanks to its vast geographical spread, dispersed island topography and ethnically-mixed population of over 215 million, Indonesia is a country seldom seen whole. After more than fifty years of independence, many – millions of its own people included – still do not think of it as a single nation, but rather as a group of territories with distinct cultures and histories reaching back through the centuries.

More to the point, for hundreds of years, but most especially during the latter half of the twentieth century, the external view of Indonesia has been as an 'area of influence', more than as an established geographical entity with a sovereign people. Too often labelled an 'emerging market', Indonesia is perceived, shaped and directed by the forces of globalization: exploitable raw material resources, cheap labour, a growing middle class of 'consumers', crudely manipulated through client power groups, endemic corruption, and – not always as a last resort – the ever-present threat of the gun.

Speaking in 1967 before his notorious term as US president, the late Richard Nixon once described Indonesia as 'the richest prize in South East Asia'. It was a typically hollow, Nixonian phrase that neatly encapsulates the dreadful events of the era then unfolding in the region, mostly hidden from the world outside.

When I first went into the region, working initially for Australian and Malayan newspapers, then as the BBC's South-East Asia correspondent, in the vacuum left by the departure of the former colonial powers, the USA (with British support) was already bent on denying that 'prize' to the opposing Communist régimes and appropriating it for Western multinational capitalism. This intrusion of foreign interests into the affairs of the newly-independent Republic undoubtedly made it a much more difficult country to govern, to hold together and defend. The continuing instability and political turmoil in many parts of Indonesia today are testimony that, whatever else may have changed, Western policy has not; Western economic interference continues to this day, in a blatant attempt to create a climate favourable to corporate interests. Some would even say that a climate of tension was deliberately created by those who wanted to remove the founding president, Sukarno, in the 1960s, and who then connived at putting and keeping in place the thirty-two year tyranny of his successor, General Suharto.

With the advent of the Dulles brothers and the anti-communist witch hunts of early 1950s America, the subtlety went out of global politics. When Sukarno would not speak out against communism, the State Department immediately categorized Indonesia as a cold war battlefront. The CIA became operationally involved and, in 1957, promoted the unsuccessful Sumatra rebellion, one of its many dubious military fiascos. In 1960, it is now known, the US State Department approached General Nasution, revered as the 'father' of the Indonesian army, intimating that he would have full US support for any showdown with Sukarno and the communists; while, in 1962, a secret, top-level US–British concord spoke brutally of 'liquidating' the president.

The irony is that Sukarno, a consummate Javanese politician immensely skilled at juggling the Byzantine nationalist and economic interests of that fragmented archipelago, was no communist himself: he wanted simply to keep his nascent Republic out of the clutches either of communism or Western capitalism, and strove to pursue a middle path. However, in his opposition to the Malaysian federation he fatally misjudged the West.

Steadily, unobtrusively, the CIA infiltrated the upper echelons of the Indonesian army, identified in the young Suharto an opportunist better disposed to meet American requirements and, in 1965, assisted him in executing a phased coup leading to the murder of more than one million supposed 'communists'. Britain, seeking US support for its Greater Malaysia plan, co-operated wholeheartedly, deploying operational naval units, exploiting tribal resentments and setting up a sophisticated propaganda weapon – of which I was one of the targets – to link Sukarno with the communists and conceal the true extent of the bloodbath.

Masterminded from the shadows, Suharto's coup culminated two years later in the displacement of the ailing Sukarno, and brought Indonesia's political development to a halt for the next three decades. Under the general's crude and endemically corrupt régime probably another million Indonesians lost their lives; hundreds of thousands were arrested, many left to rot in a gulag of concentration camps scattered throughout the islands; whilst the dictator, his family and cronies grew immensely wealthy on the so-called economic miracle presented to the outside world. It was a 'miracle' that undoubtedly benefited many, but it served also to widen the gap between the haves and have-nots; and, as with so many East Asian economies, it was a paper miracle that would never withstand the vagaries of global economics.

With the ending of the cold war, however, the structures of monopoly power began to break down. The army lost its iron mask of unity and separated into factions. Modern communications technology had its part to play in undermining the rigid censorship that masked the true goings-on in places like Aceh and East Timor, where separatist movements were still being brutally supressed. The policy of transmigration – compulsory resettlement of the underpopulated outer islands – was seen to have largely failed in its aim of homogenising the ethnic mix of the archipelago. International pressure grew for recognition of basic human rights. And, with a more liberal régime in Washington, the 'political correctness' of supporting dictators like Suharto was increasingly called in question.

When, in the late 1990s, the free play of market forces generated the catastrophic East Asian economic crisis, the USA, through the agency of the International Monetary Fund, harassed the arrogant and isolated Suharto beyond endurance; until, like his predecessor Sukarno, he had no option but to step aside. His hastily-groomed successor, Habibie, was pressured into launching wide-ranging reforms: but he was fatally weakened by association with the Suharto clan. The first free elections in nearly half a century brought to power a coalition headed by the wily civilian, Abdurrahman Wahid; supported by the populist Megawati Sukarnoputri, leader of the PDI party and daughter of the founding president, whose name remains a powerful talisman in Indonesian politics even today.

In an attempt to take the heat out of the separatist ethnic and religious movements, Wahid is even now pinning his hopes on a risky policy of decentralization: devolving power to the regions. He has attempted some well-judged accommodations with factional interests: with the powerful Muslims, and with the restructured military. But in following the broadly Sukarnoist 'middle way' he risks falling foul of a new and disturbingly recidivist tendency in Washington under the Bush/Powell régime, which is already showing signs of a return to the discredited foreign policy of the Dulles era. Nor is Wahid himself free of the taint of corruption; moves are afoot as this book goes to press to impeach him over some relatively minor past indiscretions, and in the event of that happening, and a resumption of arms supplies to the military, the path to civilian reform could become blocked. In addition, the potential for destabilizing violence in the outer islands remains scarcely diminished, fomented by Suhartoist elements and old-guard military officers who perceive their monopoly land and trade sinecures to be under threat.

Thus the key question facing Indonesia as it advances unsteadily into the twenty-first century is: whether its people will be able to complete the building of their nation, or whether the historic tensions, exacerbated by external pressures, will simply tear it apart?

The following chapters cannot answer that question, but may possibly help to explain something of how Indonesia has reached this turning point in its tangled affairs.

# PART ONE

## *Shadow Play*

# ONE

## *The Jigsaw Puzzle*

*Geography in this context is no longer an end in itself but a means to an end. It helps us to rediscover the slow unfolding of structural realities, to see things in the perspective of the very long term. Geography, like history, can answer many questions.*

Fernand Braudel[1]

ASSEMBLING THE PIECES

The nation we now call Indonesia occupies the world's largest group of islands. According to the official count there are 13,677, of which around 6,000 are inhabited. Because it is a highly active volcanic area the number changes from time to time. New volcanic outcrops are a regular occurrence, adding to the number of very small islets. On the other hand, its larger islands, Kalimantan (Borneo), Sumatra and Papua (once known as New Guinea), half of which is currently Indonesian, are among the biggest in the world.

Sumatra, Indonesia's third and the world's fifth biggest island – sometimes alluded to dismissively as an outer island – is twice the size of the United Kingdom.

From west to east, straddling the Equator, the great archipelago stretches more than 3,000 miles; from north to south, some 1,150 miles. Yet its land area (including West Papua) of 575,000 square miles is less than a fifth of the total. The rest is water.

The geophysical processes that brought it to its present pass were complex. One of them is the volcanic belt that runs from the northern tip of Sumatra, the length of Java and the islands of Nusa Tenggara, then northward again through Maluku (the Moluccas); more than a hundred and forty volcanoes are active, with at least one erupting every day. Geologists say another major factor was a shifting land mass creeping in from Australia until it was obstructed by the huge island of Kalimantan, itself an extension of the north-western Indo–Malayan mountain core.

Differences between the flora and fauna of Kalimantan and Sulawesi testify still to their diverse origins.

The geologists tell us too that at the time of the very earliest human migrations the continental Asian landmass included what are now the islands of Sumatra, Java and Kalimantan; Sumatra and the Malay Peninsula, for example, were part of one region, not bifurcated as it is today by the Malacca Strait. It was South-East Asia's largest lowland until, as the result of a geologically recent post-glacial sea-rise, the South China Sea (Nanyang) submerged most of it. Thus what we see now is a relatively shallow sea with its surface punctuated by the protruding summits of thousands of mountains and highlands. Eastern Sumatra is visibly a lowland stretching from the western mountains and merging through swamp into the sea. Like the many other swampy areas in Indonesia – such as the southern reaches of Papua and eastern and southern Kalimantan – it requires major human input to render it suitable for the cultivation of food crops.

Papua, at the archipelago's eastern extreme, is the world's second largest island and not altogether typical. It has the highest mountains, packed with gold and copper, and snow-covered peaks year-round. Like most of the other islands, however, it is clad in tropical rain forest and sedentary agriculture is not easy there.

Agriculture comes easiest where the soil is enriched by lava and volcanic ash. *Par excellence*, this from time almost immemorial means Java, a long thin island with a line of active volcanoes running along its spine. Most of its jungle cover was removed centuries ago to expose its fertile soil, so much valued that even the smallest patches of only a few square feet are typically sown to rice. Some of Java's rice terraces are believed to be two thousand years old.

The archipelago has many riches, a vast array of minerals in its soil, an astonishing variety of vegetable and animal life, but in its history to date it is the easy-going fertility of Java that has generated the densest concentrations of people – and, paradoxically, of poverty – in Indonesia.

Since the decline of the Sumatra-based Sri Vijaya empire at the end of the thirteenth century there has been a functional tension, still unresolved, between Sumatra and Java. It arises from the archipelago's location astride one of the world's most important sea passages. For many centuries it has been the principal conduit for trade between Europe and the East Indies and nowadays is equally vital to Japanese trade with Europe and the Middle East. As much as forty percent of the world's international commerce is now reckoned to pass through Indonesian waters. The usual entrance to the west–east route is the Malacca Strait, so that the east coast of Sumatra is in a sense the strategic focus of the whole archipelago. It is only in relatively recent times that the growth of the Jakarta conurbation on the north-western tip of Java has come anywhere near underpinning that focal point with a major centre of population and, as some wish to believe, providing a fulcrum between Sumatra and the densely populated, hence powerful, areas of central and east Java.

No less important to the archipelago is the part the sea has played in internal, inter-island communications. Historically, the intrusive mountainous terrain and coastal swamps have impeded human movement, isolating areas of settlement from one another. The sea by contrast facilitates transport and communication. Using ships, successive power centres, Sri Vijaya, Majapahit, Malacca, Makassar, were able to project their influence well beyond their territorial bases. Consequently, whereas in the earliest times cities lay inland, the progressive tendency of economic growth to be sea-borne has promoted the growth of coastal cities and enhanced the importance of the coast at the expense of the interior.

If the behaviour of the Indonesian peoples in historical times is a matter of record, their ethnic origins are the subject of contending theories. The basic stock, in common with Malaysia and the Philippines, is Malay. The name by which its people speak of the entire region is the Malay Archipelago or, to use the politically charged Malay name, Nusantera. But merely to see the differing colours and facial characteristics of people in different parts of the archipelago, the Sumatran Bataks as distinct from the round-faced Javanese – the Melanesian Papuans as distinct from the gaunter Acehnese and so on – is to realize that the word begs more questions than it answers. Anthropologists recognise over a hundred ethnic groups and have recorded more than three hundred living languages.

The Malays are certainly the product of mixing and transhumance, about which something can be extrapolated from known history. Yet even here there are dangers. One of them is to assume that everything can be explained by the movement of people into empty lands and that there are no truly indigenous people at all. 'Java Man', whose bones came to light in Central Java in 1891, is, after all, one of earth's originals.

The late Professor D.G.E. Hall in his great and seminal *History of South-East Asia* warned that even such terms as Indonesia were open to serious objections, since they obscure the fact that the areas involved are not mere cultural appendages of India or China but have their own strongly-marked individuality. Alluding to the art and architecture which blossomed in places like central Java, he wrote: 'For the real key to its understanding one has to study the indigenous cultures of the peoples who produced it. And all of them, it must be realized, have developed on markedly individualistic lines'.[2]

Another, more contemporary and more politically charged, danger is to leave out of account the Chinese who have in fact been migrating southward into the Malay Archipelago for centuries, possibly millennia, and who were already well established there as traders when the Portuguese and Dutch, arriving from the west, bore the first European witness to its ethnic characteristics in the fifteenth and sixteenth centuries. An identifiably ethnic Chinese minority numbering upwards of three million is still a flourishing element in Indonesia's population. And still they mix their blood with that of the indigenous Malays. Chinese blood, in other words, is part of the definition of a Malay.

Whether Indian blood is to the same degree part of the definition is a more open question. Those who believe it is cite the formidable power and durability of the Hinduised states of the archipelago: Sri Vijaya from the seventh to the thirteenth century, Mataram from the eighth to the tenth century, Majapahit in the fourteenth and fifteenth centuries. The doubters maintain that the Hindu influence may have been primarily a matter of political convenience, rather as parliamentary democracy, for instance, might be imported into a society without drawing alien people in its train.

What is certain is that all the major religions of present-day Indonesia were cultural importations which, being associated with commercial power, potently influenced the definitions of identity, if not of ethnicity itself. The Hinduism of those early states almost certainly arrived as an inherent part of the socio-political system. At about the same time came Buddhism, first in an Indian guise but destined to evolve over the centuries because it was one of the religions favoured by the Chinese, hence in the eyes of many Muslim Indonesians a symbolic label with ethnic overtones.

Islam seems not to have begun taking root until the Arabs who brought it had been plying the eastern trade for a considerable time. It has to be borne in mind that in the late seventh century when Arab traders first established settlements in Sumatra and other locations on the route to China Islam was a new religion not yet fully consolidated on its own home ground. Six hundred years later, when Marco Polo reached what we now call Banda

Aceh – carrying the seeds of yet another imported religion, Christianity – he reported that the whole town had been converted to Islam.

All but about ten percent of Indonesians now profess to be in some sense Muslim. And the senses do vary; although all are Sunni, the relatively unadulterated Islam of Sumatra in the west is of a different character from that in east and central Java where it entered into a kind of symbiosis with the beliefs and conventions of local *adat*.

The Portuguese were the first Europeans to penetrate the archipelago and enter the spice trade in the Moluccas (Maluku). To a greater extent than the Dutch and British who followed, they both inter-married locally and created enduring communities; Timor is the salient example and there is even now a colony of Portuguese-speaking Malays in Malacca. Which is not to say that the Dutch and British did not inter-marry with Indonesians; Eurasians occupy a distinctive and sometimes fraught place in contemporary Indonesian society, easy victims when inflamed mass sentiment requires whipping-boys. But the more noticeable effect of European intrusion on ethnic identification has been the introduction of various forms of Christianity which, among other things, is used by some like Buddhism as a label of opprobrium to attach to non-Muslims.

Nearly half the people of South-East Asia are now Indonesian. Yet despite its great size, Indonesia is under-populated. Indeed until the end of the nineteenth century the so-called outer (i.e. non-Javanese) regions, making up ninety-three per cent of the land, were by present-day standards all but unpopulated and produced only a fifth of the goods exported by the Netherlands East Indies. Even Java, now home to 150 million people, had barely four million at the end of the eighteenth century.

During the next hundred years Java's population increased almost eightfold to thirty million. In the same period the population of the outer regions barely doubled. The cultivation of indifferent soils that were either swampy or swathed in tropical jungle would have required inputs that were not available and, in any case, not necessary so long as Java produced a food surplus.

The situation in Java itself was altogether different. Under Dutch administration the rich soils that had supported inland cities and a relatively large population across the centuries were found also to be highly suitable for the cultivation of cash and estate crops for export. The consequent acceleration of economic activity generated rich export revenues but also severe demographic pressure. Its population grew another fivefold in the twentieth century, to produce a world record population density of eight hundred people per square mile (308 per square kilometre). Java was becoming a burden to the national economy.

Simultaneously, other factors conspired to turn attention to the outer regions. Stimulated by expanding world markets and the population problem, both the skills and the capital needed to make them agriculturally productive became available, especially in Sumatra. By the beginning of the Second World War, the population of the outer regions had risen to twenty-five million; they were producing two-thirds of Indonesia's agricultural exports and virtually all its minerals, including oil.

This reversal of the economic roles of Java and the rest of the country, together with the way population responded to it, has already had weighty political implications. In the inter-war period, to take an important example, many Malay nationalists in Sumatra and neighbouring Malaya were tempted by the thought of joining to form a nation that would be rich, religiously homogeneous and disencumbered of Java. And Sumatran separatism – to the accompaniment of audible applause from Malaya – raised its head again in the American-inspired Sumatra rebellion of the late 1950s.

Today Indonesia's population is around 215 million and still growing. About sixty percent of its people live on the island of Java; of those about two thirds are Javanese and one third Sundanese. The distribution of population has long since ceased to reflect either its bearing capacity or its needs. It is therefore a fundamentally destabilizing factor, and underlies the historic constitutional experiment which is now being attempted in Indonesia.

KINGDOMS COME AND GO

At considerable risk of over-simplification the recorded, dynamic history of the Malay Archipelago may be said to begin nearly two thousand years ago. It consists of successive kingdoms and régimes aspiring, sometimes successfully, to be empires. For the most part their economic infrastructure was founded on international trade and command of the sea-lanes running west–east and north–south through the islands; generally their power was derived from monopoly of locally produced commodities, such as the cloves and nutmeg grown in the Spice Islands of the Moluccas (Maluku), camphor, cardamom, pepper, perfumes, timber, pearls, precious stones and much more.

Trade was plied with China to the north and first India and Persia then Arabia to the west. And always with the foreign traders came religious affiliations, nurtured within the foreign trading communities and/or in symbiotic union with administrative and political systems.

The imperatives of travel in small ships necessitated the formation of settlements on the coasts or in river-estuaries. Near the present-day city of Palembang in south-eastern Sumatra there arose in the seventh century the Hindu-Buddhist kingdom of Srivijaya. It was the first of the great Hinduised states and some – but not most Indonesians – would say the greatest. For hundreds of years it was a radiant centre of Mahayana Buddhism, the resort of scholars from both India and China.

Its international trade was controlled principally by businessmen from China and southern India in whose hands it became an elaborate and highly successful entrepôt. With the later and less imposing exception of Malacca, on the other side of the water, Srivijaya was alone in juxtaposing a major population centre with domination of the Malacca Strait. Perhaps for that reason it lasted longer than other states, six centuries. Another factor may have been that, although its commercial reach was widespread throughout the archipelago and its kings did demand tribute from dependencies, it was compact politically. It was not an empire in later senses of the term.

During Srivijaya's long history, other Hinduised states rose and fell on the neighbouring island of Java and coexisted with it. Benefiting from the fertile soil, they generally flourished inland, were based on inland cities and enjoyed plentiful manpower.

Supreme in Java between the eighth and tenth centuries was Mataram, based on the Solo river in the vicinity of the important modern city of Yogyakarta. The kings of Srivijaya and Mataram were related and seem to have been both active and competitive trading partners. As between Hinduism and Buddhism, Mataram leaned more towards the former, though not so emphatically as to prevent it collaborating with Srivijaya to construct the mighty Buddhist temple at Borobudur in central Java, one of the world's most majestic religious structures.

Mataram's prominence dwindled in the tenth century, while Srivijaya still had nearly three more centuries to go. Then, near the end of the thirteenth century, there arose in central Java the last of the great Hinduised states, Majapahit, following hard on the final gasp of Srivijaya's dominance. Destined to survive barely a hundred years, Majapahit nevertheless came to symbolize the glory and confidence of a supposedly united past when seen from the perspective of twentieth century nationalism.

Its appeal to President Sukarno was obvious. It was a powerfully-led kingdom, it was rich, it was largely though only briefly successful in integrating large parts of the Malay Archipelago and it embodied Javanese ascendancy.

There are doubts about the solidity of the Majapahit achievement, but it is clear that, whatever that achievement was, it is primarily attributable to one exceptional political leader, a politician, not the king. He is known as Gajah Mada ('wise elephant'), a Napoleon of his time. Like Napoleon, his most lasting achievement was the codification of law and the creation of an administrative framework that endured into the nineteenth century. Also like Napoleon, he had (and briefly realized) wide-reaching imperial ambitions.

If we are to credit a sycophantic court poet – better perhaps to be described as official historian – by the name of Prapanca, Majapahit under Gajah Mada imposed vassalage on states all around the archipelago: in Sulawesi (Celebes), Maluku (the Moluccas), Bali, Lombok, Sumbawa, Kalimantan. In Sumatra, around which they arranged a ring of coastal vassals, they installed a king of Malayu (not to be confused with Malaya) whose Minangkabau dynasty outlived Majapahit itself. They also, of course, maintained trading relations with China and seem to have paid particular attention to the kindred Hinduised mainland kingdoms of Siam and Indochina.

Simultaneously with the rise of Majapahit the infiltration of Islam from northern India had begun to escalate as a political force. Under cover of Majapahit negligence this fresh cultural and commercial invasion found fertile ground among local rulers. One of those, a prince driven by Majapahit forces from his court at Palembang in the heart of old Srivijaya, was one of several who conceived the plan of reestablishing control over the Malacca Strait from a different adjacent base. To that end he founded a settlement at Temasik in what we now call Singapore. It could not last, but around the turn of the fourteenth and fifteenth centuries a dogged remnant from Temasik headed north to Malacca (a few hours' drive now) on the west coast of Malaya, there to found a Muslim trading settlement which would rival the great Hinduised empires in its commercial reach. As Malacca's fortunes rose it emerged in 1478 that Majapahit could not even resist a fragile coalition of Muslim states on its own nearby north Javanese coast; the once proud empire tottered and in 1515 fell apart definitively.

By then Islam had been the ascendant religion in the archipelago for the best part of a hundred years. Malacca had been officially converted in

1414, since when the religion simply conformed with the age-old pattern of following the trade routes. Those now ran along the northern coast of Java, past the strategic port of Makassar in south-west Sulawesi and up to the Moluccas, still at that time the only known source of the cloves and nutmeg so ardently desired in India, Arabia and parts of Europe – and the source, in fact, of such wealth as gained Malacca a reputation as one of the biggest ports in the world.

Malacca's virtual spice monopoly did not stay unchallenged for long. In 1498 a Portuguese fleet under Vasco da Gama, having rounded the Cape, reached India and got wind of the fact that the sought-after spices were to be had at Malacca. Thirteen years later another Portuguese admiral, Alfonso d'Albuquerque, turned up in Malacca, captured it and at once despatched three ships to the Spice Islands. Thus began the European penetration of the Malay Archipelago.

When they reached the Spice Islands the Roman Catholic Portuguese were perhaps not altogether displeased to find Muslims installed ahead of them. Their violent measures to seize control and construct a fortress on the little island of Ternate off the west coast of Halmahera placed the spice trade firmly in their hands and at the same time struck a blow against an old and familiar religious rival. But they too over-reached themselves, so that local rulers finally formed a coalition to drive them off Ternate.

So for about a hundred years Portugal's trading clout first rose then fell, its missionaries barely more sensitive than its rapacious businessmen. Seeing its dwindling influence, more and more local rulers turned to Islam and, although it took time, the Portuguese were driven back to a single stronghold on the island of Timor, slowly to decay into a post-colonial anachronism which would occasion much pain in the twentieth century.

The situation in the wake of Portugal's brief and ferocious commercial sally into the East Indies trade was a free-for-all, the very opposite of regional unity. It was the Dutch who, together with the English, the Spanish and the French, were probing South-East Asia in search of commercial opportunity, who delivered the next substantial wave of European penetration and with it the first makings of an Indonesian nation.

It may, as has been said, be true that the Dutch did not set out to find or found an empire in the East Indies, that their motive was commercial profit. As much might be said of all the Europeans who made their mark there. There was politics in the air nonetheless. It was when the old enemy, Spain, occupied Portugal in 1580 that Holland began to show a serious interest in

Iberian trading enterprise in the Malay archipelago, and took the initiative of consolidating a multiplicity of independent companies into the United East India Company.

Exhibiting the familiar Indonesian propensity for competitive disunity, local rulers lent themselves to divide and rule tactics. The Dutch paid well for the spices and other commodities they exclusively shipped back to Europe and it was scarcely to be expected that they would build their local suppliers into a potential foe by encouraging them to unite. In the very different circumstances of northern Sumatra the Sultan of Aceh, profiting from his pepper monopoly and protected by the British, merely did what all his successors did – defended the idea of Acehnese independence.

Meanwhile the Dutch, in heavily armed fleets that bespoke something more than commercial ambition, occupied themselves to the east in flushing the Portuguese and English out of the spice-bearing Moluccas and to the west in opening up a new trade route that was to have a major geo-political impact. Instead of relying wholly on the north–south passage through the Malacca Strait, they pioneered an alternative approach from the south Indian Ocean, affording them entry into the Java Sea northward through the Sunda Strait which lies between the tips of Sumatra and West Java. Malacca declined in relative importance as they developed a new port-settlement close to the new passage at Jacatra, which they renamed Batavia and is now the Indonesian capital, Jakarta.

Here was the fulcrum between the spheres of geo-political power formerly wielded by the Srivijaya and Majapahit empires, the link between the Straits and the agricultureal resources further east – in Java and the spice gardens of the Moluccas. After the seizure in 1667 of Makassar (later called Ujung Pandang) in south-western Sulawesi, the Dutch enjoyed a monopoly of the shipping lanes that was even more important than the spice monopoly. They were well-placed on the one hand to exploit the proliferating trade in mixed goods passing through Indonesian waters and on the other to generate the plantation industries which used the rich soils of Java to produce large exportable surpluses of sugar, tea and coffee.

Operations of this order, however, demanded more sophisticated administration than the simpler exploitative activities of earlier days. Successful business required peace, stability and either collaborative or compliant local administration. In 1755 the United East India Company, acting as agent of the Dutch government, engineered the division of the kingdom of Mataram into two: Surakarta (usually known now as Solo) and Yogyakarta. Together with several smaller Javanese states they became effectively vassals of the Dutch.

Increasingly the company was preoccupied with financial and fiscal rather than commercial management and shareholders were taking far too big a share of the profits. So when, at the very end of the eighteenth century, it turned to the Dutch government for a rescue operation, there was only one feasible remedy: the company was wound up and a trading empire was taken over as a colony.

GOING DUTCH

The transition from company to direct Dutch colonial rule was neither smooth nor simple. It would in any case have taken time to unravel the corrupt and often incompetent company bureaucracy, but the whole process was overtaken by the Napoleonic wars. It was a British administration, not Dutch, which inaugurated the most important early reforms.

British interest in the East Indies was not new. As the eighteenth century ended, British ships were insinuating themselves increasingly into the trade of the archipelago, both through smuggling and by means of concessions extracted from the Dutch authorities. Then, when France occupied Holland, the British, encouraged by the exiled Dutch monarch William V, first began the naval harrassment of Java and in 1811 took it and several other Dutch possessions over.

A contemporary account describes the Java discovered by its British occupiers as 'a country completely disorganized and virtually bankrupt: a mass of depreciated paper money; and almost complete absence of a silver currency, or indeed, any currency other than paper; a large army requiring payment in silver, the export trade dead and difficult to revive; an inadequate civil service of dual nationality . . .'[3]

The British take-over was executed under an agreement between the British government and the British East India Company whereby, once the Franco-Dutch forts, batteries and works of defence had been destroyed, the territories would be returned to the occupation of the natives.

Thus the British interregnum lasted only five years, after which control was restored not to the natives but to the Dutch. It was, however, an episode of singular significance, distinguished by the reforming endeavours of a Lieutenant Governor appointed by the British administration in India,

Thomas Stamford Raffles. In the course of his five years in Java he addressed problems that the Dutch had not tackled in two hundred; there was too much to do, the problems were too complex and many of his schemes failed. His central concept was that government required contact with the governed and must serve their interests if they were to be economically motivated.

Raffles' most important work was his attempt to abolish the system of so-called 'contingencies'; these were compulsory deliveries of produce exacted from growers through the agency of middlemen, often Chinese, employed by local rulers. His aim was to replace it with a land-tax system in which the growers would have direct title to their land. Although he did not succeed in getting the new system satisfactorily established, his thinking permanently coloured subsequent debate about the responsibilities of government and taxation.

In 1816, the Napoleonic wars now ended, the Dutch took up where they had left off in the East Indies and quickly restored the well-known scenario of high profitability allied to deepening debt, all at the disregarded cost of poverty, injustice and stifled incentive among those who actually produced the valuable crops.

Dissatisfaction was intense. Uprisings and rebellious disturbances became endemic, and in two cases, the Paderi War in Sumatra and the Java War in Central Java, extended into guerrilla campaigns that lasted in one case seventeen years and in the other five. The Java War alone brought about the deaths of some 200,000 Javanese and 15,000 members of the Dutch army. There were other costs that had to be taken seriously: it was a drain on the exchequer, and it provoked the early symptoms of a unifying national identity expressed through Islam.

The Java War was brought to an end in 1830 by a stroke of treachery. Diponegoro, a prince of the royal family of Yogyakarta who was leading the Javanese, offered to negotiate a surrender. When he turned up for talks the Dutch army arrested him and despatched him to Sulawesi to languish in exile and become a national legend.

It was a turning point. The Dutch at last settled to the task of consolidating and organizing their East Indian colony. In the context of Raffles' half-digested land reforms, they could not go back to the contingencies system of compulsory deliveries. So they introduced the notorious *cultuurstelsel*, or culture system. Instead of levying a prescribed quantity of produce or a percentage of the value of a crop, it constrained the peasant farmer to use a proportion of his land, seldom less than two-fifths, for the enforced cultivation of prescribed crops.

Its application, never widespread, yielded oppression, injustice and poverty, but also generated high and reliable financial returns. Irrigation was improved, rice production soared, the colony became self-financing and by the end of the nineteenth century Java's population had multiplied sevenfold.

But discontent went on growing too. For the great majority who did not benefit from the culture system the economic situation steadily worsened. There was hardly ever a time when there was not violent conflict somewhere. Active colonialism meant assailing the independence of non-Javanese territories which were not already under Dutch control. What had briefly been a policy of non-intervention in the affairs of Indonesian states evaporated as the Dutch rediscovered the advantages of dividing to rule; a fast-track treaty system was perfected whereby any local chief or ruler who recognised the authority of the centre would be confirmed in his rule and, in theory at least, protected. By 1911 some three hundred self-governing states had been brought under Dutch control by this means, planting the seeds of an antipathy towards federalism which deeply affected political sentiment during and after the independence era.

It was in the north Sumatran state of Aceh that the Dutch met the stiffest resistance. Until 1871 the sultanate, which had once held sway over much of the rest of Sumatra, enjoyed implicit British protection, but in that year the British government intimated it would no longer raise objections to Dutch occupation. Thereupon the Dutch declared a war against Aceh which lasted officially until the surrender of guerrilla remnants in 1908; in fact guerrilla resistance to rule from the centre never ceased there.

Coincident with the great administrative and territorial drive in the latter half of the nineteenth century, the Dutch rulers introduced economic policies designed to attract investment into the region. But again it was mainly the Dutch people living in Indonesia (208,000 of them in 1930) who benefited. For most Indonesians, the new policies spelt further hardship. Understanding of this fact in sections of public opinion in Holland led to the introduction of social and other policies aimed at helping Indonesians both at a welfare level and by enhancing their spending power. Policies were elaborated for providing relevant infrastructures for agriculture and smallscale industry. Some of them, however, were never put into effect at all; and where they were it was done in a spirit of paternalism which labelled them as mere palliatives. The infrastructure projects that did flourish had to do with communications – railways, port installations, telegraph – the essentials of a colonial private-enterprise economy. Consequently, as the nineteenth century drew to a close, there was a groundswell of refusal to acknowledge Dutch authority, and the Netherlands East Indies entered the twentieth century in ferment.

## Notes

1 Braudel, Fernand *The Mediterranean*, London, Collins 1972.
2 Hall, D.G.E. *A History of South-East Asia*, London, Macmillan 1955.
3 Crawfurd, John *Descriptive Dictionary of the Indian Islands and Adjacent Countries*, London 1856.

# TWO

## *One Nation and Free*

Until well into the latter half of the nineteenth century the Netherlands East Indies comprised the densely populated and tightly administered nucleus of Java and a loosely-controlled hinterland of non-homogeneous outer regions. While parts of that hinterland had been under some kind of Dutch control for as much three centuries, other parts of the archipelago were still not controlled by the Dutch at all. When Dutch people spoke of their eastern colony Java was what they had in mind.

That perception changed abruptly after about 1870. The Netherlands embarked on a new and purposeful empire-building drive which, at its culmination, placed them in the same imperial league as Great Britain, France, Spain and Portugal. The motor that impelled them was the industrial revolution which was transforming Europe and reaching out for new export markets and raw material supplies.

In the Malay Archipelago the new imperialism was a unifying force. Administration had a homogenizing effect. Modern communications, by improving access and bolstering central authority, made the emerging nation aware of itself. Out of the gathering unity of the Indies was born the novel idea of nationhood and out of that came nationalism. Because of the way it evolved, largely in the thinking of a small educated élite, that conceptual construct was at least as instrumental in carrying the nationalist movement forward as was grass-roots resentment.

It is even arguable that in Indonesia, as in British India, the first tender shoots of nationalist leadership were nurtured not in the land where it belonged but in the academies and public debate of the metropolitan power. The reformed and more benevolent attitudes that seeped into Dutch administration of its colony and came to be known as the Ethical Policy were bred in European soil.

The Ethical Policy meant different things to different people. Some undoubtedly envisaged progress towards home rule; but the official Dutch view never did admit the prospect of withdrawal from an independent Indonesian nation.

To some the provision, albeit inadequate, of education was regarded as a specific against an Islamic take-over. Islam was by now the prevalent religion throughout the region and, although it had assumed different complexions according to the cultures it encountered, the simplifying and modernising currents blowing in from Egypt at the beginning of the twentieth century overcame those differences and informed a sense of collective identity which appealed not only to intellectuals but to all who considered themselves Muslims.

Language too was a unifying factor, not only the Malay which was ultimately adopted as the national language, but Dutch which was the language of government and, at that level, bridged the gap between the many regional language groups. For many years Dutch alone challenged the Javanese spoken by that socially presumptuous people. As late as 1966, when the process of toppling President Sukarno was well in hand, I sat near a room where a cabinet committee was meeting under the chairmanship of the Sultan of Yogyakarta and was intrigued to hear them all speaking Dutch.

Hence the intellectuals who set about rallying the discontented under-classes – rural and urban – were equipped with potent tools.

Movements, associations and societies proliferated, often with educational rather than explicitly political preoccupations. Limited by their regional and class appeal, many groups were eclipsed by one of two Muslim organizations formed in 1912. One of them, Muhammadiyah, was a modernising educational body that was to be of considerable significance later; but of greater immediate importance was Sarekat Islam (the Islamic Association).

The offshoot of what might now be called a chamber of commerce which had been formed to resist the sodality of Chinese traders, Sarekat Islam rapidly gathered a mass following and, despite its prudent denials of political intent, was the chief standard-bearer of nationalism for a decade. Recognising its importance, the Dutch leader of what was to become the Indonesian Communist Party tried to subvert it; he set up the Indies Social Democratic Association which, led by Semaun and the legendary Tan Malaka, penetrated Sarekat Islam and attempted to promote a revolutionary agenda. Although the strategy failed, they were fighting on other fronts as well and successfully fomented trade union unrest; in spite of brutal official suppression it never really ceased.

The government's stern anti-communist measures produced a brief remission in political activity, but it was almost immediately compensated for by another development in the Netherlands, where in 1922 a distinguished generation of Indonesian students started a nationalist group called the Indonesian Union which was to play a major part five years later in creating the Indonesian Nationalist Party (PNI). Seizing the nationalist initiative, the new party brought those Dutch-educated intellectuals into effective collaboration with an indigenous Study Group movement in which Indonesia's future president, the young Ahmed Sukarno, was already taking the lead.

Sukarno came to the chair as the man of the moment: conciliator, syncretist, orator, equally well-read in European political philosophy and the Javanese classics, and with a sophisticated understanding of what Indonesian nationalism must mean if it was to win through to independence. 'The vessel that will bear us to a free Indonesia,' he declared in a famous article, 'is the ship of unity,'[1] in writing which he well understood the necessity of finding common cause between Marxism, Islam and – keystone of his personal philosophy – nationalism. In a land of such diversity he recognised from the outset that the idea of the nation as an entity would take time to evolve and attached more importance to arousing the spiritual will to be one than to prescribing particular and potentially divisive institutional goals. The exception which has latterly returned to challenge the nation was his early opposition to the unitary organization of the Indonesian state: 'the motto therefore should be federation', he recalled later in the autobiography he dictated to Cindy Adams, federation which 'must leave intact the personality, the individuality, the character of the cooperating parties'.[2]

Seeing the PNI's mounting strength, the Dutch outlawed it, made mass arrests and in 1930 sent Sukarno for his first term of imprisonment. Later two other giants of the nationalist movement, Muhammad Hatta and Sutan Sjahrir, returned from Holland and after only two years of political activity were in their turn arrested and sent to the vile conditions of the Boven Digul political concentration camp in what is now called West Papua (New Guinea). It was left to the invading Japanese to release all three (and many others) in 1942.

Deprived of its three principal leaders, the nationalist movement fell into factions. The fundamental issue was whether nationalists should cooperate with their Dutch rulers and negotiate their way towards independence, or cease all cooperation.

The solution was pre-empted by the Second World War, the German invasion of the Netherlands and, in 1942, the Japanese invasion of the Netherlands East Indies. As early as 1928 Sukarno had begun predicting conflict caused by Japanese imperialist expansion. Many Indonesians were sympathetic towards Japan's projection of itself as the Asian leader against European colonialism in South-East Asia and so accorded its army a guarded welcome. While Sukarno himself may have harboured reservations, he set about turning the new situation to his country's advantage. From the Indonesian perspective the enemy was Dutch rule and Dutch resistance to Indonesian independence and, for three years, it was reasonable to act on the presumption of a prolonged Japanese stay; non-cooperation with them was not a realistic option – they made sure of that.

They also, however, introduced Sukarno to the theme of Japan as liberator, and it was on that basis that he agreed to act as an intermediary between the military administration and the Indonesian people.

Hatta and Sukarno set aside for the time being their differences over approach. The question of whether or not to cooperate no longer offered them real options; the terms of the old debate were no longer relevant. As things fell out, Sjahrir played a clandestine role, organizing an anti-Japanese underground movement and doing his best to keep Hatta and Sukarno informed about the world beyond Java, while they served as advisers to the occupiers.

The Japanese could not, of course, be seen to offer less in the way of political benefit than the Dutch had before them. They in fact went much further; they initiated widespread political organization by setting up a number of regional advisory councils, and a Central Advisory Council situated in Jakarta with Sukarno as its president, hence the most senior Indonesian under the occupation régime. They did not, as Hatta and Sukarno certainly wished, do anything to promote the idea of a united Indonesia. On the contrary, the prime minister, General Tojo, addressing the Japanese Diet at the beginning of 1943, promised post-war independence for Burma and the Philippines but avoided the very word 'Indonesia', speaking only of the southern areas and citing Malaya, Sumatra and Java as separate entities. Japan too intended to divide in order to rule.

Nevertheless, the new political organizations gave Sukarno and his colleagues access to the country's grass roots which he tried to turn to nationalist advantage. In March 1943, for instance, he cooperated in the creation of a body (Putera) to mobilize public support for the war effort within the framework of the Greater Asian Co-Prosperity Sphere. Tojo spurned this conciliatory gesture but did set in train the accelerated transfer of important administrative posts to Indonesians who thus found themselves in seats once occupied by Dutch civil servants who were now interned. Coupled with the creation of a corps of Indonesian military auxiliaries called PETA, this helped build a national resource beyond anything the Dutch contemplated.

Unlike the Dutch, the Japanese recognised the potential of Islam as a possible source of sympathy for aspects of their rule. They sponsored the formation of a new Muslim consortium that was to continue as an important element in Indonesian politics long after their departure. This was Masjumi (Consultative Council of Indonesian Muslims) which brought together the modernising, urban-based Muhammadiyah and the supposedly apolitical, largely rural Nahdatul Ulama (Religious Scholars' League).

The faster the tide of war turned against them, the quicker-footed the Japanese occupiers became. In September 1944 Sukarno's persistent demand for a nationalist-led propaganda organization was rewarded by the creation of the Pioneer Corps, and 'the nationalist élite was thus for the first time during the occupation given an organizational weapon of the first magnitude'.[3] Three months later, in a decision pregnant with future consequence, the Japanese, now clearly preparing for defeat, allowed Masjumi to set up its own military force which was able by the end of the occupation to field thirty thousand troops.

The implicit change of policy became explicit in September 1944 when Japan's new Prime Minister, Koiso, unexpectedly stood up in the Diet and promised future independence for the whole of Indonesia. Suddenly it was permitted to fly the red and white Indonesian flag and sing the Indonesian national anthem. The motivation was exposed in a Japanese government statement: 'National consciousness must be aroused to the utmost degree and used to strengthen our defences and cooperation with the military government so as to forge Japan and Java into an indivisible unit. No drastic changes are to be allowed in the political and economic structure created by the military government . . .'.

To chart the way towards the independence which was now a realistic prospect, a widely representative investigative body, the BPKI, was assembled. It was in effect a constituent assembly. Partly due to their own inertia, the Muslims, though represented, came through under-weight, enabling the proponents of secular nationalism to speak as the pre-eminent voice of the emerging nation. At first their deliberations drifted; but in July 1945 Sukarno galvanised the process with what might well be considered the most important speech in modern Indonesian history. In it he propounded the philosophy of Pancasila (five principles) to which even those who have most grossly betrayed it swear allegiance to this day.

The five principles, in the order in which he then presented them, were: nationalism, internationalism (or humanitarianism), democracy (or mutual consent), social prosperity and belief in one God. Subsequently, in response to Muslim pressure, belief in one God was promoted to first place. The speech was a call to 'all human beings who . . . live throughout the entire archipelago of Indonesia from the northern tip of Sumatra to Papua' to transcend ethnic, regional, religious, every kind of sectional interest and build a single national state. It challenged some of the strongly-held convictions of many of his countrymen and has been at the centre of many a raging controversy since and yet remains the doctrinal core of the near-consensus that still holds Indonesia together.

The result of deliberations by the BPKI and its constitutional sub-committee was the 1945 Constitution defining a unitary rather than a federal state; and the so-called Jakarta Charter, which endeavoured without much success to resolve the vexed issue of Islam's role in politics. More than half the Indonesian members of the BPKI, Sukarno among them, voted for the inclusion of Malaya, the British North Borneo territories including Brunei, Portuguese East Timor and New Guinea (West Papua) in the new nation, but Japanese influence led to acceptance of a definition confined to the former territories of the Netherlands East Indies. Hatta and Sukarno could justifiably claim that their strategy of accommodation with the Japanese invaders had achieved the best attainable results for their country.

The end was signalled by the detonation of American atomic bombs over Hiroshima and Nagasaki in August 1945. On 11 August the Japanese military governor in South-East Asia, Field-Marshal Terachi, summoned Sukarno to his headquarters in Saigon and urged him to return at once and set up an independent republic. On his return to Jakarta (still called Batavia at that time) Sukarno came under pressure to make an immediate declaration of independence in an anti-Japanese vein. But he and Hatta held out for a more cautious approach, one likely to avoid bloodshed and confrontation with the crumbling Japanese régime. Their counsel prevailed, and it was in a subdued ceremony outside his own house that he proclaimed the independence of a united Indonesia on 17 August with

Muhammad Hatta at his side. They raised a home-made red and white national flag coloured with their own blood, unaware of how much more Indonesian blood would be spilled before independence could be made real.

## TURBULENT DAWN: THE GREAT LEADER

Japan was in no legal position either to acknowledge or reject the declaration of Indonesian independence in August 1945, having surrendered to the allies several days earlier. Its military administration was, nevertheless, in effective control of the Indies.

The allied purpose was to remove Japanese forces from the territories they had invaded and restore effective sovereignty to the Dutch. More than just a legal posture, it was in British eyes the best prescription for securing free passage through the Malacca Strait and in American eyes for safeguarding the Sumatran oilfields. Four weeks slipped by after the surrender before allied forces made their appearance off Jakarta in the shape of ships of the Royal Navy.

The Malay Archipelago had only just passed under Mountbatten's command as the result of a decision taken at the end of July by allied leaders meeting at Potsdam. Previously the Indies had come under the South West Pacific Area command within the purview of General Douglas MacArthur. An early discovery was that MacArthur had failed to organize the gathering of intelligence about the territories he was handing over.[4] As a result Mountbatten had no idea of the political situation he was about to encounter in Indonesia.

So began Britain's second intervention in Indonesia's political history, once again in preparation for the return of Dutch rule, curiously echoing the Stamford Raffles episode at the end of the Napoleonic wars. British troops landed in the latter half of September, soon followed by Australians responsible for the eastern islands. They found the country in a state of high excitement with the Indonesian national flag flying everywhere.

In the capital, Sukarno's republican leadership group had a firm grip on the political situation. Continuing the process begun under the Japanese, they had adopted transitional regulations under which Sukarno was voted president and Hatta vice-president. Arrangements were made to secure the administration throughout the regions. By the end of August the preparatory committee had been dissolved and its members coopted, together with another 135 representatives of political and ethnic groups, into a Central

Indonesian National Committee (KNIP) which became an essential prop of government and was in effect the Republic's first parliament.

Important compromises were made in those early months. The non-Javanese Sutan Sjahrir, whose power base was in the revolutionary anti-Japanese community which had sustained an underground movement during the occupation, agreed to support Sukarno in return for a commitment to multi-party democracy. Sukarno would have preferred a single-party system but was obliged to accept that a revived nationalist party (PNI) would be one among many. Sjahrir was made prime minister at the head of a cabinet more pronouncedly anti-Japanese than Sukarno might have wished and, although day to day executive authority was vested in the presidency, the principle of cabinet responsibility was adopted and the president was divested of his initial extraordinary powers.

The Japanese, it will be remembered, had formed a home defence corps (PETA) which had attracted good Indonesian support and turned into a rallying place for nationalist sentiment. Together with armed struggle groups, the Masjumi militia and tens of thousands of semi-trained irregulars, this now became the nucleus of Indonesia's national army. To the weaponry already provided to them was now added a steady stream of arms handed to nationalists by the defeated Japanese to be used in local conflicts which British forces had to control. The most noted of these was the battle of Surabaya in East Java, where it took a British force more than three weeks of fierce fighting to subdue nationalists who had taken control of the city. Plainly other conflicts on that scale could not be sustained, and although heavy fighting did occur elsewhere, the battle of Surabaya confirmed the British view that the Dutch would have to negotiate with the republican government.

Had Mountbatten's allied forces, comprised largely of Indians, been able to restrict their activities to de-activating and evacuating the Japanese, their presence in the infant nation might have been remembered with some affection. Sukarno and the republican government started out by being highly cooperative. Initial suspicions were briefly allayed when the Dutch Deputy Governor, who arrived with the British, repeated a war-time speech given three years before by the Queen of the Netherlands adumbrating advances towards self-government. However, the Dutch government immediately repudiated the broadcast, whereupon Sukarno ended all cooperation, threatened to oppose Dutch landings and fight the British should they provide them with military cover.

Where ground forces were concerned, Mountbatten was ill-provided for the tasks he was given. His solution was to make use of large elements of the Japanese army which he was there to dismantle and disperse. Thanks to a still unpublished paper by Dr Andrew Roadnight[5] the full extent of this highly controversial measure has now come to light:

Between September 1945 and November 1946, up to 35,000 surrendered Japanese troops were incorporated into Lord Louis Mountbatten's South East Asia Command (SEAC) in the Netherlands East Indies (NEI). Although under the ultimate control of British officers, the Japanese were led by their own officers, were allowed to retain their wartime unit structures and remained armed.

In Sumatra, where there were strategic economic assets to be secured, the use of Japanese troops was even greater than in Java. Roadnight records that the Japanese 25th Army had retained its discipline and, crucially, its weapons; and '. . . even before the arrival of the allies it had helped in evacuating all Allied prisoners-of-war and about 1,000 internees'. Some 24,000 surrendered Japanese personnel came under allied orders in Sumatra, he wrote, of whom 10,500 were deployed as a screen around the major city of Medan to protect it against Acehnese marauders.

While South East Asia Command provided cover and Indonesian politics gathered pace the Dutch set about destabilizing the new Republic and built up their own military presence. By the time the last British troops left towards the end of 1946 some 55,000 Dutch replacements had been landed on Java, and the Sumatran cities of Medan and Palembang were being bombed in preparation for Dutch reoccupation. For the next three years, in the face of hostile world opinion but encouraged by a certain secret ambivalence in the American attitude, they pleaded the menace of communism as their reason for trying to cling to their huge economic assets in Indonesia.

Communism already had mature roots in the land. A body called the Indies Social Democratic Association and founded in 1914 by a Dutchman named Hendrik Sneevliet turned into the PKI in 1920. The Dutch expelled its first chairman, Tan Malaka, from the country in 1922 and he subsequently spent long years in the coils of international communism. Probably he owed his life to his exile, since he was absent during the 1926 communist rebellion in western Java which the Dutch suppressed with nine hangings and thousands interned. He found his way back during the Japanese occupation and after the war re-emerged to build up a following among opponents of Sukarno's and prime minister Sjahrir's policy of negotiating with the Dutch.

Sukarno recognised the danger and went on preaching his old theme, the importance of unity and the avoidance of class struggle. So-called Marxists did not understand socialism, he said. Indonesia was living through the revolution of a people, not the revolution of one or another class. The time for social revolution would come, but not yet. 'First we must tear power away from the hands of foreigners and build up our national armed forces to completely destroy colonialism. We must unify all the islands of Indonesia within one independent state and make Indonesia strong in modern technical know-how. We must devise a diplomacy calculated to secure *de jure* international recognition'. It was the counsel of a prudent and clearly non-communist leader.

Tan Malaka, frustrated dreamer and would-be national leader, wanted the communist revolution there and then. Working from the Central Javanese town of Madiun with the idea of setting up his own government, he pressed for Sjahrir's replacement as prime minister and in February 1946 forced his resignation only months after the new Republic had begun work. When Sukarno called on Tan Malaka to form a government his band of followers fell to pieces in contention over cabinet appointments, opening the way for Sukarno to take back some of the prerogatives he had so recently surrendered and re-appoint Sjahrir. Tan Malaka was placed in detention, but within four months a group of his communist supporters, including a section of the army led by a general, kidnapped the prime minister. Again Sukarno acted decisively, assumed emergency powers and successfully demanded Sjahrir's release.

The policy of negotiating with the Dutch therefore survived, and in November 1946 an agreement was signed, named after Linggadjati, the Javanese hill station where the talks were conducted. Its one enduring virtue was Dutch recognition of the principle of Indonesia's independence. The Indonesians, on the other hand, were called upon to accept that the Republic did not include the whole country and agree to the formation of a federation jointly administered by the Netherlands. The Dutch meanwhile had set about creating fifteen small, semi-autonomous states, which they intended to introduce as puppets into the new federation. Intentional obscurities led to almost immediate argument over interpretation of the Linggadjati agreement. The Dutch, with American acquiescence, issued an ultimatum declaring that *de jure* sovereignty over the Republic remained with the Netherlands pending its transfer to the proposed United States of Indonesia.

It was a moment of political confusion, and the Dutch availed themselves of it by launching a full-scale military attack on the Republic. They called it a police action. Driven by the heavily armed Dutch army, the republicans withdrew into the Sumatran and Javanese countryside, resorting to mobile warfare and guerrilla tactics. By the time a ceasefire was called at the behest of the United Nations the Dutch had taken hold of large parts of Java and its north-coast island of Madura. Resumed negotiations led to the signature of a truce aboard the American warship Renville. The terms were humiliating and, although Sukarno, playing as always the unifier and conciliator, retained the allegiance of the PNI and the Muslim Masjumi, it was an opportunity for the communists to pick up the nationalist card.

The distancing of the Indonesian communists from the nationalist mainstream in 1948 has to be seen in the context of the famous Calcutta conference (of Youth and Students of South-East Asia Fighting for Freedom and Independence). Generally recognised as the starting point for a wave of communist activism in Asia, in pursuit of a new line transmitted from Moscow, it was followed by violent eruptions in Burma, India, Indochina and Malaya. Not long after the Calcutta conference, a former communist leader, Musso, who had lived for years in Moscow, returned to Indonesia. He immediately became party secretary and went on tour opposing Sukarno's cautious handling of the Dutch. A pro-PKI military force occupied key areas in the city of Madiun, branded Sukarno and Hatta 'fascist collaborationists' and purported to form a rival administration.

Sukarno's decisive handling of this so-called 'Madiun affair' bears heavily on the interpretation of events nearly twenty years later when communists were alleged to have hatched another anti-government rebellion. Declaring martial law in the area, he accused the PKI, in an oft-quoted broadcast, of high treason. 'I call on you at this extremely critical moment', he told his listeners, 'when you and I are experiencing the greatest test, to make a choice between following Musso and his communist party, which will obstruct the attainment of an independent Indonesia, or following Sukarno–Hatta . . . who will lead you on the road of independence for Indonesia and freedom from all oppression'.

In the fierce fighting that ensued, Musso and possibly thousands more were killed. As many as 25,000 communist troops were said to have been engaged and roundly defeated by the Police Mobile Brigade and the Siliwangi division commanded by Colonel (as he then was) Abdul Haris Nasution, the creator, many would say, of the Indonesian army. A huge casualty toll included hundreds of Muslims – this at a time when the Darul Islam secessionist movement was coming to life and trying to found an independent Muslim state farther west in Java.

The PKI was for the time being disabled, and it was the government of the Indonesian Republic – not the Dutch – that had done it. Horrified, Sukarno castigated the affair as a social revolution that was forced years and perhaps decades before its time.

So long as republican forces were tied up fighting communists the Dutch, under American influence, had abstained from exploiting the government's discomfiture, but their restraint ended once the Madiun fighting was over. In December they launched their second 'police action', this time against Yogyakarta which was serving as the Republic's administrative capital. With the choice of vanishing into the countryside to lead guerrilla resistance or staying to face capture, Sukarno, Hatta and several others chose the latter and were duly arrested and sent into detention in northern Sumatra.

It was to no avail. To the accompaniment of unremitting guerrilla resistance, belying Dutch claims to have pacified the country, global censure continued and grew. An alternative republican government was formed in Sumatra. The USA turned up its diplomatic and economic pressure on the Netherlands until, in July 1949, a ceasefire was ordered, and Sukarno was flown triumphally back to Yogyakarta to pick up the reins of government and recommence negotiations.

The Dutch yoke was at last thrown off in 1949 as the result of a round-table conference in the Netherlands at which the republican delegation was led by Dr Muhammad Hatta. Unconditional sovereignty passed to the United States of Indonesia, under a constitution providing for multi-party parliamentary democracy, proportional representation and a presidency with largely nominal powers.

Within months, once Indonesian independence was secure, the federal constitution was abrogated in favour of a unitary structure. Under a provisional constitution Sukarno continued as president and Hatta as prime minister in a balance of power that had again swung against the president.

For many Indonesians Sukarno was one of two co-equals, and at this juncture it was the man who became prime minister, Muhammad Hatta, who emerged with the greater institutional power. Not only were his personal credentials in the fight for independence comparable with Sukarno's, but both the 1949 constitution and the provisional one with which they replaced it put him at the head of a cabinet answerable only to parliament. Although some important prerogatives still rested with the president – his was the power to issue decrees on vital matters like declaring war and emergency, the dissolution of parliament and the formation of new cabinets – the role was designed as essentially that of a ceremonial figurehead.

Plainly it was not a system compatible with the views of the man who had habitually pointed out the inappropriateness of western parliamentary democracy, with its adversarial conventions, to the realities of a perilously fissiparous nation. Sukarno's talk had long been of consultation (*musjawarah*), consensus (*mufakat*) and mutual cooperation (*gotong royong*). In a nation divided between the Javanese and the rest, between strict Muslims, hybrid Muslims and non-Muslims, between a social establishment and the rest, he never lost sight of the need to unite, to foster tolerance, to eschew western conventions which might pull society apart instead of binding it together. Nevertheless, he went along with the choice of a multi-party parliamentary system, accepting his presidential role within the provisional constitution.

However, it did not work. All the early governments – five of them in the first five years – were party-based. Parties proliferated, jockeying for the cabinet positions that would give them the coveted power of patronage. The two that really mattered in that earlier independence phase were Sukarno's favoured nationalist PNI and Masjumi, the nationalistic concatenation of Muslim groups. Rivalry grew between them. The trouble was that they were not even stable within themselves; Masjumi especially had the problem of bestriding urban and rural Islam, and finally lost the battle in 1952 when the traditionalist Nahdatul Ulama (Religious Scholars League), powerful in the villages of Java, withdrew from it, objecting to the modernist sentiments of its 'socialistic' leaders. Thenceforth no-one could pretend to speak for Indonesian Islam as a whole.

Yet Islam, like nationalism, then as now, although never a monolithic force, was one of the fundamental elements in the Indonesian power spectrum. Others were the Marxist left, the army, the civilian bureaucracy and a multifarious tendency to separatism in the regions. Among the last was the campaign of Darul Islam (House of Islam) in West Java. From the moment of Indonesia's independence in 1949 into the early 1960s this body of militant zealots deployed its army in support of a self-proclaimed Islamic State of Indonesia.

Witnessing its persistent dissidence from his ideals of inter-religious tolerance, notwithstanding the care he had taken to give it a prominent place in his Pancasila philosophy, Sukarno began to view Islam as a threat to national unity. But equally he recognised the danger posed by doctrinal socialism. Although the mainstream communist party, the PKI, was badly mauled in the Madiun affair and was thus not a factor in the early post-independence governments, it remained a disciplined body and a new generation of well-indoctrinated leaders was already burgeoning: D.N. Aidit, the future chairman, Njoto, Sudisman and M.H. Lukman – all destined to figure prominently and suffer in the story of Indonesia. They castigated both Sukarno and Hatta for their wartime collaboration with the Japanese, denounced Hatta's round-table agreement with the Dutch as a capitulation and dubbed their followers lackeys of American imperialism. The PKI had deep roots which it was able to cultivate anew; it worked to foster support among the Central Javanese peasantry and in both the plantation industries and the new urban industries, where its labour federation, SOBSI (the Central all-Indonesian Workers' Organization), soon accumulated a mass following.

The PKI had a Marxist rival, the Partai Murba (Proletarian Party). Founded in 1948 shortly after the suppression of the PKI revolt at Madiun, it rallied followers of the former PKI leader, Tan Malaka, and described itself as a Marxist-Leninist, national-communist party. Its credentials for doing so were strong, many of its adherents having led mass organizations during the Japanese occupation and fought with their feet in the mud during the revolutionary struggle. Its economic policies were radical – collectivisation and/or nationalization of key economic assets such as minerals, transport facilities and of course Dutch properties and plantations. Adam Malik, the first foreign minister in the Suharto régime of the late 1960s, belonged to Murba, and there was to be more than a hint of American collusion in sustaining it as a counter-force to the PKI.

Also prone to describe itself as Marxist but less doctrinaire in its approach to the pressing political and economic problems of the era, there was a small but intellectually influential Socialist Party (PSI) led by former prime minister Sutan Sjahrir. It was a primarily urban party with its strongholds in the army and the upper reaches of the bureaucracy, where it was a serious rival to the PNI. Concerned more with good administration than with national psyche, the PSI reflected its leader's disaffection from Sukarno, largely on the pretext of his collaboration with the Japanese.

The interaction between the army and politics, and increasingly the animosity between the military and the politicians, sprang from the roots of Indonesia's life as an independent nation. In the very nature of the war that had to be fought to disempower the Dutch the assortment of forces engaged in the armed struggle between 1945 and 1949 could properly be described as a people's army. The army could in a real sense claim to be the embodiment of the revolution.

Its strength in 1950 was estimated at around 200,000, of which the largest bloc, some 35,000, were members of the Japanese-raised self-defence force PETA. Many others belonged to former guerrilla units adhering to a variety of local leaders who had been awarded senior rank in return for their loyalty to the national cause. Others, though few officers, had served in the Netherlands Indies Army (KNIL); one such was the impenetrable, ambitious and intensely political Abdul Haris Nasution. The different traditions did not blend well, as was demonstrated by demands from PETA stalwarts that Nasution should be dismissed.

Dr Muhammed Hatta had started the necessary task of rationalizing and homogenising the army even before the independence treaties were signed. It was a controversial and painful process. Thousands of veterans were demobilized; many regional warlords were divested of the rank they had enjoyed during the revolutionary conflict.

Amidst embittered confusion two trends gradually crystallized: civilian parliamentarians were drawn into the various controversies, sharpening the rivalry between military and civil, and the army fell into factions, each with its own political agenda. The triumvirate of top defence leaders, which included Nasution and the Sultan of Yogyakarta who was defence minister, had great difficulty controlling the armed forces; Nasution especially grew impatient with the factional rivalry among the political parties. Recognising the seriousness of the situation parliament attempted to impose order by voting to set up a commission to study and report, but the voting was confused and the exercise further aggravated the military.

Nasution meanwhile was preparing his first attempt to manipulate President Sukarno into becoming the figurehead leader of, in effect, a military junta. On 17 October 1952, the day after the parliamentary vote, some thousands of demonstrators, blatantly mustered by sections of the army, marched first to parliament and then to the presidential palace demanding the dissolution of parliament. Although Sukarno was himself losing patience with the anarchic parliamentary process, he rejected the officers' demands and instead consulted his vice-president, prime minister and parliamentary speaker.

The October 17 affair, as it inevitably came to be known, was an omen of military behaviour to come, a warning to Sukarno of the danger an unbridled army might pose, yet at the same time its failure was a demonstration of the authority his own status as a national symbol conferred on him. Aspirants to political power would always want him on their side.

No review of the elements of power in post-independence Indonesia would be adequate without reference to the bureaucracy. Government was the biggest employer of educated people and as such bestowed both status and economic security. Herbert Feith, the veteran Australian scholar of Indonesian affairs, wrote:

> To be a government servant in 1950 was not only a matter of high prestige, as it had been all the century. It was seen as being literally in the service of the nation, as being part of the spearhead of national progress . . . Government had long been the great provider and protector. Now it was also the great leader. To be employed as its servant, civil or military, was to share in this leadership rôle. It was to be close to the sacred symbols of nation and nationality.[6]

Most business activity was dependent on the favourable application of rules and regulations by bureaucrats who thus wielded great coercive influence. The same went for a multitude of voluntary social organizations which relied on the bureaucracy for consent and often for subsidy. Add the blurring of borders between bureaucracy and political parties and you have a system vulnerable to the perversion and corruption which quickly took hold of public and economic life.

The bureaucracy was and is still many times larger than all the armed services. Its single disadvantage in comparison with the army is that it is not armed. Which is not to imply systematic rivalry between the two constituencies; on the contrary, as time went on, and particularly after the nationalization of Dutch enterprises in the late 1950s when some four thousand army officers moved in on their management, they tended to overlap and coalesce, corroborating Feith's allusion to public servants 'civil or military'.

President Sukarno tried to avoid alignment with any of the contending forces in the nation's political life. He strove always to defuse or counterbalance the power-hungry instincts of, for instance, the Javanese and of institutional Islam. He would have preferred a single movement rallying all tendencies to the national cause but, given the situation as it was, he acknowledged the equal right of all parties to play their part in public life. This, of course, included the communists, reduced after the Madiun débacle to a membership of fewer than eight thousand. Preoccupied with their own recuperation, they attenuated their policies and public positions and worked to give themselves a more nationalistic image by drawing closer to the PNI and to Sukarno himself – and greatly harmed both in the process. At the time they seemed of small importance except to the US Central Intelligence Agency, quietly watching.

As successive governments lost control of the economy in the post-Korean war slump and put off promised general elections, Sukarno spoke of a loss of national will-power. Indonesia needed to recapture the revolutionary spirit that had won it independence. Every nation, he once observed, needed an enemy. And at this moment of national floundering a new – though in fact old – enemy came on stage as it became obvious that, instead of observing its treaty obligation to negotiate the transfer of sovereignty in West New Guinea (now West Papua) within a year, the government of the Netherlands intended to hold on. For several years the USA, while pretending to support the United Nations position on this, furtively gave the Dutch moral support, not wishing to compromise the new cold war structure that was being pieced together in the North Atlantic.

Here, Sukarno argued, was the old colonialism in a new guise. 'NEKOLIM' he called it in one of his famous neologisms, 'neo-colonialism and imperialism'. It was the common cause he needed to rally the feuding parties; the PNI and PKI especially took up the cry. No less important, the issue of West Irian, as it was then called, was a useful preoccupation for an army that was actively learning and applying the lessons of the divisive October 17 affair.

As Sukarno steadily strengthened his position in public esteem, devotees of multi-party democracy weakened theirs by mishandling the parlous economy – twice failing to strike an annual budget – and repeatedly delaying the Republic's first general elections. Several reasons have been adduced. Many MPs owed their seats to the special circumstances of the transition to independence and could not expect to be re-elected. Local and princely leaders from pre-independence times who had already seen their positions threatened by the new dispensation feared the further evolution of the political scene that an election campaign would inevitably cause. The outer regions, over-represented under the independence constitution, would be weakened, while Javanese representation would grow in the election. On the other hand, there were those who were wary of an expected swing in favour of the Islamic parties. All the same, an election bill was at last enacted and the newly independent nation prepared for its first general election in September 1955.

Two important things happened in the months and weeks preceding it: the Bandung conference of non-aligned nations and President Sukarno's 1955 Independence Day speech. By assembling the leaders of twenty-nine African and Asian powers, including India and China, the unexpectedly successful Bandung conference brought Indonesia – and Sukarno especially – into unprecedented prominence as a standard bearer of non-alignment in a world increasingly riven by cold war politics. It also saw the fruition of diplomatic efforts to improve relations between China and Indonesia.

For the USA, currently paranoid with the anti-communist obsession of the Dulles brothers (Secretary of State John Foster and CIA chief Allen), Bandung was proof that Sukarno was leading Indonesia into the arms of the Chinese Communist Party. For Sukarno it was a triumph nicely timed to embellish his domestic leadership status at a moment when, thanks to economic drift and conspicuous corruption, the faith of the political public in party politics was wavering. He devoted a large part of his Independence Day speech to a trenchant critique of parliamentary democracy, a theme he was to develop with redoubled energy after the election.

The results of the long-awaited election merely demonstrated how evenly the political spectrum was divided between Muslim and non-Muslim parties and promised nothing but further muddle and weak government. The unexpectedly diminished Masjumi, in spite of receiving American financial support, got only twenty-one per cent of the votes; the Nahdatul Ulama which had defected from it got eighteeen per cent. The nationalist PNI won twenty-two per cent and the resurgent communists sixteen.

The election fortified Sukarno's position by weakening Masjumi, which was hostile towards him, and leaving the PNI and PKI, which supported his views, relatively strong. Reinforced by this knowledge and still riding the wave started by the Bandung conference, Sukarno toured the country preaching his philosophy of Pancasila and laying the groundwork for his alternative to multi-party democracy. 'In western countries', he said, 'there is no economic democracy; we use the concept of guided economy. So why not speak of guided democracy . . . leadership that suits our situation?'

Meanwhile, the army, in disarray over its political rôle, continued in ferment. Some regional commanders who had been encouraged by the Americans to see the result of the Bandung conference as the start of a slide into communism now saw the post-election confusion as a pretext for separatist ambitions. Before 1956 was out colonels in West, North and South Sumatra and northern Sulawesi (a centre of military smuggling) had attempted to take over the administration in their local provinces.

Nasution, however, himself a Sumatran, now a general and back in post as Army Chief of Staff, was pressing ahead with his old ambition of forming an alliance between the army and the president. Sukarno was not averse.

In October 1956, back from overseas travels which further enhanced his personal standing, Sukarno started campaigning in earnest for guided democracy and the president's pre-eminent leadership role within it. In the Indonesian context, he argued, minuscule parliamentary majorities which might be acceptable in a Western democracy were damaging and divisive. 'My dream is that party leaders should deliberate with one another and then decide, "let's bury all the parties"'. Later he drew back from that radical threat to the parties, but only to ease the passage of an even more innovative feature of his presidential concept – the creation of a National Council comprising functional groups: religious bodies, youth and women's organizations, peasants, workers, big business and, yes, the armed services.

To lead the nation's refashioned democratic institutions he wanted a mutual help (*gotong royong*) cabinet representing all major parties including the communists and above that, of course, the president. Vice-President Muhammad Hatta, Sumatran, practical administrator, other half of the duo that had held Indonesia together hitherto, grew steadily more dissatisfied with the trend of the political debate. In 1956, as military commanders in Sumatra were making their bids for some kind of local autonomy, Hatta washed his hands of Sukarno by announcing his resignation. It was a gesture full of portent for the future course of events.

The next move by the ever cautious Sukarno was to convene a conference of nine hundred political and other leaders to whom he made a formal and detailed presentation of his concept, asking them to consider his plan and react within a week. Only the PNI and the PKI liked it. The others were opposed, none more robustly than the Muslim Masjumi, strong in Sumatra.

Most of the territorial military commanders also disliked it. Within less than two weeks the commander in Sulawesi had promulgated a state of war and siege and the one in South Sumatra had firmed up the effective military takeover of three months earlier.

General Nasution had been working quietly for a reconciliation between central government and the territorial commands. He now finessed them all by recommending Sukarno to declare a state of war throughout the whole of the Republic. At a single stroke – for Sukarno agreed – the various military coups in Sumatra and Sulawesi were legalized, civil administration passed under army control and a new partnership was born: the army Chief of Staff, General Nasution, and the army Commander-in-Chief, President Sukarno.

One political drama led to another. Sukarno kept his profile high by harping on the West Irian issue and threatening economic reprisals against the Dutch if it were not resolved to Indonesia's satisfaction. Then in November 1957 he was the target of the first of five unsuccessful assassination attempts. The year ended with the threatened economic measures against the Dutch, banks, businesses and estates taken over bloodlessly – mainly by the army – and a mass exodus of Dutch nationals.

As the new year broke, the flame of rebellion in Sumatra began to burn higher. A formidable group of Sukarno's critics came together in Padang on the west coast to confer with the military commanders who had usurped the administration of their areas in Sumatra and Sulawesi. Among them were former prime ministers, the governor of the national bank and the highly influential Professor Sumitro Djojohadikusumo, the Berkeley-educated professor of economics at the University of Indonesia upon whom the Americans reposed their hopes of promoting acceptable economic management. In due course the group broadcast an ultimatum calling on the government to resign in favour of a new cabinet headed by Dr Hatta and the Sultan of Yogyakarta; five days later, when the ultimatum was ignored, the group announced the formation of the 'revolutionary government of the Republic of Indonesia'. The coup failed, notwithstanding substantial military support from the USA, as a result of serious miscalculation and because General Nasution stood firm by Sukarno.

While the Sumatra rebellion rumbled on, politicians in Jakarta tangled in a tortuous debate about the constitution in which the key issue was whether or not to accept Sukarno's idea of re-introducing the 1945 constitution. When at last it came to a vote in 1959, the motion failed to achieve the necessary two-thirds majority. In Sukarno's absence abroad, Nasution acted instantly; as chairman of the Supreme War Authority governing the state of emergency, he banned all political activity and called on the president to promulgate the 1945 constitution by decree. On his return to Jakarta Sukarno followed Nasution's advice, dissolved the constituent assembly and issued his decree.

Thus ended the era of parliamentary democracy. 'Guided democracy' took its place and, together with the 1945 constitution, was to remain the order of the day throughout the rest of Sukarno's and his successor's terms of office.

OUT INTO THE COLD

Indonesia's unsteady emergence into effective independence in the period from 1945 to 1950 was not an isolated event. Western colonial régimes tottered and fell like dominoes; the Philippines achieved independence from the USA in 1946, India and Pakistan from Great Britain in 1947 and Burma in 1948.

In the paroxysm of war the European imperial powers and Japan, following broadly the predictions of Karl Marx, had driven themselves to exhaustion. In Asian eyes, notwithstanding their final victory, they had been shown not to be immune from defeat. Sooner in Britain, later in France, Portugal and the Netherlands, it was acknowledged that the brand of imperialism born in the nineteenth century was unsustainable.

This did not imply abandoning secure access to South-East Asia's, and especially Indonesia's, huge raw material resources, bearing in mind the competing economic ambitions of the Soviet Union and its satellites. The question was how to maintain capitalist control of the South-East Asian mercantile economy; Western political strategists were no less doctrinal in their approach to the problem than were their Soviet protagonists. Britain and the USA came early to the view that the framework most conducive to preserving their interests – and the easiest to achieve and influence – would be economic collaboration with politically independent nations. The requirements of trade, investment and relevant skills would yield interdependence.

France, with its stake in Indochina, and the Netherlands in Indonesia saw things differently. Both were recovering from the humiliation of wartime invasion. Both regarded their dependencies as parts of their territory rather than colonies. Both needed the income they had been used to derive from those colonies. Their instinct was to hold on, conceding minimal political advances, as they had been doing since the early years of the century.

The circumstances of the Dutch re-entry into Indonesia after the war did not favour their aspirations. Their rearguard action was fought in the face of a hostile international tide. Not only had the Japanese given rein to

Indonesian nationalist sentiment during their occupation, it was plainly understood in the Hague that the British, whose armed forces reoccupied the country, wanted Indonesia to advance towards independence. In 1948, the year of tumbling colonial dominoes, Soviet spokesmen at the Calcutta conference urged colonial peoples everywhere to throw off their oppressors. Communist insurrections forthwith erupted in Burma, the Philippines, Malaya and around the East Javanese city of Madiun.

On the other side of the cold war confrontation then taking shape, the USA, starved of intelligence about Indonesia thanks to MacArthur's negligence, was floundering in ignorance of the strength of national feeling and knew nothing about the party political scene in the country.

Its primary interest in Asia was the rehabilitation of Japan and to the extent that it had any attitude towards Indonesia it was merely a local application of its fast-fading and, in all senses of the word, sentimental anti-colonialism. It had, on the other hand, emerged from the war with an enhanced appreciation of the value of Indonesian rubber, metals, oil and timber; but there was a flabby assumption that it could be left to others – Japan, the Netherlands, even Britain – to find the right way of keeping them within the capitalist system. Above all, America's attention was focussed on Europe where Marshall Aid had become an important instrument of persuasion and preparations were afoot for the inauguration in 1949 of the North Atlantic Treaty Organization, NATO, of which the Netherlands would be a member.

Broadly, then, the American post-war policy began by being non-interventionist, holding up a public façade of anti-colonialism and quietly nudging the Dutch along hoping they would contrive to maintain a sufficient presence to stabilize both the economic and the political situation.

After the events of 1948 that policy was increasingly questioned. The accession to power of the Chinese Communist Party in 1949 cast an urgent new light on the east and south-east Asian strategic landscape. Perceiving a communist threat to Japan and to the archipelago in which it must find resources and a large part of its market, the Americans now thought in terms of securing the east Asian island chain running all the way southward from Japan, through Taiwan, the Philippines and Indonesia to Australia. In the State Department voices which were formerly ignored when they called for greater pressure on the Dutch now made themselves heard advising more sympathetic attention to Indonesian nationalist sentiment as a means of keeping Soviet influence out.

No longer were the Dutch regarded as guarantors of American interests in the area; indeed their behaviour in Indonesia was stigmatised as the principal threat to the Western position there. Writing to the US Ambassador to the United Nations in December 1948, the then Director of the Office of UN Affairs, Dean Rusk, said the USA must avoid association with colonial rule and project an image to Asians of American interest in *self-rule*. This doubtless lay behind the Ambassador surprising the Security Council a few weeks later with the assertion that the Indonesian Republic was 'the heart of Indonesian nationalism'.

It was at this juncture that the Dutch, bent on crushing that very Republic, launched their attack against Yogyakarta and captured President Sukarno. This second so-called police action triggered the final failure of Dutch policy in Indonesia and spelled the end of the USA's low profile tactics. Friendly countries all the way from India to Australia closed their ports and airports to Dutch military traffic. The USA openly rebuked the Netherlands in the United Nations and the Security Council ordered the Dutch force to cease fire and withdraw. They refused.

Acting in the spirit of a radical policy review, the USA, although restrained at first by Britain and France, finally threatened to withhold both economic and military aid; only then did the Dutch government capitulate. Between August and November 1949 the round-table conference in the Hague worked out terms for the transfer of sovereignty. In December 1949 Dr Muhammad Hatta, as head of delegation, accepted the freedom of the Federal Republic of the United States of Indonesia. Within eight months the Indonesians repudiated the federal arrangement and incorporated all the former Netherlands East Indies territories into a unitary Republic.

With one exception. The status of West Irian, the western half of the huge island of New Guinea now known as West Papua, was left for resolution at the end of another year. In fact, thirteen tortured years were to pass before the Dutch let go. Their argument in behind-the-scenes discussion with the Americans stemmed from domestic political considerations, although they had already identified the massive mineral resources that were at stake; they said they needed a sop to public opinion if they were to raise the necessary two-thirds parliamentary majority for the constitutional amendment ceding sovereignty over their former territories to Indonesia. The Americans and Australians, acknowledging this problem of Dutch self-esteem, persuaded the Indonesians reluctantly to concede.

The result was that the US State Department was furnished with a new issue over which to vacillate in dealings with Indonesia, perhaps little realizing how major it would become in Sukarno's thinking – no less major, in fact, than their own doctrinal anti-communism during the Eisenhower and Dulles era that was soon to begin.

The lines of American thinking in Asia were, nevertheless, becoming clearer. In 1950, hard upon the communist accession to power in China, came the start of the Korean war. The USA and its allies, including Australia and the Netherlands, engaged in a bloody conflict against a communist army. The Europeanists in the State Department no longer had everything their own way. Asia had to be taken seriously.

All the same, Indonesia, now independent and, as they supposed, grateful to the USA for having helped it along the way, relapsed into a lower priority. The Americans awarded a niggardly aid package – $5 million – and left the Indonesian government to revel in the commodity price boom that quickly grew out of the Korean war; at that time about a third of US tin and rubber imports originated in Indonesia. The State Department took it almost for granted that Indonesia would concur with their plan for an anti-communist defence pact.

Both assumptions were wrong. The war boom concealed dire economic problems; the treasury, burdened with debts transferred from the Dutch administration, was bare, exports were at half their pre-war level, fundamental cash flows were still at the mercy of foreign-owned estates. As to the ideological confrontation with China, Indonesia opted for an 'active and independent' foreign policy, in other words a sort of neutralism. President Sukarno did discreetly convey a promise of stability and, in a broad sense, alignment with the West in return for support on the West Irian question, but when it came up again for negotiation in 1950 the State Department chose publicly to stay out of it and privately notified the Dutch it would prefer a long-term Netherlands trusteeship under the United Nations.

Yet again the USA was vacillating. To make matters worse, a mission was sent to Jakarta to prepare the way for the hoped-for defence pact. When the Indonesian government stated a preference for outright arms purchases rather than deals which might compromise them with the PKI, the American mission-leader haughtily announced that the USA would not tolerate this vacillation. Later there was tension over the small non-military aid package, with the Americans insisting they were obliged to administer it while President Sukarno demanded 'aid without strings'.

And yet, by dint of secret, sensitive and painstaking negotiation the first American Ambassador in Jakarta, Merle Cochran, very nearly did clinch a comprehensive aid agreement in 1952 in which Foreign Minister Subardjo was ready to accept a condition that Indonesia would 'make a full contribution . . . to the defensive strength of the free world'. As soon as they heard of it the PNI and Masjumi partners in the government renounced it and the government fell as a result, plunging US-Indonesia relations into temporary crisis.

A detailed and probably definitive account of how American policy towards Indonesia evolved over the next ten years is given in a thesis completed in 1999 by a British scholar, Dr Andrew Roadnight. Relying mainly on American official documents now publicly available, he demonstrates that to the exclusion of all else, cold war priorities formed the basis of US policies towards Indonesia and that this translated into an overweening concern to secure access to its raw material resources and protect them against subversion.

When President Harry Truman came to the end of his second term in office he was succeeded in January 1953 by the former wartime general Dwight Eisenhower. Senator Joseph McCarthy's frenetic witch-hunt against 'un-American activities' was in full cry; American public opinion was being whipped into an anti-communist hysteria. In this climate Eisenhower appointed as his Secretary of State John Foster Dulles who, for the next six years, was to conduct foreign policy with a rare disregard of advice discrepant from his own perceptions. His brother Allen, whose counsel he did usually accept, was made head of the Central Intelligence Agency (CIA) at the same time.

Cochran, the ambassador in Jakarta who was beginning to have some grasp of the nuances of Indonesian politics, was replaced by Hugh Cumming. John Allison, who argued in favour of the Indonesian claim to West Irian on the ground that it would inevitably prevail in the end, left office as Assistant Secretary for Far Eastern Affairs. Differences between the few in the State Department who knew about Indonesia and those who did not but thought they knew what was best for it became polarised.

There was a short-lived respite when Vice-President Richard Nixon went to Jakarta to talk to President Sukarno. Roadnight quotes him as calling the Indonesian leader 'our main card . . . a good card, a strong card because he is a strong man'. There was talk of issuing a much desired invitation to Sukarno to visit Washington. Unhappily, though, Nixon had fouled his own nest in Jakarta by harping on about a Pacific pact.

Meanwhile the PKI used the USA's feigned neutrality on the West Irian issue as an opportunity to reinforce its image as an essentially nationalist party. American policy was helping to promote the very force it meant to weaken.

The Dulles mafia, professing to see 'leftists' in almost every cranny of the political scene, began towards the end of 1954 to worry about elections due the following September. Zest was added to their anxieties with the announcement that Indonesia was to host a Conference of the Non-aligned Movement – the great Bandung Conference of April 1955. They began, on a basis of stupefying ignorance, to take sides in the local political scene. Their fancy, and not a little of their money, inclined towards Masjumi, the predominantly middle class Muslim coalition formed during the Japanese occupation.

Simultaneously, the US Secretary of Defense, Charles Wilson, secured the agreement of the National Security Council '. . . to employ all feasible covert and all feasible overt means, *including the use of armed force* [my italics] if necessary and appropriate, [to prevent Indonesia] or vital parts thereof from falling to communism'. As Roadnight points out, despite Ambassador Cumming's reports that the situation was manageable, the NSC opted in effect to categorize the Indonesian government as unfriendly and decided to authorise the use of extreme measures to prevent Indonesia from going communist. Secret planning for possible overt intervention against the PKI began at about the same time under cover of the ANZUS (Australia, New Zealand, USA) treaty.

Nevertheless, thanks largely to British persuasion, Dulles kept a level head over the Bandung conference. Everyone exploited it as a propaganda opportunity and, from the Western perspective, it produced the satisfactory result of buttressing a view of communism as a new form of colonialism. By giving prominence and respectability to the idea of neutrality in cold war politics it did, however, represent a head-on challenge to the Dulles doctrine.

A revised policy document was adopted by the National Security Council just weeks after the Bandung conference. While acknowledging a perception of reduced risk, it still allowed wider scope to take covert and overt action, together with allies in the newly formed Southeast Asia Treaty Organization (SEATO), 'as appropriate'. Resolving to promote the election of governments which would not be dependent on the PKI – of which there had been none so far – the NSC, says Roadnight, decided that it would forge closer links with the Indonesian military and police forces by providing them with equipment and training and by ensuring that the West was the 'principal source' of matériel to both.

All this marked a momentous turning point in relations between Indonesia and the USA, knowledge of which must inevitably colour the interpretation of subsequent events. Mounting disarray among Indonesia's dozens of political parties played to the Dulles brothers' prejudices. The September 1955 elections failed to produce the Masjumi triumph the Americans had expected and felt they had paid for. Instead the biggest share of the vote went to the PNI, bastion of nationalism, the party routinely associated with Sukarno and, so far as Dulles partisans were concerned, the left.

Sukarno too was fretting over party disarray, thwarted by the limited prerogatives of his presidential office and as anxious as anyone to keep the PKI in check. Whichever way he looked there was dissatisfaction and division. The army was seething with anti-politician sentiment. Military commanders in Sumatra and Sulawesi successfully defied government attempts to curb the illicit export trade in which they were indulging to supplement inadequate central funding. Talk of imposing military rule came to nothing, only because the army itself split into two factions, the larger of which was headed by the army chief, General Nasution, the President's man.

Faced with such turmoil, Sukarno chose to continue his 'Pancasila' theme, demanding an end to the Western-style party system in favour of what he called 'guided democracy', or 'leadership suited to the situation'. In October, he chose a gathering of youth delegates to deliver a key speech about 'the very great mistake in 1945, when we urged the establishment of parties'. The Americans, who had their own stake in the Indonesian party scene, were deeply unhappy. Sukarno's game plan was clearly to accommodate the many rival tendencies in Indonesian political thought by building them into one centrally-managed structure – and that meant including the communists.

Unyielding rehearsals of their respective positions formed the grist of discussions during a one-day stop in Jakarta by Dulles and then a visit to Washington by Sukarno in 1956. Dulles chanted his mantra about the immorality of neutrality; Sukarno appealed for US support over West Irian and asked for more aid. Neither got what he wanted. Indeed, a suggested $35 million aid package was pared down to $15 million later in the year as a mark of displeasure at the success of two profitable state visits by the Indonesian president to China and the Soviet Union.

In November 1956 came Dr Hatta's announcement that he would quit the vice-presidency before the end of the year, thus dismantling the unifying duumvirate in which he was seen as the embodiment of non-Javanese

Indonesia and Sukarno as the embodiment of Java. Everyone knew his reason for going was his loss of patience with the gathering momentum of Sukarno's assault on liberal democracy.

By the end of 1956, Roadnight writes, the CIA had become actively involved in the implementation of what had become the Administration's very personalized opposition to Sukarno. In November, Frank Wisner, the CIA's Deputy Director Plans, signalled the beginning of eighteen months of undercover operations against Sukarno when he told Al Ulmer, the chief of the CIA's Far Eastern office, that 'it's time we held Sukarno's feet to the fire'. This new phase in the build-up of US intervention in Indonesia was accompanied by a purposeful programme of persuasion to ensure that the British and Australian governments were on-side – a vital precaution for practical as well as political reasons, since Singapore was where the Americans had their contacts with the rebellious Indonesian colonels who were about to break loose.

The stage was now set for one of the CIA's more spectacular fiascos. The opening scenes were played in Sumatra. A reunion of several hundred officers who had fought in the revolution assembled in a somewhat agitated mood and came out with a set of demands, including the immediate implementation of progressive and radical improvements in all fields, especially in the leadership of the army and also in the leadership of the state. Days later a specially summoned meeting at the Army Staff and Command School at Bandung in Java called for comprehensive change in the make-up of functionaries in the army leadership. Clearly they had Nasution in their sights. Then on 20 December, a Lieutenant-Colonel Ahmad Husein, military commander in West Sumatra, took over the government of the province of Central Sumatra from the seemingly compliant civilian governor, who just happened to be a member of Masjumi. Two days later, the military commander in North Sumatra, Colonel Simbolon, a prince among smugglers, tried to do likewise in Medan but was quickly thwarted by a series of well-calculated military moves by Nasution, who obviously had foreknowledge of what was afoot.

Nevertheless, as time passed, similar challenges to the central government erupted in many parts of the country. Two more colonels made their move in March: Sumual in East Indonesia and Barlian in South Sumatra. All made the same demands: the return of Hatta and a range of reforms. At no stage did they represent their movement as being aimed against the communists.

On Nasution's recommendation Sukarno responded by declaring a state of war and siege throughout the Republic. The rebellious colonels were out-manoeuvred, but it was in effect the death-knell of liberal democracy: the political parties were incapacitated; the army, under President Sukarno, was now in charge everywhere.

But the contest went on and by the end of 1957 there was full-scale rebellion in Sumatra and Sulawesi. The Dulles brothers were delighted, John remarking disingenuously that if the movement had not happened it would have been necessary to promote it. Favouring autonomous regions and a weak central government, he and his brother Allen encouraged renewed thinking about the possible break-up of the unitary republic, contrary to expert advice that even the rebels would not rally to such a cause. In spite of all this the NSC initiated a flow of money and arms to the rebels.

Their position hardened further when, in response to a United Nations rejection of Indonesia's claim to West Irian, the remaining 40,000 Dutch were expelled and more than 500 Dutch enterprises expropriated. The Dulles brothers wanted Sukarno overthrown, with back-up by American land forces if necessary. At their instance Eisenhower moved a naval force out of Philippine and into Indonesian waters ready for any contingency. Forces of a different kind, known as the Padang group, assembled in Sumatra: a prominent US-educated economist, a former governor of the Bank of Indonesia, former prime ministers, one of them the chairman of Masjumi, and others.

In February 1958 Allen Dulles, the CIA chief, notified Eisenhower that the rebellious colonels were about to put an ultimatum to the Indonesian government demanding a national government headed by Hatta and the Sultan of Yogyakarta. A satisfactory outcome, he advised, would make it feasible to mount guerrilla activity in Java with the expectation of support in Sumatra and Sulawesi. The ultimatum was duly presented but his judgement about what would follow, in this as in his misperception of the whole affair, was wrong. The government, headed by Dr Djuanda, a non-party man, and supported by Nasution, did not agree to resign; army leaders did not rally to the support of the colonels; negotiations did not ensue.

Neither did Dulles desist from his conspiracy. Immediately after the ultimatum he went public with a press conference. Describing the rebels as 'anti-communist' – which was true but hardly relevant – he supported their cause, denounced Sukarno's ideas about guided democracy and professed a deep desire for 'constitutional democracy' in Indonesia. Everyone else knew that Hatta, Nasution, Djuanda, even Sukarno himself were looking for compromise; Dulles refused to take cognizance of it.

Four days later the rebels formed their own government in Padang on the west coast of Sumatra. It came to be known by its initials PRRI (Revolutionary Government of the Republic of Indonesia). They took up arms and set about consolidating their authority around the Sumatran oil installations and in major cities. Nasution acted decisively. In a series of surprise attacks the Indonesian army struck hard at a number of rebel strongholds, regaining control of them and making other sweeping gains before the US navy could move in on the pretext of protecting American lives.

One might have thought that the unambiguous defeat of the Sumatra rebels – for that was what it was – would have brought Dulles's military adventure to a halt. It was not as if better informed and more cautious advice was not reaching his ears. In addition to State Department specialists, indignant at being overlooked in favour of their CIA rivals, successive ambassadors, eventually including even the hard-line, pro-CIA Howard Jones, who was there at the time of the disaster, warned the Secretary of State that he was acting in ignorance of political realities. Jones in particular came to realize and report that Nasution was the strongest anti-communist force in the country.

Yet the Dulles brothers soldiered on. CIA war-planes were sent from Clark air force base in the Philippines to the island of Sulawesi. For several weeks they flew bombing missions, denied by US spokesmen, which helped the rebels to make small and temporary gains, until in May 1958 Indonesian forces struck again. They recaptured a few islands and destroyed five American aircraft at Manado on the northernmost tip of Sulawesi, revealing remarkably detailed knowledge about the presence there of American, Taiwanese and Filipino pilots. Dulles, with characteristic courage, assigned to one of his deputies the privilege of repeating the lie that US forces were not involved. His reward was the shooting down almost immediately thereafter of an American B-26 bomber over the East Indonesian island of Seram and the capture of its CIA pilot.

Andrew Roadnight in his 1999 thesis concludes:

The swift defeat of the Sumatran revolt revealed the extent of Washington's failure to analyse correctly virtually every aspect of the situation. In the first place, policy-makers did not treat seriously the possibility that Jakarta would take a tough line with the rebels . . . The

Sumatran revolt was also linked with the struggle to recover West Irian for, unless Jakarta could assert its sovereignty over its own rebellious provinces, Sukarno could hardly exert a serious military threat against the Dutch . . . Dulles failed even to understand the effect of the rebellion on the PKI . . . Once the rebellion had begun the PKI was able to cloak itself in nationalist garb and gain prestige by allying with Sukarno, Nasution and others opposed to the rebels. The further adjustment of US policy which necessarily followed the bungled intervention in Sumatra and Sulawesi by no means spelled abandonment of its underlying focus or philosophy . . . The Dulles brothers still wanted to bring the Indonesian leader down and maintained their anti-communist obsession, here as elsewhere in the world. The question in their minds was not how best to manage Indonesia's intricate political jigsaw, but more simply how to isolate and suppress the Indonesian Communist Party (PKI) at any cost.

In terms of power the events of 1958 left behind a simplified and more focussed structure, with Sukarno, the PKI and the army as its salient points. Picking over the ruin of its failed policy, and exasperated by Sukarno's determination to press ahead with his guided democracy concept, Washington accepted the judgement of ambassador Howard Jones that the Indonesian army would be its best ally against the PKI. Four short months later, the Americans delivered fifteen large arms shipments; no heavy weapons were included, but there were enough small arms to equip twenty-one Indonesian battalions.

From that moment may be dated the syncretistic relationship that developed, sometimes slowly, sometimes by leaps, between successive US administrations and factions within the Indonesian army. Years later, Nasution revealed how detailed and intimate the sharing of ideas became when he recounted in an interview with the *Straits Times* how he had talked to General Maxwell Taylor in the late 1950s about putting military pay and allowances on a realistic basis and equipping the army for the 'civic mission business'.[7]

It was a relationship that survived periods of sharp disagreement between US ambassadors on the ground and the NSC and fluctuating assessments concerning the reliability of General Nasution.

Sukarno's ingenious efforts to build a political structure that would hold the PKI visibly in place without either sending it dangerously underground or precipitating an open challenge to the government perplexed the

Americans and ultimately exhausted their patience. Their instinct was to draw the communists into open conflict and hit them hard – or preferably to get the Indonesian army to hit them hard

Such was the sentiment behind an assurance communicated to General Nasution when he visited Washington in September 1960 for talks with the US State and Defense Departments and unearthed by Andrew Roadnight in the course of his researches. In a declassifed preparatory memo, marked secret, Graham Parsons, who was Assistant Secretary of State for Far East Affairs at the time, proposed that since army leaders had banned communist activities in parts of Indonesia, it was possible that the situation might result in a final confrontation between the army and Sukarno on the communist issue. He added: 'we believe that before Nasution would act, he would want assurances from us that we would support him if he found himself in need of military or economic aid in a struggle to reduce the influence of the Communists in Indonesia and eliminate Sukarno as an effective force in the country'.

On that premise, Parsons sought and obtained authority to tell Nasution that: 'we are aware of and heartened by recent actions which the Army has taken to curb Communist power. . . . We know from our experience elsewhere that sometimes when there is strong opposition to a strong Communist party in a given country there can be a showdown . . . If American help is wanted in the form of military or economic assistance, the United States in such circumstances does its best to be helpful and quickly . . . We would like General Nasution to feel that the United States would wish to be helpful to Indonesia too in such circumstances.'

In a handwritten note recording a subsequent conversation with the Defense Secretary, William Gates, on the basis of his memo, Parsons said: 'Mr Gates expressed full agreement with this line and asked if he should say anything. I said that would be helpful . . .'[8]

It is hard not to see that démarche as an incitement to what in fact happened five years later in an episode of coup and counter-coup allegedly provoked by the PKI.

## Notes

1 'Nationalism, Islam and Marxism' in the journal *Indonesia Muda*, 1926.
2 *Sukarno, An Autobiography*, as told to Cindy Adams (Bobbs-Merrill Co. Inc, 1965).
3 Benda, H.J. *The Crescent and the Rising Sun*, 's-Gravenhage, 1958.

4 Dennis, Peter, *Troubled Days of Peace: Mountbatten and South East Asia Command 1945–46*, Manchester University Press, 1987.
5 Roadnight, Andrew, *Sleeping with the Enemy: Britain, Japanese Troops and the Netherlands East Indies, 1945–1946*. Unpublished paper, 1999.
6 Feith, Herbert, *The Decline of Constitutional Democracy in Indonesia*, Ithaca, Cornell University Press 1962.
7 The *Straits Times*, 30 October 1972.
8 US National Archives, RG 59 Records of DOS, Decimal File 1960–1963, Box 2204, NARA 212 and 494, located by Andrew Roadnight.

# THREE

## *Confronting the Neighbours*

The international arena in which he was now seeking to bolster Indonesia's ambivalent sense of nationhood proved to be treacherous ground for President Sukarno. On the broad scene of macro-politics both his theories and his rhetoric struck a chord. Among peoples sickened by the capitalist-communist bipolarity of the North Atlantic confrontation the appeal of non-alignment was high. But when it came to practical relationships with near neighbours, where he could neither manipulate and cajole as he did at home nor feast on global generalities, his mastery failed him and he made mistakes.

Neither the declaration of the Republic in 1945 nor the Dutch admission of Indonesian independence in 1949 had spelled the end of European imperial influence in the Malay Archipelago. Within Indonesia itself West Irian, a recognised part of its sovereign territory, remained under Dutch administration throughout the fifties, with the Netherlands showing every sign of wanting to hold on – doubtless with a view to exploiting the gold and copper deposits which have since been opened up.

Hundreds of miles to the west another remnant of European colonialism posed an equally untidy but legally different problem. The eastern half of the island of Timor was still under Portuguese rule. No-one could argue that it was part of the package inherited from the former Netherlands East Indies. Few in the early years of independence gave it much thought. Impossible to ignore, however, was the major British presence in the Malay Peninsula, Singapore and three territories in northern Borneo.

The British aim ever since the end of the Second World War had been to forge a single political unit out of the various states and protectorates of Malaya and the island of Singapore, thus to create a friendly, defensible and economically buoyant nation astride one of the world's strategic crossroads. Similarly, there had been some thought of bringing Sarawak, North Borneo and the protected sultanate of Brunei together so that they too could ultimately face the prospect of independence as one.

There were some common features in the two areas as well as important differences. Ethnically all had populations composed of indigenous races mixed with immigrants, mainly overseas Chinese; but the proportions differed. In Malaya and Brunei the Muslim Malays and their royal houses were dominant. In Singapore the great majority were Chinese. In both North Borneo (later to revert to its pre-colonial name, Sabah) and Sarawak indigenous races akin to the Malays predominated but, unlike the Malays, were not Muslim. Their economic resources and potential were similar and formed part of a mercantile system controlled from Europe. In these ways and in life-style they closely resembled nearby parts of their powerful Indonesian neighbour. The thousand-mile land frontier demarcating the northern Borneo territories from Indonesian Kalimantan was virtually meaningless to the native peoples living in the jungle through which it ran. Likewise, the Malacca Strait between Sumatra and the west coast of Malaya was more a thoroughfare than an obstacle to thousands of migrants, smugglers and fishermen, many of them close blood relatives, who regularly crossed it in small boats.

Politically, the principal difference which set the British territories apart was the experience of British rather than Dutch colonial administration. They used English as the language of government; their legal systems were founded in English law; the British officials who 'advised' their governments came from the same Whitehall ministries. A banknote issued by the Board of Commissioners Malaya and British Borneo and dated 21 March 1953 says it all: 'This note is legal tender for five dollars in the Federation of Malaya, Singapore, Sarawak, North Borneo and Brunei'.

The drive towards a comprehensive federal solution, or rather dissolution, of Britain's remaining colonial problems in South-East Asia never faltered. The constitution which brought the Federation of Malaya to independence in August 1957 included the unobtrusive but important provision that Parliament could admit other states to the federation. In neighbouring Singapore, granted self-government in January 1959, non-communist politicians had high hopes of gaining full independence by merging with Malaya. The Chief Minister at the time, Lim Yew Hock, described it as 'the prime interest of both peoples to merge into a single political unit within which, as one people with one outlook and purpose, all may share'. And when he was defeated in elections held under the new self-government constitution in May of that year, the man who succeeded him, the People's Action Party leader Lee Kuan Yew, sang the same song.

The response from the Malayan capital, Kuala Lumpur, was cool. The People's Action Party (PAP) was a classic united front, embracing communists and democratic socialists. Malaya was only just emerging from a bruising twelve-year war – the so-called Emergency – involving British forces – against a communist and mainly Chinese insurrection. For this and a deeper ethnic reason there was fear of a new communist threat, this time from Singapore. However much inter-dependent economies and the common inheritance of British colonial institutions argued in favour of merger, the Malay establishment saw that the introduction of a million and a quarter Singapore Chinese into their federation would turn the Malay majority into a minority.

What they did not at first comprehend was that Singapore's PAP government was a bastion against communism. For three years the Malayan Prime Minister, Tunku Abdul Rahman, although he personally understood Lee's predicament in Singapore, set his face against merger. Britain kept on trying to persuade him, insisting at the same time that there would be no independence for Singapore without it. The Singapore communists argued for going it alone and fighting for absolute independence. But it was the non-communists led by Lee Kuan Yew who prevailed, and the communists left the PAP to form a new front party, the Barisan Sosialis.

At the end of April 1961 an event occurred to give pause to those Malays in Malaya whose anti-Chinese sentiment had dictated Tunku Abdul Rahman's resistance to merger. A pro-communist candidate inflicted a humiliating by-election defeat on the PAP candidate in a Singapore constituency previously regarded as a party stronghold. In Kuala Lumpur the Tunku saw at once the likely implications of any further erosion of the PAP's position. Speaking a week later to the United Malays National Organization, he sounded a warning: 'There is a section of the Chinese in Singapore who do not want a good government working for the good of the people. What they want is a communist government, or a communist-oriented government'.

Shortly after, on 27 May 1961, the Tunku was guest speaker at a luncheon given by foreign correspondents in Singapore. After a wry disclaimer that he had anything important to say, he announced a policy initiative that not only reversed his previous position on merger but led to profound change in the entire Indonesian archipelago. Sooner or later, he said, Malaya should have 'an understanding with Britain and the peoples of the territories of Singapore, North Borneo, Brunei and Sarawak'.

Thus was launched the Anglo-Malayan plan for an enlarged federation, to be known as Malaysia. It was designed to serve the interests of everyone involved. Singapore would achieve its merger with Malaya. The Borneo territories would cease to be colonial dependencies. An overall majority of Malay and other indigenous people would remain, with the power to contain the Chinese minority. For Britain the Malaysia plan promised the closing of an imperial chapter without the loss of economic influence, and without compromising its military obligations to the Southeast Asia Treaty Organization (SEATO) – in short, it was an adroit evasion of the anti-imperialist tempest which Sukarno was stirring up on the international scene.

This was a key year in Sukarno's attempt to contain the communists in his own quite different way. In order to counter-balance communism – an undeniable reality in his country – with the equally undeniable realities of religion and nationalism, he concocted the composite formula known as NASAKOM. Less than a year before, he had described to the UN General Assembly his growing disaffection from the world model, as defined in European cold war terms. Now he was rampantly preaching his own conception of a world where the essential ideological conflict was between the old-established imperial forces (OLDEFO) characterised as NEKOLIM (neo-colonialism, colonialism and imperialism) and the newly emerging forces (NEFO) like Indonesia itself. The enthusiasm he aroused for this view of things was not the least of the factors behind Britain's haste to be rid of its South-East Asian colonial dependencies.

Arguably, the Malaysia plan was a pragmatic attempt to accommodate the world-view Sukarno was propagating. The involved British diplomats I spoke to were clear that, with the third world membership of the United Nations steadily growing, international opinion would require decolonisation within ten years at most. History, however, had laid a number of traps. Through the centuries, as its spotlight shifted to and fro across the archipelago, the territories earmarked for the Malaysia project had all at one time or another been part of one or other of the regional precursors of the Javanese empire currently known as Indonesia. A map in the presidential palace at Bogor showed the entire archipelago, including the Malay Peninsula, as undifferentiated Indonesian territory. And no map could disguise that, whereas nearly a thousand miles of sea separated the northern Borneo territories from Malaya, they had direct or close land frontiers with Indonesian Kalimantan.

It was only three years since the back of the separatist rebellion in Sumatra had been broken, and it rankled in Jakarta that there had been evidence of fraternal sentiment between Malaya and the Sumatran rebels. More immediate still, the Dutch were holding on grimly to West Irian; it was in this same year that President Sukarno put a promising young general, Suharto, in command of total mobilization to liberate that territory.

Even without the additional factors which were soon to come into play, it can therefore be seen that the Malaysia plan presented serious food for thought to Sukarno and his foreign minister, Dr Subandrio.

They did not react hastily. Six weeks after Tunku Abdul Rahman's first allusion to the plan, a Sarawak delegation visiting neighbouring West Kalimantan received an assurance from the provincial governor that Indonesia had no territorial claims on the north Borneo territories. Another four months passed before Foreign Minister Subandrio made any notable reference to the subject. He mentioned (during a UN debate on West Irian) that the Malayan government had informed Indonesia of its plan to incorporate the three territories into the Malaysian federation, and that he had told them Indonesia had no objection. While in part this was integral to the argument that Indonesia's West Irian claim was posited on its treaty right to take over former Dutch territories, probably it also reflected the attitude of the Soviet Union, upon which Indonesia was depending for military hardware.

In the meantime, however, the Tunku had toured the north Borneo territories spelling out his further thoughts about the future shape of the proposed federation. He met with almost unanimous opposition.

One Sunday morning following the Tunku's July visit, while I was still in Jesselton (the Sabah capital now known as Kota Kinabalu), I received a 'phone call. Donald Stephens, leader of the dominant Kadazan community and the force behind the imminent formation of North Borneo's first political party, invited me to what turned out to be a sparsely attended press conference. With him were the chairman of the Sarawak United Peoples' Party, Ong Kee Hui, and the president of Brunei's Partai Rakyat (People's Party), A.M. Azahari.

They told me they had agreed to adopt a united front on the Tunku's 'Mighty Malaysia' plan. So far as the wishes of the people in the three territories were ascertainable, they wanted Britain to know that any plan in accordance with the pronouncements made by Tunku Abdul Rahman in Brunei and Sarawak would be totally unacceptable. It wasn't that they spurned the thought of some future association with Malaya, but they wanted independence first and perhaps a federal arrangement among themselves before going on to talk of a confederation with Malaya and Singapore.

There followed a British-led campaign of education and persuasion to alert public opinion to the external issues and urgency that lay behind the Malaysia plan. Within months, attitudes in North Borneo and Sarawak evolved strongly in favour of Malaysia, to the extent that in May 1962 Tunku Abdul Rahman and the British prime minister, Harold Macmillan, signed an agreement naming 31 August 1963 (subsequently deferred into September) as the 'birthday' of Malaysia. But in Brunei things took a different turn.

In August 1962 Brunei's first-ever election placed all the elected seats in its new legislative council in the hands of Azahari's Party Rakyat, confirming that he enjoyed a real power base which had not previously been ascertained.

Born of an Arab father and Malay mother, Azahari had been sent to Java to study veterinary science during the Japanese wartime occupation and soon involved himself in guerrilla activity against the Dutch. Politics became his life. No doubt inspired by Sukarno's oratorical powers, he too became a rousing public speaker. He befriended another exile, Ibrahim Ya'acob, the pre-war founder of a Malay nationalist party which had campaigned for incorporating Malaya into a larger Indonesian union. During the early 1950s Azahari based himself in Singapore. He set up a number of companies, usually financed by the Brunei government on conditions which he regularly disregarded and whose failure never seemed to bankrupt him personally. Among his associates was the Singapore politician who was to lead the communists out of the united front with the PAP, Lim Chin Siong. Closely watched by British security agents, he travelled frequently between Singapore, Jakarta and Brunei and in 1956, against the wishes of the Sultan's British advisers, founded Brunei's first party, the Partai Rakyat.

The party manifesto described its purpose as to oppose colonialism in all its forms, safeguard the position of the Sultan and his heirs, fight for the freedom of the Malay homeland and bring about the formation of one Malay nation and state covering the whole Malay Archipelago – a greater Indonesia. It might have been the young Sukarno speaking, except that Azahari's vision was founded in Malay nationalism rather than the multi-ethnic realities which Sukarno always recognised. It was by no means a communist formulation, but it had features which the Indonesian Communist Party (PKI) could support. In the last days of 1961 the central committee of the PKI adopted a resolution describing the Malaysia plan as an unacceptable colonial intrigue. It went on: 'By unifying their colonies in Kalimantan with Malaya, the military agreement in force between Malaya and Britain will safeguard Britain's position in these colonies, especially now that Malaya and Britain have agreed that this military agreement must be extended to include Sarawak, Brunei and North Borneo. . . . The Federation of Malaysia will strengthen the position of the imperialists in South-East Asia in implementing their SEATO activities which are also aimed against Indonesia . . .'.

The position of the Brunei Partai Rakyat, now more than 25,000 strong, was also in tune with that initially adopted in Jesselton by the tripartite United Front, that the north Borneo territories should draw together among themselves before thinking of anything as ambitious as the Malaysia plan. On the other hand, with Azahari propagating his views ever more conspicuously, while opinion in North Borneo and Sarawak was shifting more emphatically in favour of Malaysia, the Front was falling apart. To complicate matters for the Sultan, who was personally in favour of joining Malaysia, the ruling clique of nobles by which he was surrounded was overtly opposed to the project; any thought, therefore, of going in against the wishes of the Partai Rakyat as well would be foolhardy.

This was the context in which the Partai Rakyat decided on violent action. On the morning of 8 December 1962, several thousand uniformed Brunei Malay rebels seized key positions in Brunei town and seven other places in Brunei and adjacent areas of North Borneo and Sarawak. Among them were the oil-producing centres of Seria and Miri. Azahari described his force as the Tentara Nasional Kalimantan Utara (North Borneo National Army), a name with a decidedly Indonesian ring to it – the Indonesian army being known as the Tentara Nasional Indonesia (TNI). His objective was to turn the three north Borneo territories into a unitary state ruled over by the Sultan of Brunei with himself as prime minister.

In Jakarta the government, including Sukarno himself, hailed what they represented as a people's uprising against NEKOLIM. Although the Indonesians claimed to have no foreknowledge of what was happening, British police and military intelligence already knew better. Nine months before, the British High Commissioner in Brunei, Dennis White, had warned Whitehall of a situation arising beyond the ability of the Brunei police to control, and there had been rumours since June 1962 of the existence of a Borneo Liberation Army. Preparations for the revolt were detected several weeks before it erupted: large quantities of khaki material passed through the market, a cache of made-up uniforms was uncovered, a training area was discovered and numbers of Brunei Malay employees went missing as they crossed into Indonesian territory for military training.

Two Gurkha companies were put on standby before the action even began. Before nightfall of the first day they were deployed in Brunei town and 300 other British troops were on their way aboard Royal Navy vessels. Within a fortnight the revolt was suppressed without any serious harm done on the ground.

On the political plane, though, it was a turning point. Not just Azahari's Partai Rakyat but Indonesia also had shown their hand. Although the communist press in Jakarta went on for another three years proclaiming Azahari prime minister of the Revolutionary Government of the North Kalimantan Unitary State, his destiny was now contingent on the success or failure of Indonesia's policy. The Sultan also was compromised and it would soon be apparent that Brunei could no longer be regarded as a secure partner in the Malaysian project. Public opinion in North Borneo, and to a lesser extent Sarawak, moved further in favour of Malaysia. In Singapore, following tense discussions between the Malayan and Singapore prime ministers, more than a hundred members of the pro-communist Barisan Sosialis were arrested on the ground that they had consorted with Azahari four days before the outbreak of the Brunei revolt.

Seen from Jakarta the suppression of the Brunei revolt did not represent a policy reverse either for Sukarno or for the PKI. On the contrary, its occurrence and the manner in which it was handled by British troops demonstrated the validity of the PKI analysis and Sukarno's thesis about the opposition between the Old Established Forces (OLDEFO) and the New Emerging Forces (NEFO). In the broad context it came as a gift from Allah.

The interplay of international forces at the time was complex. The developing ideological rift between the Soviet Union and China – the one wanting peaceful nuclear coexistence while the other needed ongoing confrontation – was proving an embarrassment to the PKI, which had traditionally followed Moscow leads. The obvious tactic for the Indonesian communist leader, D.N. Aidit, and his colleagues was independence and equidistance. Sukarno's redefinition of the confrontational model offered a way through, though even that could be and was seen in both Moscow and Washington as a move towards the Chinese camp.

Central to American policy in Asia was fear of the communist Chinese colossus. Washington's concern in Indonesia was still to prevent its cornucopia of raw materials falling under communist – and increasingly that meant Chinese – control. Great hopes were invested in Japan, emerging from its post-war recovery period as a bastion of capitalist ideology. The American view of Japan's rôle was to buy Indonesian raw materials and sell Japanese manufactured goods in return. The proposed system was in fact triangular: American investment would stimulate Japanese industry which would sell its marginal product in Indonesia and other parts of South-East Asia. There was also a military-strategic vision behind American policy, the securing of the island chain off the east coast of the Asian mainland as a bulwark against feared Chinese expansionism and the denial of naval base facilities in Indonesia to either of the major communist powers.

So far as they related to Indonesia, these American concerns had translated during the late fifties into an obsessive anti-communism. Under Eisenhower (US President from January 1953 until January 1961) the Dulles doctrine, that all who were not unambiguously pro-American must be regarded as pro-communist, was given free rein. Although isolated voices had urged the importance of Indonesian nationalism as an antidote to communism, their message had not been heeded. The policy-makers had gone on judging Sukarno by the touchstone of their global dogma, their dislike of him compounded by the prim attitudes Eisenhower and the Dulles brothers had evinced towards his sexual exuberance.

If the public rhetoric changed with the advent of President Kennedy, the essential thinking behind American strategy did not. Meeting in April 1962, the British prime minister, Harold Macmillan, and President Kennedy were recorded as agreeing that it was desirable to 'liquidate' President Sukarno, depending on the situation and available opportunities. Co-authors Paul Lashmar and James Oliver quote the CIA memorandum revealing this remarkable meeting of minds in their book *Britain's Secret Propaganda War*. They quote the CIA officer who wrote it as saying 'it is not clear to me whether murder or overthrow is intended by the word liquidate'.[1] Neither does it much matter. The sentiment was clear.

Meanwhile Sukarno had a touchstone of his own by which he was judging the Americans. In spite of the hard-won agreement in August 1962 that the Dutch should hand West Irian over to Indonesia in May 1963, the wrangling over details and modalities sputtered on. Washington under the new Kennedy administration could in fact take some credit for forcing the Dutch to the 1962 agreement, but preferred as ever to play publicly neutral on the issue. This was not enough for Sukarno who, indeed, had learned how to exploit American ambivalence to his own political advantage. He could perfectly well argue that the real impetus behind the achievement of the 1962 agreement was the 'total mobilization' he had ordered in December 1961 for the taking of West Irian – the same month in which India had invaded the enclave of Goa, another colonial relic. Clearly, confrontation of the Old Established Forces by the Newly Emerging Forces was the order of the day. It worked. What was more, it helped to keep the unruly Indonesian army occupied.

## GANJANG MALAYSIA

A contained military confrontation of Malaysia would keep the armed forces occupied and, by channelling more resources in their direction, keep them happy. In the more focussed political scene following the abortive rebellion in Sumatra the army – together with the PKI – was more clearly than ever one of the pre-eminent forces requiring the President's constant and firm attention. Its decisive success in Sumatra and Sulawesi had raised its reputation to a level comparable only with what it had enjoyed during the final stages of the independence struggle. Already in April 1962, recognising a potential threat in the enhanced prestige of the author of that success, General Nasution, Sukarno had judged it necessary to trim his authority by promoting him out of the post of Army Chief of Staff to that of Chief of Staff of the Armed Forces. Coincidentally, one of Nasution's first acts in his new position was to place an officer just back from commanding the 'total mobilization' in West Irian – one Major-General Suharto, a man he had once removed from a command on suspicion of corruption – in charge of KOSTRAD, the Jakarta-based rapid deployment force tasked with keeping a look-out for insurrectionary movements.

While the president may not have known about the secret undertaking given to Nasution by the Americans in September 1960, that they would support the army in a final confrontation with Sukarno, he obviously was aware that the US administration now counted the senior commanders of the Indonesian army as their friends. No other conclusion could be drawn from the establishment during 1962 of the American Military Training Advisory Group in Jakarta.

With every year that passed, the delicate task of offsetting the army and the communists was being made more difficult by the intrusion of external influences: the USA on one side and, as was now becoming evident, China on the other. It made sense to identify policies in which these forces could be counterpoised. One such was mobilization against the Dutch in West Irian; might not resistance to the formation of Malaysia be another?

Indonesia's other important neighbour is, of course, the Philippines. There a new president, Diosdado Macapagal, had come to power in 1961, a protégé of the Americans. President Garcia before him had shown historical prescience by combining with Malaya and Thailand to launch the Association of South East Asia (ASA). Rather than consolidate this friendly tie with Malaya, Macapagal resolved instead to lay claim to North Borneo. It offered Sukarno and Subandrio another sign amongst many that the Malaysia project might not work, that there might be an alternative more in harmony with Indonesian interests and that the USA might go along with such an alternative. Macapagal further encouraged the idea by advocating a different regional grouping – Malaya, Indonesia, the Philippines, Singapore and the northern Borneo territories – pandering to Sukarno's known sentiments with the thought that an Asian scheme was preferable to a European one.

Then came the Brunei uprising, signalling a measure of public support for Azahari's North Kalimantan ambitions. While in neighbouring Sarawak, a complicated political picture was evolving in which a hard core of mainly Chinese communists was opposing the Malaysia plan with vocal support from China and the pro-communist Barisan Sosialis in Singapore.

The British and Malayan governments did nothing to reverse the trend of thinking in Jakarta. In December 1962, responding to the trouble in Brunei, they acted well ahead of the game by appointing General Walter Walker, a British Gurkha commander with unparalleled jungle warfare experience in Burma and Malaya, as commander of Commonwealth forces in Borneo. Elevating Walker to the overall directorship of Borneo Operations four months later was a formality. Operations were by then well on the way; the SAS had begun patrolling the thousand-mile frontier between Sarawak and Indonesian Kalimantan in January, weeks ahead of Nasution's first cross-border marauders, and were soon cooperating with the Gurkhas to train a network of friendly intelligence contacts in Iban villages. Helping them was the elusive Tom Harrisson, known at the time as the likeable and bibulous curator of the Kuching Museum, but in fact an experienced jungle fighter, organizer of Iban headhunters against the Japanese during the 1939–45 war and, at that particular time, the leader of an Iban force pursuing the remnants of the Brunei rebels.

Perhaps the most provocative gesture, as Sukarno would have seen it, was the stance adopted by Malaya on the West Irian dispute. Having had an offer to mediate brushed aside in Jakarta, Tunku Abdul Rahman announced in parliament that Malaya would observe strict neutrality. A leader in the *Straits Times* on 12 January 1963 spelled out the Tunku's reasoning: 'Although the Malayan Government has always believed that the persistence of Dutch sovereignty in the western half of New Guinea was a vestige of colonialism, and thus by implication held that it ought to end, it enjoys friendly relations with both Indonesia and the Netherlands; the resolution of their dispute is necessarily their own problem and one in which Malaya ought to remain strictly neutral. It is merely an extension of this position to say that Malaya would continue neutral in the event of hostilities over West Irian.' It was a skilfully modulated slight; while punctiliously warning the Dutch against any expectation of being able to use military transit facilities in Malaya (or Singapore), it put Malaya firmly in line with the long-standing American posture of neutrality which the Indonesians regarded as implicit support of the Dutch.

The arrest of more than a hundred communist front politicians in Singapore at the beginning of February 1963 prompted the Indonesian Foreign Ministry to brand Malaya – although it was not *overtly* implicated in the Singapore arrests – as a 'police state'. It was the first public sign of the policy switch which the Foreign Minister, Dr Subandrio, was to declare outright on 11 February. Speaking of Tunku Abdul Rahman's hostility towards Indonesia, he threatened armed conflict if it were to spread into the Borneo territories.

Two days later Sukarno elaborated the theme. 'What is the reason for our opposition to Malaysia?' he asked rhetorically. 'Indonesia's opposition to Malaysia is not because of communist influence but because Malaysia represents the forces of neo-colonialism. Malaysia is being set up to save tin for the imperialists; Malaysia is being formed to save rubber for the imperialists; Malaysia is being launched to save oil for the imperialists . . . and we do not agree with this. If the Malayan leadership continues its present policy, Indonesia will have no choice but to face it with political and economic confrontation.'

General Nasution, the armed forces chief, added his voice to the anti-Malaysia chorus and forthwith infiltrated military units across the border into Sarawak, raising the military stakes at a steady pace which allowed time for a parallel tactic of playing hot and cold on the diplomatic front. It was April before an Indonesian squad of some sixty uniformed and well-armed men ostentatiously raided a police station three miles into Sarawak territory, killed a policeman and made off with the contents of the armoury. Days later there was an attack on a British jungle patrol.

In the meantime, Britain was making progress in defusing Macapagal's territorial claim to North Borneo. During a well-tempered round of talks in London in January the British government managed to swathe its reiterated refusal to countenance the Philippine claim in an agreement to exchange further documentation and to cooperate in handling the piracy and smuggling which were a perennial problem in the waters between Borneo and the Philippines.

While Britain pressed on with the technicalities of the Malaysia project, Macapagal went ahead with his search for a rôle. This he saw as trying to promote a settlement of the Malaysia dispute, and there was a series of meetings between representatives of the three countries – Indonesia, Malaya and the Philippines – in Manila, during which his spokesmen went on promoting the conciliatory idea of forming the three nations into a permanent confederation.

But no sooner would the mood improve than Sukarno would do something to embitter it, and the urbane, clear-thinking and much underrated Tunku Abdul Rahman knew well how to respond in kind. Both men were experts in applying balm with one hand while delivering bodyblows with the other. At one stage in June Sukarno suggested a face-to-face encounter in Tokyo, in the course of which they appeared to achieve a good-natured meeting of minds on the modalities of ascertaining that the people of North Borneo and Sarawak did really want to join Malaysia. Within weeks Sukarno was complaining because the Tunku would not agree to a simple voting process, which led him to come out at a palace reception with the invocation which became the acknowledged slogan of the whole dispute – 'Ganjang Malaysia', crush Malaysia!

Another two weeks and the mood sweetened yet again. Sukarno and the Tunku accepted Macapagal's invitation to a tripartite meeting in Manila. They agreed to ask the UN Secretary-General, U Thant, to conduct a rapid consultation of public opinion on the Borneo territories. Thant reported 'there is no doubt about the wishes of a sizeable majority of the peoples of these territories to join in the Federation of Malaysia'. But even before he did so the Tunku announced a new date for Malaysia Day, September 17 – whereupon Sukarno declared that the 'crush Malaysia!' campaign would continue.

The events of those summer months in 1963 were followed with intense interest in Beijing. Despite the defeat of the Malayan Communist Party in the so-called Emergency, China never abandoned its ambition to use overseas Chinese communities throughout South-East Asia as a basis for communist or communist-leaning movements. Sarawak and Singapore in particular were regarded as promising ground for its strategy. The realization of Malaysia would stand in its way.

In the midst of the political wrangling over the Malaysia plan, in April 1963, China's President Liu Shao-chi paid a visit to Jakarta. Following in the footsteps of the Soviet Defence Minister Marshal Rodion Malinovsky, his purpose was to consolidate China's improving relationship with Indonesia after a period of anti-Chinese sentiment. At stake was the orientation of the Indonesian Communist Party (PKI); as we have seen, it was the Russians who lost the contest. Liu pledged that China would remain reliable comrades in arms to the Indonesian people, and a joint statement spoke of resolute support for the people of North Kalimantan in their 'courageous struggle for the right of self-determination and independence and against falling into the trap of neo-colonialism in the guise of Malaysia'.

Soon after these prestigious visits, which the USA could easily have matched had it not rejected repeated invitations by President Sukarno, the Indonesian communist leader, D.N. Aidit, led a party delegation on an extended and unprecedented tour of nearly all the communist capitals in the world. When they returned to Jakarta in September, a few days after Malaysia had actually come into being, the PKI's lopsided pro-Soviet allegiance was a thing of the past and there was a new solidarity between the Chinese and Indonesian communist parties on the Malaysia issue. From then on, as the former Malaysian Minister of External Affairs, Tan Sri Mohammed Ghazali Shafie, explained, the PKI went all-out to prove that Malaysia was hostile, and their propaganda was that the concept behind Malaysia was taking over Sumatra and Sulawesi. In fact the PKI agenda was to create a fifth force after the army, navy, air and police forces, who should be sent out of Jakarta to defend the country from Malaya's annexation with the help of the British. Once Jakarta was clear of the four forces the fifth force would take over and, using Sukarno, the whole of Indonesia would be under the control of the PKI.[2]

On balance it looked as if the PKI was having a good year, the army not so good. On 1 May 1963, the day West Irian was at last delivered into provisional Indonesian sovereignty, President Sukarno had ended the state of martial law that had been in force since the Sumatra rebellion, thus constraining military authority in the land. In subsequent weeks he removed General Nasution from the chairmanship of the so-called Committee for Re-tooling the State Apparatus, and in its stead set up a new body under Dr Subandrio; then he went on to reduce Nasution's status within the command organization which had been set up to prosecute the West Irian campaign.

Sukarno's call to 'crush Malaysia!' was the signal for coordinated attacks against British diplomatic and business properties throughout Indonesia. The first, five days before the birth of Malaysia, was in the East Javanese city of Surabaya, where the Union Jack was pulled down and replaced by the Indonesian red and white. Four days later, in the North Sumatran city of Medan, just across the Malacca Strait from the Malayan mainland, both the British and Malaysian consulates were virtually destroyed by government-marshalled mobs.

While showing their hand in Surabaya and Medan, the orchestrators of these manifestations were also gearing up in the capital, Jakarta. Guests at the nearby Hotel Indonesia were regaled with the hauling down of the British Embassy's Union Jack, the stoning of diplomatic personnel, cars and premises and at last the egregious tones of a marching embassy bagpiper making the hour – and the general situation – hideous with his airs. Whatever secret joy the performance may have bred in the Scottish heart of the then ambassador, Andrew Gilchrist, it stirred the mob to further endeavour, and by the evening of 18 September his chancery was a smoking wreck.

Even at its peak, in the latter half of 1964, the military commitment was never vast. Certainly it never attained the tenacity or professionalism of the Vietcong in the culminating years of the Vietnam war; nevertheless it was holding down Commonwealth military resources (there were New Zealanders and Australians as well as British and Malaysians) costing money which the governments concerned would have preferred to save.

Most of 1963 was devoted to low-key probes as the forces confronting each other along the Sarawak frontier penetrated the jungle areas and reconnoitred each others' deployments and lines of communication. The Indonesian objective was to enter North Borneo and Sarawak, join up, where they existed, with elements of what was referred to as the Clandestine Communist Organization (CCO), attack a police station or some similar target then hastily withdraw. Reviewing the Borneo confrontation in March 1964, almost a year after the first Indonesian incursion, the British Admiralty's secret Quarterly Intelligence Report commented: 'The tactics of the border raiders have varied and have been unpredictable. Recently they seem to have been concentrating on military targets. They have been well led and equipped and participation by Indonesian Regular Forces has been confirmed. To date, however, the Clandestine Communist Organization (CCO) within Sarawak has not caused much trouble, but the police and many well informed local people are convinced that active CCO operations will start before long.'[3]

The British-Malaysian side had an advantage in the local knowledge of Tom Harrisson, the special operations specialist-cum-museum curator, who rallied the Kayans and Kenyahs and Kelabits and Muruts of the inland hills to hound the rebellious Brunei rebels across the border into Indonesian Kalimantan in 1962. In her book *The Most Offending Soul Alive* the American author Judith Heimann quotes from the minutes of a working group set up, with Harrisson as chairman and note-taker, by the Sarawak Defence Committee in April 1963. It decided to establish 'Border Scouts, Tom's idea, . . . "to serve as an auxiliary, with expert local knowledge – aggressive within Sarawak's own territory and opposing any intrusion by outsiders".' She continues:

Tom quickly moved to the next stage: preparing secretly to move the war into the enemy's camp. Beginning in mid-1963, groups of at most seventy men, but often far fewer, penetrated into Indonesian Borneo to carry out specific aggressive tasks assigned to them by British military intelligence. At first they were all indigenous and thus more easily deniable by the British and Malaysian governments . . .[4]

When infiltration by regular Indonesian formations began in 1964, the activities of what Harrisson himself described as 'the army I had the privilege to command' faded away and were left to the Gurkhas, SAS patrols and others. On the Malaysian side there was great emphasis on befriending villages and long-houses where possible and in any case establishing permanent contact. The 'hearts and minds' campaign, as it was called, yielded invaluable dividends in the forms of military intelligence and a propaganda grapevine.

Probably the most psychologically telling Indonesian exploit was in December 1963, when they landed near Tawau on the remote south-eastern coast of Sabah (the former North Borneo) and wiped out a force of the

Malay Regiment. Typically, Sukarno followed up this relative success with hints of a willingness to talk peace, but nothing came of it. By March Indonesian forces, now made up entirely of army professionals, were back to full-scale operations. Troop strengths on either side were approaching their peak. To meet the Indonesian build-up the Commonwealth army force was increased from ten to twelve infantry battalions in January 1965, by which time there were some 22,000 Indonesian regulars plus an unkown number of volunteers facing 14,000 Commonwealth soldiers.

SAS infiltrations became deeper and more targeted, but were still limited to locating and assessing Indonesian troop deployments. General Walker, characterising the situation as undeclared war, pressed the Malaysian government, as he had before, for permission to enter Indonesian territory both in hot pursuit and for purposes of interdiction. And at last, as Sukarno offered another spurious peace initiative, they agreed. In an operation convivially named 'Claret', he was now at liberty to send his men first five thousand metres and ultimately twenty thousand metres into Indonesian Kalimantan.

Whether or not operation 'Claret' was the cause, it marked a turning point and a seeming loss of resolve in the Indonesian campaign in Kalimantan.

Less complicated politically and militarily than the confrontation in northern Borneo – but scarcely less expensive to contain – was that round Singapore and the west coast of the Malayan peninsula. The Indonesians began low-level harassment of Malayan fishermen in the Malacca Strait during 1963 and sporadically deposited small packages of explosives on Singapore's southern sea wall, including one where I lived. There was also one act of sabotage in the city centre, the perpetrators of which were captured and subsequently hanged.

Up until August 1965, when, to Indonesian delight, the Malaysian prime minister, Tunku Abdul Rahman, forced Singapore out of the new federation for ethnic reasons, the larger proportion of this coastal marauding was concentrated on Singapore and the southern Malayan state of Johore. However, as the Royal Naval flag officer then in command of the fleet at sea, now Admiral of the Fleet (retd) Lord Peter Hill-Norton, has recalled, there were ultimately far more landings and landing attempts than has been generally recognised, extending along the Malayan coast as far north as Penang.[5]

There were also two more ambitious landings, one seaborne and the other airborne, in 1964, coinciding with the growing Indonesian army presence opposite the Sarawak frontier. Both were disastrously unsuccessful. The first, on Indonesian Independence Day, 17 August, brought more than a hundred Indonesian regulars to the beach at Pontian in south-western Johore with orders to establish a guerrilla training base in the jungle. The second was a bungled parachute drop onto an agricultural area in the middle of the state. Interrogated after they had nearly all been captured, the soldiers confessed with astonishment that they had expected a warm welcome from the local Malays, instead of which they were immediately handed over to the Malaysian security forces. In Jakarta the foreign minister, Dr Subandrio, explained to the French and American ambassadors that these two raids were in retaliation for repeated British and Malaysian assistance to rebels in Sulawesi and Sumatra. It appears relevant that in a conversation some weeks later between the American secretary of state, Dean Rusk, and the British foreign secretary, Patrick Gordon-Walker, Rusk pointed out the weakness of the Indonesian position from a military point of view: 'They could not possibly defend the hundreds of islands, and hit-and-run tactics on our part would present them with insuperable problems'.[6]

The Naval Intelligence Report for 12 April 1965 records that: 'After the initial sea landings in August and the air drop in September, Indonesian infiltrations in West Malaysia were, so far as we know, very limited. The next sizeable landing was of 52 men south of Malacca at the end of October; they were undetected on passage across the Straits, but were mopped up in 36 hours. . . . Thereafter infiltration intrusions increased, mostly in small parties of one or two sampans . . .'.[3]

The report continues: 'The problem of preventing infiltration by sea is a difficult one, and the close vicinity of the Indonesian staging posts in the Rhio Islands and off Sumatra gives advantage to the Indonesians'. 'Consideration' was to be given to the 'problem' of Indonesia's claim to a 12-mile sea limit.

Another problem for the naval patrols was the saturation of their radar screens by fishermen and smugglers who carried on their business with little regard for President Sukarno's campaign against neo-colonialism. They too contributed to tying down a Commonwealth naval force recorded in December 1964 as including two aircraft carriers, one commando ship, four destroyers (two carrying guided missiles), twelve frigates, seven coastal minesweepers, three submarines and a variety of support ships and launches.

The best informed estimate to reach the Ministry of Defence was that four in every five attempted crossings were intercepted at sea. The sorties originated from three main bases: Belawan near the city of Medan to cover the sector up to Penang, Bengkalis on the Sumatran coast opposite Malacca and Tandjung Pinang on Bintan island in the Riau archipelago immediately south of Singapore. The last of these, the probable command centre, attracted the attention of British special forces and, together with the Surabaya naval base in East Java, was the object of an attack plan that was abandoned at the end of 1964.

On paper, the Indonesians now had enough forces deployed on both fronts to sustain a large number of frontier raids in Borneo and simultaneously keep the Commonwealth navy busy indefinitely in the Malacca Strait. And yet it was at this juncture that Indonesian military resolve seemed quite suddenly to falter.

We know now that during 1964 Major-General Suharto, the man who was to oust President Sukarno and was then commanding KOSTRAD in Jakarta, had made his own secret contacts with Malaysia through intermediaries. And we have the evidence of the general he sent to command one of the combat sectors in Kalimantan that some of the troops dispatched there to fight had not in fact been deployed. General Supardjo, a key army figure in the October 1965 coup affair, testified at his 1967 trial:

Under instructions I sent troops to Kalimantan Barat (West Kalimantan). But when I visited Kalimantan Barat, I observed that the troops were not deployed. I thought then that some army leaders were not keen on the confrontation.

The President had spoken also about the NEFO and OLDEFO. But some military leaders in the army did not hold the same view as the President. Although the President spoke of an enemy from the north, by which he meant Malaysia, some army leaders were of the opinion that that enemy was China.

Documents at the Public Record Office chronicle a flurry of secret Indonesian feelers in October 1964, aimed at finding a way out of the military confrontation. An intermediary known as Mrs Leon Soh was quoted as saying that the Indonesians had 'sent out nine horses in the hope that not all would come to grief'. One of the first, and perhaps the most significant, was Brigadier-General Ibnu Sutowo, who made his approach to the Singapore government and met one of its representatives in Cairo. One of General Suharto's oldest and closest friends and financial advisers, Sutowo was already president-director of the state oil company Permina and later, after Suharto's accession to the presidency, was at the centre of one of the régime's most dramatic corruption scandals. His message was that, in return for Malaysian agreement to hold a plebiscite in Sabah and Sarawak within five years, Indonesian guerrillas would be quietly withdrawn.[7]

At about the same time, the British Embassy in Jakarta reported contacts with the third deputy premier, Chaerul Saleh, who suggested secret informal talks to find a face-saving solution on Malaysia.[8] This was significant because Saleh, a non-party politician, was seen as a potential successor to Sukarno and rival as such to the leftist Dr Subandrio. Reportedly, his approach had President Sukarno's agreement.

Next, within the same few days, came an approach in Paris by Major-General Parman, the director of military intelligence, who chose for his purpose 'a British official whom he regards (*sic*) as a personal friend'. Parman was one of six generals destined to be murdered in the putsch in the early hours of 1 October 1965. Expressing concern over the Indonesian predicament, he wanted to know Britain's view about the conditions needed for negotiation. The best way to end confrontation, he suggested, would be for Britain to announce her intention to withdraw from bases in Malaysia at some date in the longer-term future. Even in the absence of such agreement, while military operations would have to go on, they would not be on a large scale; the Indonesians, he conveyed, were at a loss what to do next.[9]

Another half dozen approaches were made to Malaysia – some of them to well-connected senior officials in the Ministry of External Affairs.

In London meanwhile, the foreign secretary, Patrick Gordon-Walker, brought the matter to Cabinet. The Indonesians, he told his colleagues, had privately renewed their overtures for a peaceful settlement, and it was minuted that the approach seemed sufficiently serious in intention to justify a tentative response.[10]

By November, Western diplomats in Jakarta were convinced that Sukarno wanted a way out of confrontation. It had become a highly political issue and top army échelons were seething with controversy as ideological differences between rightists and national communists sharpened. From Washington the British ambassador, Lord Harlech, reported in a letter to the Foreign Office that Dean Rusk had 'again' pointed out that the Americans 'have recently been warning Sukarno that if he continues to misbehave over Malaysia he may find himself tangling militarily with the US . . .'[11]

As 1964 gave way to a new year, the scale of military activity was declining. The new federal state of Malaysia had been accepted into the

United Nations in November. British diplomats and military experts spent most of 1965 trying to ascertain whether the confrontation really had run out of steam.

General Walker relinquished his Borneo command in March 1965. In a long talk I had with him a few days before his departure I found him unperturbed by the Indonesian threat but pessimistic about the threat to Sarawak posed by some twenty-three thousand ethnic Chinese members of the Clandestine Communist Organization. So far as the undeclared border war was concerned, he predicted – accurately – that units of the Indonesian army would mount one more substantial attack, which Commonwealth forces would be able to handle. General Suharto had by then already been in touch with the Malaysians for months, and the Indonesian general staff had decided to phase out the military side of confrontation.

Walker left as the victor. On the Indonesian side, there were at least six hundred killed and seven hundred captured . . . hundreds more died of malnutrition and starvation. On the Commonwealth side he reported 114 killed and 200 wounded.[12]

There can be no more authoritative verdict than that delivered by Dr Subandrio at his trial in 1966: 'The British, the USA and Malaysia won against Indonesia'.

## Notes

1  Lashmar, Paul and James Oliver *Britain's Secret Propaganda War*, Thrupp, Sutton Publishing 1998.
2  Letter to author, 12 May 2000.
3  Public Record Office ADM 223/727 and 732 Quarterly Intelligence Report, March 1964, No 39.
4  Heimann, Judith, *The Most Offending Soul Alive*, University of Hawai'i Press 1999.
5  Interview with author, June 2000.
6  Public Record Office IM 103145/2 Record of conversation between Rusk and Gordon-Walker.
7  Public Record Office FO371/176460 Inward Telegram to Commonwealth Relations Office from Kuala Lumpur, marked secret, 12 October 1964.
8  Public Record Office FO371/176460.
9  Public Record Office FO371/176460 Outward Telegram from Commonwealth Relations Office to Kuala Lumpur Approach by General Parman marked secret, 15 October 1964.
10 Public Record Office CAB128 C.C.2 (64) Cabinet meeting 22 October 1964.
11 Public Record Office FO371 176454 Letter from Washington to the Foreign Office, 31 December 1964.
12 Walker, Walter *Fighting On*, London, New Millennium, 1997.

# FOUR

## *Living Dangerously*

In 1965 the tide turned suddenly and irreversibly against Sukarno. Making the speech famously preparing his countrymen for 'a year of living dangerously' (vivere pericoloso) some months earlier, even he could not have supposed that in little more than a year his authority would be fatally compromised, his system of checks and balances overturned and his personal fate in the hands of a coalition of forces fronted by the right-wing Major-General Suharto.

Many of the factors that now began to affect him adversely had their roots in the international arena where he had taken to performing with such bravado in an evident attempt to reinforce unifying nationalist sentiment at home. As early as December 1963 it was becoming clear that the new Johnson administration in the United States, gearing up for all-out anti-communist (and implicitly anti-Chinese) war in Vietnam, would abandon the previous Kennedy policy of granting the Sukarno formula the benefit of some doubt.

Secretary of State Dean Rusk told Dr Subandrio in person of his government's expectation that Indonesia would not seek to settle the Malaysia dispute by military means; President Johnson himself affirmed his support for a free and independent Malaysia.

Reacting and thereby contributing to this sudden collapse in Indonesian-US relations, Sukarno turfed out the Peace Corps, shrugged off the sacking by the mob of some USIS libraries and, as a crowning gesture, in March 1964 publicly brandished his finger at the US ambassador, Howard Jones, and told him to 'go to hell with your aid'. Non-military aid was duly suspended, although covert assistance to 'friendly elements' within the armed forces continued and in fact grew. Two months later Jones left, to be followed in July by Marshall Green, a former deputy assistant secretary of state for Far Eastern Affairs, who came bearing a revised brief.

Had he adhered to the Moscow stance of acquiescing in the formation of Malaysia, Sukarno might have spared his country a lot of trouble and his armed forces a bitter humiliation. Arguably he might even have been able to sustain his political balancing act for several more years. Instead he played into British hands by confirming the American perception that he was yielding more and more ground to Aidit's communist party (PKI) and its Beijing backers. From Washington's perspective he conclusively discredited whatever credentials he might have had as an obstacle to communist take-over in Indonesia. Mortifyingly – and in retrospect perhaps surprisingly – he received no significant international support for his confrontation policy, except from China. Malaysia was accepted as a member of the United Nations in November 1964 and then as a non-permanent member of the Security Council, whereupon in January 1965 Sukarno indignantly withdrew Indonesia from the world body. Seven months later he was to sever links with the World Bank and the International Monetary Fund, further reinforcing the impression of drift into the communist camp.

As so often in Indonesian history, external forces now played back into domestic politics. Instinctively, Sukarno pressed on with what he had always done best, whipping up a renewed frenzy of revolutionary sentiment, arousing the spirit of national self-reliance, preaching endlessly the need for unity among the diverse elements of his people – and disregarding the catastrophic state of the economy.

Wholly dependent on the export of raw materials for foreign exchange earnings, Indonesia's economy was a classic example of the colonial mercantile system. It was inherently vulnerable to fluctuating world prices; and the prices of such commodities as petroleum, rubber, tin had fluctuated enormously in the years since independence. The domestic economy was also out of control. By 1965, the collection of taxes was in chaos. While civil servants attended to their own fortunes, public services lapsed; thousands of miles of roads reverted to earth tracks; telecommunications in the major cities became so bad that heaving traffic systems were further congested by hundreds of message-bearing *betjaks* (pedicabs); ships were unable to put to sea for want of spare parts; Jakarta was dotted with abandoned building projects; starved of raw materials, manufacturing industry was running at a fifth of capacity.

And yet the government went on recklessly spending. For want of proper regulation much of the expenditure went into the pockets of officials and the military. The wages of the mass of office-workers, teachers, drivers, workmen fell routinely into arrears. At the same time, thanks to the disintegrating distribution system and the dearth of imported goods, the swelling flood of printed money lost all touch with the quantity of goods available for purchase. The familiar scourge of inflation touched new heights, reaching an annual rate of 650 per cent in 1965.

For town-dwellers, although there was usually rice to be had, its price suddenly doubled. Other household necessities like sugar and kerosene all but vanished from the shelves. In rural Indonesia, which means most of it, the people's concerns were of a different kind: the requisitioning of their land by big businessmen, most often military officers, and the interminable burden of sustaining an army obliged to live off the land. The only people spared some of these deprivations were those who lived by subsistence and barter and thus had no part in the monetised economy.

By the beginning of 1965 foreign exchange earnings covered barely half the required outgoings, including debt repayment. At home the predicted budget deficit, as everyone knew would be the case, again bore no relation to the actual deficit. The rupiah, Indonesia's national currency, officially valued at 45 to the US dollar, entered the new year at 8,500 to the dollar on the open market.

Although the army high command had in fact tried to limit the scale of confrontation operations, the people increasingly blamed for the economic mess were the blatantly corrupt military. The people doing much of the blaming were the communists (PKI) who, by dint of sound analysis, effective organization and not a little coercion now had three million full members plus, it was reckoned, up to 20 million supporters in communist-controlled trade union, youth, women's, artists', veterans' organizations and the like. It was the biggest and best disciplined party in the land. Aidit's boast that the PKI would now come out on top in a general election was sufficiently credible to alarm its rivals.

The counter-balanced structure that Sukarno had built so carefully over the years was coming unstuck under the pressures of the global cold war dynamic. Aidit's communist party, emboldened by its firm roots in rural and industrial discontent, was pressing for a 'fifth force' armed with weapons from China for a class-based showdown against reactionary forces. On the other side of the equation the army, uniformly imbued with the conviction of its so-called civic mission, was united in nothing else.

As well as being factionalized along all the old lines, the army was now ideologically divided over its fundamental mission. From its origins as a national revolutionary body, many aspiring leaders on its right wing had been working since the late 'fifties to transform it into a counter-insurgency agency, that being perceived as the only real threat to national security. The doctrinal and intellectual debate behind this process was centred on the Army Staff and Command School (SESKOAD) in the city of Bandung. The key figure there was the US-trained General Suwarto whose agenda, actively nourished by the CIA, the Pentagon and a couple of well-known American propaganda corporations, was the ultimate seizure of political power by the armed forces. Among his students was the quiet but ambitious Suharto, fated to be the Republic's next president; who, although he never went to the USA for training, was already being nurtured as a likely candidate for US sponsorship should it appear necessary to replace General Nasution; the same Suharto who would declare in August 1966 that the army must play a leading role in every field.

The significance of Suharto's ideological proclivities seems not to have been widely recognised for quite a long time. Sukarno is unlikely to have known, for instance, that by August 1964, communicating through intermediaries, he had established political contacts with Malaysia, Britain, Japan and USA. At the beginning of 1965 the military name that mattered was still Nasution; despite having been promoted upstairs to Chief of Staff of the Armed Forces in 1962, and despite American misgivings over certain ambiguities in his ideological stance, he was for all that Minister of Defence and an acknowledged symbol of army antagonism towards the communists. Nevertheless, amidst the factional tensions of 1965, it must be supposed that the Javanese Suharto, encouraged by his American and British contacts, viewed his older Sumatran superior as an impediment to his ambitions.

Setting aside his considerable personal ambition, what differentiated Suharto essentially from Nasution was that he favoured an unambiguously right-wing, militaristic power structure for Indonesia with no space for the communists, whereas Nasution, no less anti-communist, still thought Sukarno's formula offered a realistic hope of containing them. As we shall see, this did not mean that Suharto's political analysis differed much from Sukarno's; he simply drew different conclusions from it.

At this time Nasution's view was in the ascendancy. The army was led by a group of generals headed by General Yani, the soldier whom Sukarno had appointed to replace Nasution as army chief of staff in 1962. In the power spectrum of the period, Yani and his men were regarded as pro-Sukarno centrists. To their right were men of Suharto's stamp. To the left a number of army formations including the Brawidjaya and (in Central Java)

Diponegoro divisions and a host of impatient junior officers scattered throughout the land.

Whatever their political allegiances, they all wanted to be on-side with President Sukarno. The PKI supported him because his doctrine of combining nationalism, religion and communism (NASAKOM) legitimised their proselytising activities. Believing, as they did, that the end of the process would be the collapse of rival political forces, the mistake they made was to press too hard for formal implementation of NASAKOM at all levels of government, and in the armed forces.

On the other hand, all who were opposed to communism and alarmed by its evident success in East and Central Java preferred to stress another of Sukarno's doctrines, Pancasila, the five principles of nationalism, internationalism, consensus, social prosperity and belief in God – but no communism!

A more tangible expression of their concern was the formation at the end of 1964 of an organization called the Body for the Promotion of Sukarnoism. The prime architect of this short-lived coalition was Adam Malik, then Trade Minister and a leading figure in the Murba party, which had been set up eight years earlier as a pseudo-Marxist alternative to the PKI. Its obvious intention was to provide a vehicle for the state philosophy of Sukarnoism which might in time draw away from Sukarno himself. Unsurprisingly Sukarno saw through this, banned it and within weeks, to the delight of the PKI, suspended Murba as well.

At about the same time two other themes wove their way into the intricate play of events that were to mark 1965 as pivotal in Indonesia's post-independence history: President Sukarno's health, and the plottings of a shadowy group that came to be known as the Council of Generals.

In September 1964 Sukarno, then in his sixty-fourth year, went to Vienna for a medical check on a kidney complaint that had troubled him on and off for several years. Legend has it that he declined surgical treatment because a seer of some kind had predicted that he would die by the knife. Instead his highly developed instinct for self-preservation led him towards traditional Chinese medicine and Chinese doctors.

From then on speculation about his health escalated, spurred not least by Western propaganda; in my own hearing British official observers in the area would urge the importance of encouraging Indonesians to think ahead to the 'post-Sukarno' era. They needed no prompting. The military especially had had it on their agenda for five years or more. Military order of a kind had been imposed on the awkward north Sumatran province of Aceh since 1959; Darul Islam dissidence in West Java had been silenced by the capture of its leader Kartosuwirjo in 1962; West Papua, where Sukarno had at first put Suharto in command, was ceded to Indonesia in 1963; and as 1965 dawned there was reason to believe Muslim rebellion in South Sulawesi had also been suppressed. The next item on the unwritten military agenda, as many analysts then and since have supposed, was to address the communist challenge which they saw coming.

A note of urgency may have been injected into such thinking in the first few days of 1965 when Dr Subandrio, the foreign minister and not himself a communist, spoke of the new year as the most critical yet to be faced by Indonesia and speculated that some former comrades-in-arms might have to be discarded because they had become counter-revolutionary.

Hence there were multiple factors behind Suharto's suggestion of convening an army unity meeting in January 1965. It coincided, significantly, with such a crescendo of rumour about his health that President Sukarno laid on a special ceremony in his palace at Bogor to honour his Chinese doctors and proclaim how well he was.

As commander of the Army Strategic Reserve (KOSTRAD) Suharto was the officer designated to step in as army chief of staff should anything happen to the incumbent General Yani. Subsequent analysts have seen that January meeting as a stepping stone on his path towards taking over from his rivals Nasution and Yani.

Three months later, in April, the unity meeting was followed up with a seminar at SESKOAD, the high temple of the army's civic mission theology, with the object of defining a compromise strategic doctrine.

In a painstaking rehearsal of the events of that period in the journal *Pacific Affairs* (Summer 1985) Peter Dale Scott quotes an article by the *Washington Post* journalists Evans and Novak claiming to know that already in March 1965 the [Indonesian] army had (*sic*) 'quietly established an advisory commission of five general officers to report to General Yani . . . and General Nasution . . . on PKI activities'. Rumour was spreading about the Council of Generals. Brigadier-General Supardjo, the most senior army officer implicated in the coup attempt at the beginning of October, stated during his 1967 trial that he first heard of it in March; his informant had been Colonel Latief, one of the putsch organizers, who had characterised the council as being opposed to the government. The air force chief Air Vice-Marshall Omar Dhani, at his trial, said he heard about it from

General Supardjo in April; and he was sufficiently convinced to convene a meeting of air force officers in June at which he distributed discussion papers on the subject.

The supposed members of the Council of Generals – Nasution, Yani and several others, but not Suharto himself – persistently denied its existence. In the contrived atmosphere of the post-coup trials in 1966 and 1967, an armed forces special committee would dutifully concur that there had been no such council. So strong and pervasive was the rumour of its existence, however, that Sukarno summoned key figures to the presidential palace to throw light on it. They included the leader of the PKI, D.N. Aidit, who was also a cabinet member without portfolio, and the army commander, General Yani. They circled round the subject for three quarters of an hour. When pressed by Sukarno, General Yani conceded that there was indeed a council of generals but that its remit was to vet candidates for promotion to the rank of general. Aidit was said to have laughed outright on hearing this. The implausibility of Yani's explanation was later addressed more tellingly by General Supardjo when he told his military trial judges that he assumed the Council of Generals was political because there was already another committee in being to deal with senior promotions.

Whether or not there was a group calling itself the Council of Generals in so many words is of small consequence. That the army was split into factions, and that one of them was a right-wing group spoken of as the Council of Generals, is incontestable. Drawing on the 1990 memoirs of one of Suharto's close army colleagues, Michael Vatikiotis says:

In the months before September 1965, Suharto drew together close associates from his days in Central Java, building up a core of trusted deputies. Ali Murtopo, his trusted territorial assistant in Central Java, became his intelligence chief in KOSTRAD. Yoga Sugama, another of his trusted deputies from the 1950s, was recalled from duty overseas to join Suharto in Jakarta in March 1965. According to Sugama, the three of them began working as a team again in early 1965, making moves to counter PKI influence.[1]

The clear and persistent evidence of the Council's existence was blurred rather than reinforced by the insinuation into the web of rumour of an undated secret letter allegedly written by the then British Ambassador, Andrew Gilchrist, to the Foreign Office in London. Said to have been recovered from the house of a staff member at the time of the embassy sacking in August 1963, this text spoke of 'our local army friends' and was construed by some as implying a conspiratorial connection between the British and the Council of Generals. In fact, Dr Subandrio, who fed the text to Sukarno at an opportune moment in 1965, never made that precise connection.

The phrase 'our local army friends' is of a kind that must have been used hundreds of times by diplomats and defence attachés of many nationalities reporting back to their superiors. Rapport of that nature is the daily stuff of diplomatic relations, encouraged on all sides even in difficult times. The impression fostered by the British Foreign Office was that the Gilchrist letter was a forgery. Interestingly, however, Gilchrist's own reference to it in a secret letter from Jakarta in September 1965, only released in February 2001, enfolds the word 'forgery' in inverted commas.[2] Pending the delayed release of further relevant documents by the Public Record Office, it is reasonable to believe that the Gilchrist letter was authentic but tangential.

As early as May Subandrio – hence probably Sukarno also – knew of the Council of Generals and its alleged plan to stage a coup. Thanks to BPI, the intelligence organization of which he was head, he was also aware by September at the latest of the PKI's assessment of the situation. Naive as it now seems, this in the words of Aidit the party leader in a March interview with the *Hindu* was that the army would not fight the PKI 'so long as we fight for the people and not only for the PKI'.

A BPI agent in Central Java reported on 21 August that the PKI central committee had circulated all branches warning of an impending coup by the Council of Generals. Aidit told the politburo – citing information he had received from the BPI chief of staff! – that a progressive group within the army was intending to forestall the coup by the Council of Generals. There were, he said, differences between the armed forces chief, Nasution, and the army chief, Yani.

The old differences between Nasution and Sukarno were still festering too. In a pointed passage of his Independence Day speech on 17 August, the President remarked: 'Those who were progressive yesterday may today be retrogressive, anti-progressive. Those who were revolutionary yesterday may today be counter-revolutionary. . . . Even if you were a man of ideas in 1954, if you now obstruct revolutionary cooperation, if you now oppose the NASAKOM front, if you are now hostile to the pillars of the revolution, you have become a reactionary force'.

In what looked like a riposte, Nasution used a speech on National Peasant Day to reaffirm his revolutionary bona fides: 'We have now reached the final phase of the national democratic stage of the revolution and will soon enter its socialist stage', he said. 'This must serve us as an impetus further to forge our unity and determination to complete the revolution'.

A rumour spoke of a coup against army leaders on 19 September. Nothing happened. The day before, however, a BPI agent reported on the military training of several thousand volunteers, many of them communist supporters, at the Halim airforce base on the outskirts of Jakarta. Permission had been given by the air force chief, Air Vice-Marshal Omar Dhani. On 30 September, a day before the putsch, yet another BPI agent who had been infiltrated into the trainee force, gave notice that the so-called '30th September Movement', thereafter known by the acronym GESTAPU, was about to act.

Why '30th September'? The proximate cause is likely to have been the imminent celebration of Armed Forces Day on 5 October. Thousands of troops had been brought to Jakarta from all over the Republic. Plotters wishing to forestall action by the Council of Generals would be wary of such an occasion.

A deeper reason for the sudden culmination of months of manoeuvring and speculation lay in the state of President Sukarno's health. On at least one occasion he was seen to suffer a fainting spell in public. Nevertheless he still had five years to live and one may ask whose interests were best served by rumours of serious deterioration? Subandrio, whose doctorate was medical, accused the Western press of making use of those rumours. At the beginning of August, however, air force intelligence reported that Sukarno was seriously ill and on the verge of collapse. The communist leader, Aidit, told one trial witness that the Chinese doctors believed just one more serious bout would kill him.

To conspirators of every persuasion the dawn of the post-Sukarno era must have seemed unnervingly imminent in Jakarta on Thursday 30 September 1965.

COUP AND COUNTER-COUP

The GESTAPU putsch began at half past one on the morning of Friday 1 October, mosque day for most people in Indonesia. Seven army trucks carrying armed soldiers drove from the Halim airbase on the edge of

Jakarta with orders to secure seven generals: the Minister of Defence, General Nasution, the army chief, General Yani, and five other generals comprising Yani's inner circle. General Suharto was not on the hit list.

Yani and two others were shot dead at their homes. Three more were arrested and executed shortly afterwards. Nasution is said to have received a telephone warning and scrambled over his garden wall into the grounds of the Iraqi Embassy, breaking his ankle as he fell. In his place a junior officer who resembled him – and may have been a look-alike – was arrested and taken away to be shot; his availability to be mistaken thus for his boss at four o'clock in the morning is one of those details that pose questions.

Simultaneously with the purge of General Yani and his inner circle other troops surrounded the presidential palace and seized the central broadcasting station and the telecommunications centre. GESTAPU forces were thus in control of three sides of the huge Merdeka Square in central Jakarta. Much significance has been attached to the fact that the fourth side of the square was left inviolate, for there was located the headquarters of the army's Strategic Reserve Command (KOSTRAD), headed by Major-General Suharto.

Within less than five hours of the hit squads setting out, the organizers of the putsch back on the Halim base were recording the all-but total success of Phase One, barring only the uncertainty about Nasution. Interestingly, no-one judged it necessary to probe with any urgency into the whereabouts of the missing Minister of Defence. Instead they pressed ahead with their plan. Later in the day, Nasution was observed receiving medical attention for his broken ankle at KOSTRAD headquarters.

The question remains: whose coup was it? Ostensibly, the organizers of the military strike were led by Lieutenant-Colonel Untung. Seventeen years earlier he had taken part in the unsuccessful communist rising known as the Madiun affair; and still he was no more than a lieutenant-colonel, a thwarted old-stager newly embittered by the prospect of a further shift to the right in the army. Although originally from the Diponegoro division, he was conveniently placed at that time as a battalion commander in the Tjakrabirawa regiment, responsible for the presidential palace guard, hence for Sukarno's personal safety.

Senior to Untung in rank, but apparently willing to acquiesce in his leadership of the putsch, was Brigadier-General Supardjo. His background was in the famously anti-communist Siliwangi division, Nasution's early fiefdom, where he had been a regimental commander in West Java until posted to command a KOSTRAD combat group in West Kalimantan (Borneo) in the war of attrition against Malaysia.

As well as the military team led by these two men, a team from the PKI leadership, headed by Chairman Aidit himself, was installed at the Halim air force base, but at some distance in a separate building. Their role was advisory, not operational. Acting as go-between was a shadowy but important figure by the name of Kamarasuman bin Achmad Mubaidah, more often known by his alias, Sjam. Under Aidit's instructions he had been working since 1960 to establish a secret special bureau to foster support for the party among military officers. Later, giving evidence at one of the trials, a person said to be Sjam was to assert that he had master-minded the operation.

Around five o'clock in the morning, satisfied that the purge of the Yani group had been accomplished, it was time for the organizers of the putsch to bring the President into the picture. So, adhering to the pre-arranged plan, Supardjo drove to the palace only to find that Sukarno was not there; after a speaking engagement the previous evening he had picked up one of his wives, Dewi, from a reception at the Hotel Indonesia and gone to spend the night at her house. Some hours later he was awakened and told about the disturbances going on in the city. He set out for Merdeka Square but changed course on learning by radio-telephone of the troop dispositions there, repairing first to the house of another wife, Hariati, and then to the Halim airbase where his personal Jet Star aircraft was on permanent stand-by. That is where Supardjo finally caught up with him and made his report, triggering a round of unforeseen political manoeuvring in which Sukarno strove yet again to counterbalance contending forces.

Meanwhile something had to be said to the people. As the new day dawned an announcer on Jakarta Radio read out the first public statement. A thoughtfully worded document, it still merits quotation at some length:

On Thursday 30th September 1965 a military action took place within the army in the capital Jakarta which was supported by troops of other branches of the armed forces. The 30th September operation, led by Lietenanent-Colonel Untung, commandant of the Tjakrabirawa, the presidential bodyguard, was directed against generals who were members of the so-called Council of Generals. A number of generals have been arrested, and communications and other vital installations have been placed under the control of the 30th September operation, while President Sukarno is safely placed under its protection. Moreover, those prominent

leaders of society who had been the targets of the Council of Generals
have been placed under protection by the 30th September Movement.

The Council of Generals is a subversive body sponsored by the CIA,
which has been very active lately, especially since President Sukarno was
seriously ill in the first week of August this year. Their hope that President
Sukarno would die of the illness was not fulfilled. So, in order to attain
their goal, the Council of Generals was planning to stage a demonstration
of power on Armed Forces Day, 5th October this year, by sending troops
into Jakarta from East, Central and West Java. With such a huge military
concentration in Jakarta, the Council of Generals was planning a coup
d'état ahead of 5th October. It is to prevent this counter-revolutionary
coup that Lieutenant-Colonel Untung has taken the initiative of
organizing the 30th September Movement, which has proved successful.

According to Lieutenant-Colonel Untung, the operation is solely a
movement within the army, aimed at the Council of Generals which has
besmirched the army's good name and harboured evil intentions towards
the Indonesian Republic and President Sukarno. . . The steps taken
against the Council of Generals will be followed by similar action
throughout Indonesia.

An Indonesian Revolutionary Council is to be established in the
capital, together with provincial, district, sub-district and village
revolutionary councils in the regions. The members of these
revolutionary councils will be civilians and military personnel who have
fully supported the 30th September Movement.

The Indonesian Revolutionary Council will not change Indonesia's
foreign policy . . . Confrontation against Malaysia will not be changed. . . .

Lieutenant-Colonel Untung has called on army officers and men
throughout the country to show their determination to eradicate the
influence of the Council of Generals and its agents within the army.
Power-crazy generals and officers who have been neglecting the lot of
their subordinates and living luxurious and happy-go-lucky lives at the
expense of their suffering, who humiliate women and squander
government funds must be thrown out of the army and duly punished.
The army is not for the generals; it is the property of all personnel who
are loyal to the revolution of 17th August 1945. . . .

As heard by the public, then, the GESTAPU putsch was purely an army matter
aimed at forestalling an imminent right-wing coup by the Council of Generals.

Ever since the small hours of the morning another story had been unfolding in parallel. Piecing it together, it is necessary to take note of that detail about Sukarno using a radio-telephone in his car. Those parts of the Indonesian security forces favoured by the Americans were equipped with advanced electronic communications systems. These were easily monitored both within the country and at nearby listening stations on land and at sea. Throughout this period, for instance, Britain's General Command Headquarters (GCHQ) ran a monitoring organization in Singapore under the direction of an agent who later became the head of GCHQ at Cheltenham before moving on into the defence industry.

What American and British monitors could hear, the KOSTRAD commander, Major-General Suharto, could also hear. He had never been mentioned as a member of the Council of Generals, neither was he selected for elimination by the GESTAPU strike units. Stories of his whereabouts during the hours of the purge varied. One had him sleeping tranquilly at home until awakened with news of things going on and shots being fired. Another had him out on a night fishing expedition. Yet another depicted him sitting at three and four in the morning by the bed of a sick child in Jakarta's military hospital. Like his arch-rival, Aidit, he appears to have had Macavity's cat-like gift of not being there. Even eighteen months later, purporting to present what he termed complete factual data about the GESTAPU affair to a session of the MPRS (Provisional People's Consultative Congress), Suharto's elaborately detailed account contained not a word about his own movements on that fateful Friday morning.

We know, however, that he turned up early at KOSTRAD headquarters on the one unoccupied side of Merdeka Square, from where he would have enjoyed a clear view of Untung's men guarding the palace, the radio station and the telecommunications centre. He was able to ascertain that the elements used in the putsch were from the 454th and 530th battalions of the Diponegoro division, all of which were recent recipients of American assistance and most of them commanded by officers close to Suharto. By half past eight he was in touch with the injured Nasution and kept him in hiding until later in the day when he took part in consultations about the situation.

In Jakarta, at least, the day passed without further military violence, thanks in part to Suharto's cool head but thanks also to the agility of President Sukarno. It was a day of political negotiation. Supardjo's initial briefing to the President had not spoken of the blood-letting, but of 'securing' the purged generals. Sukarno learned the truth only in mid-morning. He was shocked, and ordered that all bloodshed must cease forthwith. He insisted on a broadcast announcement to the nation stating that 'the President/Great Leader of the Revolution, Bung Karno, is in good health and continues to head the state'. Untung's team could hardly refuse, since they needed the public to believe that Sukarno was on-side with them. Already he was regaining freedom to manoeuvre: he prevaricated over the projected revolutionary council; he ordered two senior officers to go to KOSTRAD and fetch the commander of the Jakarta garrison. Then he went to lunch.

It was a bizarre and sometimes theatrical occasion. The lunchers included the air force, navy and police chiefs, the Attorney General and the distinctly right-wing Deputy Premier, Dr Leimena, with supporting cast – including Sukarno's wife Dewi – making sporadic appearances from the wings. They were not all supporters of the putsch.

The conspirators now tried to force Sukarno's hand. As they sat at lunch they broadcast their Decree Number One, followed by a list of members of the revolutionary council. Everyone listening, including Suharto and Sukarno himself, realized straight away that this was no left-wing phalanx. The handful of communists named were minor figures; twenty-four of the forty-five people listed held military ranks; Deputy Premier Leimena's name was there next to Subandrio's. The only thing was, as Suharto and Sukarno quickly established, that many of them did not know they were on the list and had no wish to be there.

Much more seriously, Decree Number One dissolved the existing cabinet, stripped ministers of their executive authority and proclaimed the new revolutionary council as the temporary source of all authority in Indonesia. The President's constitutional position was challenged. What began as a military putsch had turned into a coup d'état.

Had Sukarno complied, accepting Untung's decree as a *fait accompli* and settling for a puppet role as head of state, the coup attempt would have gained new ground. But he chose a fresh tack. Acting in his unchallenged role as commander-in-chief of the armed forces, he turned to the question of who should succeed the murdered Yani as army chief? Untung's group proposed two names and Sukarno accepted one of them, Major-General Pranoto, as a quid pro quo for their accepting his order as commander-in-chief to cease all operations.

Even as an order of the day embodying this arrangement was being drafted, the two officers whom Sukarno had dispatched to KOSTRAD before lunch to fetch the Jakarta garrison commander returned with a message from Suharto. He had, he said, temporarily assumed command of the army and placed himself at the President's disposal, awaiting orders.

By this means Sukarno was presented with yet another option, and in fact his order of the day was never broadcast; Radio Jakarta was being jammed and by six in the evening Suharto's forces were surrounding the radio station as a prelude to its swift and peaceable takeover. Untung, as good as his word, had ordered the cessation of all operations, and Supardjo had withdrawn his troops from around the palace.

The coup had collapsed and it only remained to find a way out of the Halim base for Sukarno. Suharto expedited the matter by letting it be known that he intended to attack the base; he had troops already concentrating around it. At half past ten that night, after refusing both air transport and an armed guard, the ever-cautious Sukarno, his wife Dewi and several others left the airbase and drove in convoy to his palace in the hills at Bogor.

British, American and Australian diplomats in Kuala Lumpur and Singapore were doubtless abreast of all these developments. They were, however, economical with the information they were prepared to release to news correspondents who, excluded like myself from entering Indonesia, largely depended on them for an account of what was going on. While most of my colleagues stayed in Singapore to cover the story, I happened to be in Kuala Lumpur when it broke. Although I did not know it at the time, one of the diplomats with whom I dealt in the British High Commission there, Stanley Budd, was a member of the Foreign Office Information Research Department (IRD) and responsible for managing all the information coming by a variety of means out of Indonesia.

Kuala Lumpur turned out to be the better reporting base for another reason: having formerly worked there for a Malaysian newspaper, I was on friendly terms with local officials and with the staff of Radio Malaysia. During the crucial days I was welcomed in the radio station and given instant access to most – if not all – of their excellent monitoring of Indonesian broadcasts.

For public consumption the known fact of Sukarno's transfer to Bogor at the end of the coup day came across as nothing stronger than an unconfirmed rumour. It was not until two days later that Stanley Budd, possibly sensitive to the BBC's reputation for accuracy, gave me information enabling me to report firmly but unattributably that the President was indeed alive and well.

There was nonetheless considerable confusion among outside observers about the true nature of what had happened in Jakarta, and it has remained a matter of controversy. The Malaysian prime minister, Tunku Abdul Rahman, made a revealing comment to me on the day after the putsch. The coup, he said, 'could have been the right one – or the wrong one'.

## Notes

1 Vatikiotis, Michael R.J. *Indonesian Politics under Suharto*, London & New York, Routledge 1998, citing Sugama, Y. *Memori Jenderal Yoga*, Jakarta 1990.
2 Churchill Archives Centre, Churchill College, Cambridge. GILC/962/13D(ii)

# FIVE

## *Out of the Shadows*

Confused and confusing though they still are, the actual events of 1 October 1965 and the days that followed are the least controversial and disputed aspect of the affair. We all, news correspondents, diplomats, spies and academics alike, immediately began trying to interpret what was going on. Explanations have proliferated over the years and, with so much documentary evidence still withheld from public view in the USA, Australia, Britain, Germany, the Netherlands as well as Indonesia itself – and no doubt elsewhere – there are certainly more to come.

All have to be weighed in the context of what had been happening nationally and internationally before the coup and in the light of what transpired after. About one seminal factor, though, there is agreement: President Sukarno's uncertain health had sensitised everyone to the question of the succession, and the key participants in Indonesia's political discourse were all hatching their own contingency plans.

Exactly who organized what, though, is shadowed in mystery. The coup was not a single event, but rather an interlacing of three distinct strands, more or less linked according to the interpretation being placed upon them, but each susceptible to a separate analysis. There was the putsch with the fleeting appearance of its own *dramatis personae*. There was the speedily launched and brutally executed extermination of communists, presided over by sections of the army. And there was the subtle, slow-moving process of removing President Sukarno from power, a psycho-political drama with a cast of hundreds.

The official, and, for many years, the conventional interpretation, promulgated by the Suharto camp and energetically promoted by American, British and Australian propagandists, was that during the night of 30 September 1965 the Indonesian Communist Party (PKI) attempted a coup d'état and was foiled by a quick-thinking army. Hence the frequent subsequent use of shorthand phrases like 'the failed communist coup of 1965'.

In this interpretation, a special group set up secretly by the communist leader D.N. Aidit had successfully subverted a number of army officers and goaded them to attempt a coup. Proponents of this scenario point to the indisputable facts that the communists had been calling for the arming of peasants and workers as part of Sukarno's NASAKOM strategy and that China was ready to provide the arms. In further corroboration they made much of Aidit's presence on the Halim airbase on the night of the putsch and of the fact that he was one of the many people to whom the President spoke while he was trying to pick up the pieces.

That authorised version has been so widely and comprehensively discredited that the once standard description of the events of 1 October 1965 as an attempted communist coup is at least tendentious and, more straightforwardly, wrong. The phrase 'unsuccessful military putsch' does greater justice to the facts. Everything that is known about the strategy and tactics of the PKI at the time militates against any notion that it had been working for a showdown. On the theoretical level its well-known analysis was that persistent, gradualistic, painstaking attention to grass-roots problems, rural and industrial, and loyalty to Sukarno's unifying nationalism would cause the attrition of other parties and deliver Indonesia into its hands without recourse to violence. The PKI well understood the danger of provoking the military. The party was not armed and had not trained its mass following for military action.

Neither was there any significant civilian agitation in support of the putsch; it is notable that the evils complained of in the initial broadcast declaration by the putschists were not the hardships and injustices suffered by workers and peasants but generals and officers who had neglected the lot of their subordinates and '. . . lived in luxury and led a gay life. . .' . According to Carmel Budiardjo, the British wife of an Indonesian civil servant subsequently imprisoned as a communist sympathiser, thoughts of rebellion were simply not in the air in communist circles at that time, even at central committee and politburo levels.[1] British diplomats who were on the scene during the coup period and with whom I have reviewed the facts no longer contend that it was initiated by the PKI.

A more prevalent British thesis is that the putsch was the work of discontented, nationalistic and leftward-leaning army officers who received encouragement but not leadership from the PKI. It is one of several cause-and-effect theories in which the putsch was the culmination of a chain of supposed actions and reactions.

We have already seen that one of these chain reactions began with the activities of a shadowy phalanx of non-communist generals widely referred to as the Council of Generals, supposedly in league with the CIA. With men like Nasution and the army chief of staff General Yani – but not General Suharto – among its number, this group was planning action to prevent a communist takeover either in the event of Sukarno ceasing to exercise presidential power or of a communist movement armed with Chinese weapons challenging the army on its own ground. Similar army moves had been tried several times in the 1950s, with Nasution involved in all of them. To any extent that the PKI became involved, it has been argued, it was only with the intention of defending Sukarno's unifying policies against a coup by the Council of Generals.

A variant sees, not Nasution and a council of generals, but Suharto as the key non-communist conspirator, again with American complicity. Indeed, one of the chief middle-rank plotters of the military putsch, Colonel Latief, said at his curiously delayed trial in the late 1970s that he had acted on behalf of Suharto and informed him on the night before the putsch of what was about to happen. The implication of this theory is that somewhere between 1960, when the US departments of Defense and State incited Nasution to stage a showdown between Sukarno and the army, and September 1965 the Americans lost confidence in Nasution and transferred their bets to Suharto.[2]

What I can vouch from my own observation in Jakarta is that, following the military putsch and the killing of Yani and the general staff, Australian and American diplomats in particular and the British to some extent backed Suharto and went out of their way to denigrate Nasution as weak, indecisive and cowardly. The tone of Australian thinking was later revealed by a letter from the Australian ambassador in Jakarta at the time of the coup, Keith Shann, to his British counterpart, Andrew Gilchrist, in which he implicitly sees Suharto as the key player:

I think my own picture of all this never differed very much from yours. . . . For your own private information my own interpretation of events was, I have subsequently discovered, heavily attacked by the then Minister for the Navy, Senator Gorton, in Cabinet on the grounds that I completely under-estimated the central and vital role played in the defeat of the communists by General Nasution. The only role that I have been able to discover that he played was that he was protected by a brave wife and that he fell over the wall and broke his ankle and was therefore unable to compromise and wreck the whole thing as he would inevitably have otherwise done. History relates that my interpretation of events was hotly defended in the Cabinet by [Prime Minister] Menzies and by the Foreign Minister Hasluck.[3]

With hindsight it is obvious that, given the strength of pro-Sukarno sentiment in Central and East Java, the Americans were going to prefer the Javanese and well-primed Suharto to the Sumatran and independently-minded Nasution as an army strong man.

A plausible socio-economic interpretation of broadly the same facts was offered in 1968 by the Soviet commentator Boris Vetin.[4] He placed his emphasis on the army's effective control by the late 1950s of foreign trade, communications and the plantation industries. A new bourgeoisie nicknamed KABIRS (kapitalis and birocrat) and made up of military and civilian bureaucrats felt itself increasingly threatened by the main supporters of President Sukarno's NASAKOM strategy – the nationalist PNI, the huge Islamic Nahdatul Ulama and the communist PKI. The CIA, he argued, therefore persuaded the top leaders of the military land forces, Yani among them, to enter into a *ralliement* with the Muslim Masjumi and the Socialist Party (PSI) to resist the promulgation and application of NASAKOM ideas in the armed forces. In reaction a group of shocked and disgruntled army progressives came together to combat lax living and corruption among top army leaders.

Like commentators of all persuasions, Vetin had evidence conveniently available to validate his scenario. On 31 August 1965, he pointed out, the commander of the Jakarta military area, General Umar Wirahadikusuma, said his area was in a state of combat preparedness and threatened to cut short any attempt to cause disorder. On 6 September the army chief of staff, General Yani, ironically unaware that he had less than four weeks to live, declared that the revolution had entered a decisive stage and 'victory was at the gates'.

That aspect of the Vetin version that had the purist Muslims of Masjumi fomenting incidents against communists with CIA encouragement sits well with the record of unrest in many parts of Sumatra and East Java in the months before and after the October putsch. But the heart of the matter, the place above all others where the second and third strands of the coup, the slaughter of the communists and the undermining of Sukarno, were played out was Central Java. It was there, even more than in Jakarta, that the pivotal drama occurred, and it was there, as seen by two American scholars, that the first strand of the coup, the military putsch, had its origin.[5]

On the basis of an intensive scrutiny of Indonesian newspapers in the period of the putsch and its immediate aftermath, Benedict Anderson and Ruth McVey took as their starting point deep divisions within the armed services. They noted rivalry tantamount to hostility between the Dutch-speaking (at that time) Siliwangi division in outward-looking West Java and the Javanese-speaking Diponegoro division in introverted and conservative Central Java. They drew attention to the dissatisfaction of many middle-ranking officers over the decision of the army general staff in 1964 to soft-pedal the confrontation campaign in northern Kalimantan (Borneo). This, they argued, was seen as the act of self-seeking and unpatriotic generals in league with the CIA. Loyal to Sukarno and possibly inspired by revolutionary fundamentalism, such officers were more than ready to believe in the danger of an imminent coup by a council of right-wing generals in Jakarta.

Anderson and McVey and many others since attached great importance to the fact that General Suharto, the indisputable beneficiary of the 1965 coup, had roots in the Diponegoro division and close connections with lieutenant-colonels Untung and Latief, the organizers of the Jakarta putsch. Suharto had himself been the army commander in Central Java in the mid-1950s; Untung had taken part in the West Irian campaign under Suharto's command and was now with the presidential bodyguard in the palace.

As Suharto seized control of Jakarta on the day of the putsch, the soldier at the helm in Central Java was a Colonel Suherman, based in the city of Semarang. Anderson and McVey held that Suherman, who was also the chief of army intelligence in Central Java, was one of the instigators of the putsch. He was, they pointed out, firmly anti-communist but prepared to make some controlled low-level use of the PKI as a means of engaging President Sukarno's sympathy.

It was indeed a striking feature of the whole affair that, with only minor exceptions, there was no communist or in fact any civilian participation in the putsch phase of the coup. The 7 a.m. broadcast announcing the putsch on Friday 1 October was the signal for conspirators under Colonel Suherman to take over first in Semarang and then in the other Central Javanese cities of Salatiga, Solo and Yogyakarta. In every case the initiators were military men; only in Yogyakarta, where the military were weak, were radical youth groups also enlisted, but they were not communists. The brains of the affair, Anderson and McVey concluded, were strongly anti-communist. They were, however, prepared to use the PKI for limited purposes to achieve their own quite separate goals. Hence, for example, the presence on Halim airbase – but at a distance from the key players – of the communist chairman D.N. Aidit on the morning of the putsch, and the inclusion of a handful of less important communists in the revolutionary council named by the putschists.

Other investigators writing since 1971 when Anderson and McVey distributed their preliminary analysis have highlighted another significant division within the army, between followers of the centrist, pro-Sukarno General Yani, the army chief of staff who was murdered, and the right-wing opportunist General Suharto, who was not on the hit-list. Others again have stressed the strength of communist influence within the army, and especially the Diponegoro division in Central Java.

Yet another theory was that Foreign Minister Subandrio, preparing himself to assume Sukarno's mantle and continue his balancing act, orchestrated the elements involved in the putsch.

In January 1967, fifteen months after the events on which he was commenting, President Sukarno bowed to heavily orchestrated pressure and gave the People's Congress (MPRS) his verdict on who had been responsible. It remains the simplest and most succinct analysis so far offered. The September 30th movement, he said, was created by the conjunction of three causes: a blunder by the PKI (communist) leadership, the wiles of neo-colonialism (a thinly veiled sobriquet for the CIA) and the existence of 'nutters'.

Determining which of the foregoing scenarios is closest to reality must depend largely on interpretations of what happened after the putsch.

In Jakarta, Friday 1 October in fact turned out to be a rather anti-climactic day. There were no public demonstrations, no violent military encounters. Suharto's forces had no difficulty in assuming control of the city and its strategic points; come early evening the rebel forces guarding the post and telecom building more or less melted away at the bidding of Suharto's men. As for Sukarno, after his day of skilful negotiation and calculation at the Halim airbase he could so easily have stepped into his presidential aircraft and flown either abroad or to a known centre of support farther east in Java; instead he elected to drive in stately convoy to the palace at Bogor, escorted by troops under Suharto's command.

On Saturday the communist newspaper *Haryan Rakyat* made a serious misjudgment by coming out in support of the putsch and was promptly suppressed, together with the rest of the leftist press. On Sunday the head of the greater Jakarta communist organization, Njono, was arrested and the party's organization and premises subsequently immobilized. By Monday 4 October the street disturbances which had so signally failed to occur on the day of the putsch suddenly erupted, provoked by an adroitly honed anti-communist campaign in which the army newspaper *Berita Yudha* led the way.

The PKI chairman, D.N. Aidit, had flown out of the Halim airbase to an airfield near Yogyakarta in an air force Hercules shortly after the collapse of the putsch. There he met a local PKI leader and warned him to leave the military to negotiate among themselves. Communist leaders should prevent demonstrations, support the President and not arouse suspicion by going underground. From there he drove to Semarang, not to join the rebellious Colonel Suherman, but to convey the message of restraint to PKI supporters there; and so the word was rapidly spread to all the major centres in East and Central Java, and thereafter also to Sumatra and northern Sulawesi. This was hardly the action of a man plotting the overthrow of the régime.

For three whole weeks, so far as civilians were concerned, the situation outside Jakarta stayed calm. It soon became apparent, however, that that was mainly attributable to Suharto's preoccupation with the problem of division within the armed forces. Once they had Jakarta and West Java secure Suharto and Nasution sent units of the Siliwangi division and the para-commandos (RPKAD) into Central Java, where they put out a warrant for Colonel Suherman and his close supporters. It took more than that, however, to solve the embarrasing problem of two Diponegoro battalions that had supported the putsch and remained fiercely loyal to Sukarno. By a process of negotiation and the threat of force, in a series of telephone conversations, the two battalions were persuaded to accept being moved out of Java altogether. As they departed, a state of war was declared in Central Java on 26 October and Suharto, a Javanese speaking to Javanese, addressed the troops in cadenced terms that were opportunistic even by his own flexible standards:

I know, and the Indonesian people know that you the troops of Central Java contributed much to the Indonesian revolution of 1945. I know also, as do the Indonesian people, that there are those among you who have strayed and been misled by the treachery and incitement of the counter-revolutionary opportunists of the 30th September movement . . . The people reject the 30th September movement . . . because it isolates Bung (brother) Karno from the people. See the error of your ways and return to the path of the revolution as expounded by Bung Karno. To those who go on opposing and are clearly in the wrong the armed forces – the children of the people – and the people themselves will teach a lesson.

And for many more months Suharto and his mentors prudently avoided saying a word against the president whom they would ultimately displace, aware that to do so would be counter-productive.

As rebellious army officers in Central Java were rounded up, the campaign of suppression spread to the whole of Central Java in an increasingly anti-communist guise, with Muslim and other non-communist elements armed and encouraged to join in. Clearly the PKI's strategy of restraint had become untenable; with its organization and leadership collapsing under military and organized mob pressure, communist elements tried to fight back in self-defence and the situation deteriorated into violent confrontation.

As the purge was extended into East Java, northern Sulawesi, Aceh and North Sumatra, vigilante bands armed and trained by the army rampaged through the countryside in a deadly witch-hunt in which old feuds of every description were revived and murderously resolved on the pretext of rooting out communism. What had begun as an internal army affair had now, it appeared, developed into a nationwide political purge. As we shall see, however, the apparent causal link between the two was never unambiguous and has become even less clear with the passage of time. The instant and expert control of information and the media, the suppression of any reference to the intricate involvement of army and air force in events surrounding the putsch, the focussed incitement of mob demonstrations against purposefully selected communist targets and subsequently against President Sukarno himself – all point to the pre-existence of a planned campaign. And that perception is reinforced by what is known about the collusion of Western propaganda specialists.

A WAR OF WORDS

Towards the end of October 1965, less than four weeks after the GESTAPU putsch, a newcomer appeared in the Political Adviser's office at Phoenix Park, the Singapore headquarters of Britain's Far East Command. His name was Norman Reddaway, and he made a bee-line for me at the first available opportunity. 'You and I,' he announced, 'will be seeing quite a lot of each other.'

I was the BBC's South-East Asia Correspondent. The late Norman Reddaway was one of the Foreign Office's most senior and experienced information and propaganda specialists, fresh from four years in charge of information in the Middle East and an expert in military intelligence. According to notes Reddaway gave me as I began work on this book, the British ambassador in Jakarta, Andrew Gilchrist, himself a practised propagandist, had asked for Reddaway to be posted to South-East Asia to apply IRD-type tactics to counter confrontation.

The Information Research Department (IRD) of the Foreign Office had been established by Cabinet decision in January 1948 (and was disbanded in 1977) with a brief to collect information about communist policy, tactics and propaganda and to promote material for anti-communist publicity via missions and information services abroad. Its primary tasks were described as being to alert public opinion to the true nature of communism and to give leads to anti-communist democratic elements.[6]

In fact, as Reddaway's propaganda campaign in relation to Indonesia was to demonstrate, the ultimate scope of IRD activities far exceeded that economical prescription. According to his note to me, his terms of reference in Singapore were to 'do anything you can think of' to get rid of Sukarno. Bearing in mind Sir Andrew Gilchrist's dictum in an unpublished draft autobiography – that 'propaganda is an adjunct; the first thing is to have a policy'[7] – one is reminded inescapably of that minuted agreement between President Kennedy and Prime Minister Macmillan in April 1962 that it would be desirable to liquidate President Sukarno, depending on the situation and available opportunities.[8]

Alluding rather more guardedly to the same minute, newly released in 1986 by the US National Archives, the author William Blum wrote: 'I have concluded from the impressions I have received in conversations with Western diplomats that President Kennedy and Prime Minister Macmillan agreed . . . to liquidate President Sukarno'.[9]

While there is room for debate about the possible meanings of the word liquidate, there is no mistaking the sentiment, couched in more oblique terms, that was expressed nine months later in a top secret letter from the British Commissioner-General in South-East Asia, Lord Selkirk, to the then head of the Foreign Office, Sir Harold Caccia: 'I cannot say I feel much confidence that we can contain an unstable and highly armed Indonesia, except on a purely temporary basis. I think therefore that we must hope that a new régime will arrive which will devote itself to the proper task of assisting the economic strength and stability of the country.'[10]

Such was the policy Reddaway was sent to support and such the policy Gilchrist clearly had in mind in March 1966 when he portrayed a drawn, haggard and fumbling President Sukarno days after he had been driven to cede effective power to General Suharto: 'I suppose I ought to have been pleased, and in a sense I was pleased, since this performance marked and affirmed the best possible outcome of my three years' mission to Indonesia'.[11]

A remarkable aspect of Norman Reddaway's IRD mission is that it began ten months after the back of Sukarno's confrontation of Malaysia had already for most practical purposes been broken. The flurry of peace-feelers by generals close to Suharto in 1964 had left little doubt that the weight and extent of Indonesian military provocations would diminish in both Kalimantan (Borneo) and the Malacca Strait; and in spite of the build-up of Indonesian forces close to the Sarawak border at the end of 1964, by June 1965 that had proved to be the case.

There were, it is true, military and political uncertainties that kept British observers on the alert during most of 1965. In March, for instance, it came to the notice of the British Ministry of Defence that Indonesian anti-aircraft units in the Riau archipelago south of Singapore were firing at civil aircraft; by the end of the year there had been nearly sixty incidents. An Indonesian NOTAM in October warned that aircraft flying over the islands of Bintan and Batam, whence many of the coastal landing parties had originated, would be shot down.

What was happening was a change in the nature of confrontation as different factions began to apply divergent policies. The Indonesian ambassador in Bangkok, B.M. Diah, one of the architects of the short-lived Body for the Promotion of Sukarnoism, told me in June 1965 that the landings launched from the Riau islands had been planned by Beijing-trained subversive warfare experts under the command of the foreign minister, Dr Subandrio. Riau was the base of a separate organization with its own intelligence, sabotage and propaganda apparatus aimed primarily at Singapore. What he described as regular Indonesian forces had been sent to Riau and as far north as Medan to put a stop to it. Different parts of the Indonesian armed forces were thus confronting each other.

Meanwhile in Borneo, while Suharto's colleagues wound down the campaign of incursions across the Sarawak border – the last of any note was in April 1965 at Plaman Mapu in the First Division – those who were loyal to Sukarno and influenced by the PKI concentrated increasingly on recruiting and training dissident elements from inside Sarawak. Many of these were ethnic Chinese involved in the so-called Clandestine Communist Organization, but it is less well-known that there were also significant numbers of Dayaks from local indigenous communities. An attack by irregular elements of this kind against a police station on the road between Kuching and Serian near the Indonesian frontier in June 1965 gave notice of the changed security threat in that area; and as time went by British, Malaysian and right-wing Indonesian voices would speak in harmony of how PKI and Chinese elements were converging on an area including Brunei and parts of Sarawak and western Kalimantan.

The IRD propaganda effort presided over by Reddaway was not, however, directed primarily against this phase-two confrontation. That was already well in hand by military psychological warfare practitioners long before his arrival; in March 1965 a Forward Plans Working Group had been constituted within the Political Adviser's office at Phoenix Park with the aim of concentrating psywar efforts in both strategic and tactical areas. Reddaway was going to have to work very closely with military psyops specialists of whose black propaganda activities he sometimes spoke less than admiringly. He liked to proclaim that anything but the truth is too hot to handle. We shall see nevertheless that he was himself prepared to dabble in the blacker art when occasion seemed to demand.

His arrival in Singapore less than a month after the GESTAPU putsch must, then, be viewed in context of the agenda set by Kennedy and Macmillan in 1962. The slow-motion coup being effected by the Suharto group was precisely the available opportunity mentioned in the CIA minute of their conversation. Harold Wilson's Labour government was now in office but had not diverged from Macmillan's attitude towards Sukarno, witness a personal telegram drafted earlier in 1965 for Prime Minister Wilson in the Commonwealth Relations Office:

The evidence is accumulating that Sukarno is seriously ill. If he were to die or be incapacitated the internal position in Indonesia might be greatly changed. We may not have to wait very long for this. Meanwhile we do not propose to do anything which might preclude our exploiting any opportunities which a change inside Indonesia might offer.[12]

With regard to thwarting President Sukarno, who was held to be yielding to an Indonesian Communist Party which in its turn was inclining more favourably towards China, British policy was in line with the USA's – much more firmly than on the matter of Malaysia. Former British Foreign Office officials recall being left in no doubt, during talks in Washington in February 1963, that the USA's only conclusive reason for accepting the Malaysia concept was that there was no more attractive way of providing for the future of Singapore. The USA's interest in restraining the spread of Chinese communist influence outweighed its interest in supporting Malaysia, and it was up to Britain to demonstrate that the two were part and parcel of each other.

Singapore's prime minister at that time, Lee Kuan Yew, alludes to this British problem in his book *The Singapore Story*:

> I myself had complete faith in the capabilities of the British, and was blissfully unaware that their policy of active opposition to Confrontation could not be sustained if the US government took a contrary line . . . but diplomatic documents from the British archives of that period disclose grave concern over the ambivalent attitude of the Americans. Their assessment was that the Americans feared Britain would be over-stretched by Confrontation and ultimately the United States would have to shoulder the burden.[13]

Tunku Abdul Rahman's expulsion of Singapore from the new-born federation in August 1965, as well as handing Sukarno and Foreign Minister Subandrio an unlooked-for propaganda gift, made it all the more necessary for Britain to support American objectives in Indonesia as a quid pro quo for continuing US support over the newly diminished Malaysia. A June 1963 review of strategic aims by the joint planning staff of the Chiefs of Staff Committee showed how fundamentally Britain was committed. After generalities about preventing the spread of communism, it spelt out as specific aims 'd) to maintain an independent contribution to the nuclear deterrent against China' and 'e) to defend and maintain the internal security of British colonial and protected territories and the external defence of the Maldives.'[14] Britain's ability to honour these commitments rested on its military bases in Singapore and Malaysia.

Working in the office of Alec Adams, the Political Adviser to the British Commander-in-Chief Far East – and not, be it noted, from a diplomatic chancery in either Singapore or Kuala Lumpur – Reddaway mounted total propaganda war. It was not until some weeks after our first meeting that he enlightened me about IRD and its rôle, leaving me with the impression that his responsibilities were all contained within that relatively innocent, faintly scholarly context. Clearly they were not. Already a year of his professional career, 1960, had been spent at the Imperial Defence College, an acknowledged centre for the study of military intelligence.[15] At Phoenix Park his office was adjacent to that of a senior MI6 officer.

IRD's patent strategy was to target the Indonesian Communist Party (PKI), to tar Sukarno with the communist brush and provide documentary support for General Suharto's interpretation of the military putsch on 1 October. In this it was not alone. Tan Sri Ghazali Shafie, who was head of the Malaysian External Affairs Department at the time, recalls: 'There were many Malays [i.e. in Malaysia] who regarded Sukarno as a demi-god. Some were in high places. So the Malaysian side during "konfrontasi" had to debunk Sukarno and his PKI cohorts with counter-propaganda . . . Special political actions were intensified and Sukarno lost his Malay constituency. Even the Radio Republik Indonesia (RRI) was not listened to or believed by the local Malays'.[16] A team of Ghazali's own career officers, kindred spirits with Reddaway and his colleagues, contributed vigorously to the counter-propaganda campaign mounted by Radio Television Malaysia and the Malaysian Information Department.

During the weeks before the putsch, when it has to be presumed that Norman Reddaway was preparing for his Singapore mission, IRD was generous with its distribution of well-researched and tendentious background briefs: one in July entitled 'PKI-Army Duel Continues', for instance, and another in August entitled 'Communist Attitudes to Singapore'.

On 7 October IRD issued 'Background on Indonesia' which opened with the disingenuous observation that 'the extent to which the Communist Party of Indonesia was implicated in the attempted coup in Djakarta on September 30 is gradually emerging though many questions remain to be answered . . .' Not, it might be thought, all that gradual, just six days after the putsch. IRD hurried on to help with the provision of answers to support the Suharto version. In November came 'The Dilemmas of China and the PKI' and in December 'The PKI Holds its Fire'. In the last of these, written when communists were being slaughtered in tens of thousands, there was no allusion to the killings; instead a picture was painted of security forces coping with a rampant communist rebellion and thousands merely arrested (as indeed they were). Only in the final paragraph did the IRD researcher mention that most of the fighting carried out by the PKI so far appeared to have been defensive and record its apparent lack of militancy.

Recipients of these and other IRD documents, or at least those who were close to the events being treated, understood the political motivation behind them. We were able to contextualize them from knowledge of the region; we had other sources, including observers and correspondents from other countries. What most British, Australian, Malaysian and New Zealand correspondents did not have was access to Indonesia itself. I was not allowed in until May 1966 by which time General Suharto had in effect completed an army coup d'état. By keeping us out the Indonesian authorities rendered us more reliant on diplomatic sources. And yet, under cover of diplomatic passports, MI6 agents came and went at will between Jakarta and other regional capitals both before and after the putsch. Reddaway and Gilchrist between them exploited the situation to the full.

In the notes he gave me Reddaway said his main source of information was a series of top secret telegrams – about four a week by diplomatic wire service – from Andrew Gilchrist in Jakarta, dealing with the dishonesty and shortcomings of President Sukarno. He said they were given exclusively to me, and explained in a similar version of his story used in a book by Paul Lashmar and James Oliver that as the BBC's correspondent in the area I was 'the most suitable customer'.[17]

Other correspondents were in fact also receiving special attention – my colleagues, for instance, on *The Times*, the *Daily Telegraph*, the *Observer* and the *Daily Mail*. Nor was Reddaway narrowly nationalistic in bestowing his favours, for there were, to my knowledge, privileged Indian, Canadian and American correspondents too.

Information was flowing into Phoenix Park from numerous sources. There were a great variety of radio intercepts, some effected by GCHQ stations in Hong Kong and Singapore itself, the latter run by Brian Tovey who subsequently headed the whole of GCHQ at its Cheltenham, UK, headquarters. Other monitored material came from Radio Malaysia, the American Federal Broadcast Information Service (FBIS, a CIA auxiliary), and the Australian intelligence centre in Canberra. Admiral of the Fleet, Lord Peter Hill-Norton, who was Flag Officer second-in-command (i.e. the admiral in command at sea of Britain's Far East Fleet), has confirmed to me that radio intercepts were carried out by ships at sea and relayed daily to Singapore. Royal Navy submarines were also particularly active at that time, operating out of the deep-water harbour at Tawau off the east coast of Sabah (North

Borneo), picking up and delivering the right people in the right places in a sort of 'anti-communist piracy', as another authoritative informant put it to me.

One of Britain's most remarkable 'inside' sources was President Sukarno's Japanese wife, Ratna Sari Dewi. The contact was developed out of a private visit to London in June/July 1965 during which she sent Queen Elizabeth a Balinese ebony carving as a token of personal esteem. She was sent a letter of thanks via the British embassy in Jakarta, soon after which there was an exchange of social visits between Dewi and Mrs Freda Gilchrist, the ambassador's wife. At those meetings Dewi was seen as being willing to be a carrier of messages. Thereafter, until Sukarno's final eclipse in 1967, she had a number of substantive contacts with the British, some of which came to my notice at the time.

Given so much information, it is inconceivable that Reddaway and his colleagues did not know about the carnage being inflicted on real and suspected communists by the Indonesian army. The control of information was rigorous. No word of the slaughter came my way. All concerned remained silent, 'not under guidance but under direction', in the words of a former information officer for one of the armed services.

Reddaway was highly selective in the way he used the flood of information. Normally I would resort to him and other information specialists at Phoenix Park several times in a week for amplification of Indonesian news stories reported through news agencies and other channels. IRD, used with discrimination, was a useful source of background information about military figures, economic affairs and developments within the political parties. Sometimes it was remarkably prescient about the likely course of events in Indonesia.

Less often Reddaway would approach me. Once he called to say the Jakarta embassy was on a state of alert fearing an attack of some kind. Another time he told me Gilchrist in Jakarta was complaining because what he had heard me say on the air resembled too closely what he had said in his telegrams! I replied that the ambassador must not suppose he was my only source of news and comment. Despite what Reddaway said, I seldom held any of Gilchrist's despatches in my hand; occasionally he would read me passages from them. During intervals events in other parts of South-East Asia took me right away from Singapore.

Some of the material collected in Indonesia and sent to Phoenix Park was actuality recording of what broadcasters call 'vox pops'. An example was a tape recorded by a Canadian journalist which was offered to me bearing what seemed to be unedited interviews with students demonstrating outside the presidential palace in Jakarta. A lot of this material was edited in Singapore under Norman Reddaway's aegis to be broadcast to Indonesian listeners in a programme whose Indonesian title meant 'Voice from the Well', a reference to the well on the Halim airbase where the bodies of the six generals killed in the putsch were thrown. Asked for his reflections on this, Singapore's former prime minister, Lee Kuan Yew, told me 'I have no recollections of a propaganda war originating in Singapore by the Singapore or the British government during Confrontation.[18]

When I put that to a former British diplomat who had been involved at a senior level, his reaction was derisory: 'Of course he hasn't; it was a black operation'. 'Voice from the Well' was in fact safe-handed into Jakarta and transmitted from a residence close to Suharto's.

The best exposé yet of the range of Reddaway's propaganda activities at Phoenix Park is in a recently declassified secret letter now held at the Churchill Archive in Cambridge. In it he responds to a request by the late Sir Andrew Gilchrist for notes to include in his memoirs. 'This is not difficult', Reddaway writes, 'and I will send you a couple of telegrams, etc., separately under confidential cover to the CRO which you can destroy after perusal'. Implicitly confirming that his IRD role was only part of his work, he adds 'I will also send you a copy of my valedictory on the IRD side, with a list of the lessons to be drawn'.

The letter, which I resist annotating with the many explanations it deserves, continues:

The incidents which stand out in my mind are :-

(a) The story carried by Reuters about the 20th October [i.e. before Reddaway arrived in Singapore] about the Chinese keeping their flag at the top of the mast. This went all over the world and back again and was even quoted by Subandrio when arguing with the Chinese Embassy.

(b) The story of the messenger plying between Aidit and Subandrio. This was carried by newspapers, agencies and radio.

(c) The story of PKI systematic preparations before the coup – the carving up of the town into districts for systematic slaughter. This was carried by agencies.

(d) Various sitreps from yourself which were put almost instantly back into Indonesia via the BBC. You may remember complaining that the versions put back were uncomfortably close to those put out by yourself.

It was about that time that I wondered whether this was the first time in history that an Ambassador had been able to address the people of his country of work almost at will and virtually instantaneously.

(e) The facts on Indonesia's economic position. These came out in Hong Kong and Melbourne – only just in time to avoid cancellation by Dear Arthur who was against the whole ploy. The Indons themselves have used them very freely since.

(f) On the 12th March your telegram about the handover of power enabled us here to lead the world's news by several hours. After we had played this news trump newsmen would take anything from here and pestered us for copy.

(g) Gavin Young agreed to give exactly your angle on events in his article in the *Observer* of 13th March – i.e. that this was a kid glove coup without butchery, denunciations and suspension of law and order.

(h) The first really irreverent words about Sukarno were broadcast from K.L. when Don North's tape, made while the students were blockading the Palace, reached K.L. via this office.

(i) A flattering version of the night of the long knives (starring Mrs Nasution) was printed by all the Scripps Howard papers in America. We made a mock-up of the cuttings and sent them to the Embassy in Djakarta, thinking Marshall Green might like to hand them to Nasution. Stanley Budd wrote the article based on Djakarta reports of the coup. (He was rebuked by his masters for doing so!).

(j) The two articles from *Encounter* on the state of Indonesia were mailed to about 600 recipients.

(k) Details of nest-eggs accumulated abroad by Soek, Sub, Saleh and Dalam came out in Hong Kong and were widely reproduced. We were forbidden to publish the complementary story about Soek's method of collecting his U.S.\$60,000,000 by means of a 7% levy on all Japanese contracts ![19]

Reddaway added a revealing handwritten postscript: 'The outstanding impression I have of my time here and elsewhere spent on this sort of work is of the suspicion and dislike of it on the part of most diplomatic officers. Their whole instinct is to negotiate in private with the people they're accredited to and politely to turn down suggestions about exerting pressures on them. We thus get a good reporting service and a good messenger boy service between London and country X but little more. The political side has been hostile most of the time, and at best neutral . . .'

BETTER DEAD THAN RED

Within three weeks of the putsch, having reestablished relative discipline over the armed forces nationwide and fractured the communist party organization in the capital, Suharto and Nasution turned to their central purpose: the total elimination of the PKI. To help them get going the United States Central Intelligence Agency (CIA) supplied them with a list of some five thousand ranking communists; one of the agency's functionaries in the American embassy kept it up to date by scoring out their names as they were murdered or detained. Few if any legal niceties were observed.[20]

Work began in Central Java, led by the swashbuckling paratroop commander, Brigadier-General Sarwo Edhie. At first he concentrated on the communist stronghold contained within a triangle marked by Boyolali, Klaten and Solo, close to Semarang where the seeds of the initial putsch had been planted. It quickly turned into one of the bloodiest assaults on the very core of Javanese identity in the history of the archipelago.

As in Jakarta, an early priority was to eliminate the communist leadership. Mayors and other local officials, a high proportion of whom were PKI members, were among the first and easiest targets; then party officers. These for the most part were dealt with by the security forces, some to be detained for questioning as a source of further intelligence.

The prime quarry was the PKI chairman, Dipa Nusantara Aidit who, having at first urged the party faithful not to go underground for fear of arousing suspicion, now changed his mind and advised them to 'breathe the air of the countryside'. He was himself among the first to do so, going into hiding near the ancient city of Solo in a little village called Sambeng.

Still only forty-two years old, Aidit was by then one of the three or four most important communist leaders and theorists in the world. The party which he had been leading for fourteen years was the biggest in the non-communist world, and he was the acknowledged pioneer in developing an empirical basis for the development of communism in post-colonial societies in Asia and Africa. Sumatran, the son of a minor forestry official, he was schooled in Jakarta and at the age of sixteen plunged into the activities of a number of radical nationalist organizations. During the Japanese occupation he carried his activities underground and in 1943, like thousands of nationalists throughout the Malay world, he joined the communists; that same year he founded the Movement for Indonesian Independence.

Despite being arrested twice, his ascent through the party apparatus was rapid. In 1948, the year of the Madiun revolt, he joined the Politburo and became a stern critic of the old-fashioned Bolshevik thinking. Benefiting from the reappraisal that followed, he became party chairman in 1951 and began building his reputation as a cautious, approachable, thoughtful and patriotic politician. He accepted Sukarno's assessment that the time was not ripe for social revolution in Indonesia, and from 1962 on was rewarded with minor ministerial posts – though he was never, like his colleague Nyoto, appointed to the inner cabinet.

Aidit's life has yet to be chronicled as fully as its interest merits. When it is, the final chapter will not be the least dramatic. Among several versions, the one most likely to be authentic is contained in a small tract called *The Last Days of Aidit*, by a man called Soebekti.[21]

His hideaway in Solo was one of a cluster of houses close to a river-bed, down a lane so narrow that no car could come near. As well as the elderly widow who was its owner there was a lodger living there, a pensioner called Pak Kassim. After the Paras (RPKAD) regained control of Solo he stayed briefly but uneasily with a family whose son was a serving soldier – though not in Java. Once in the city of Klaten, Soebekti recounts, Aidit evaded capture only by hiding under a hollow wooden vessel used for pounding paddy. Then on to a village called Manisrenggo, but again had to move, this time to hiding places on Mounts Merapi and Merbabu to confer with other communist leaders.

The troops looking for him were no less resourceful than he was. Some disguised themselves as trishaw drivers and iced-water vendors so as to pick up gossip about his whereabouts. The hunt went on for eighteen days until they came to kampong Sambeng. All the male inhabitants were ordered into the open and checked. Finally the searchers entered widow Hardjo's house, Aidit's last refuge, searched but found only a bag of his belongings and his transistor radio. Ostensibly the search was called off, but agents were posted to keep watch. Meanwhile, as Soebekti cryptically recounts, troops finally managed to make Pak Kassim talk. They immediately removed the cupboard hiding the door to Aidit's room and captured him.

That was on 21 November 1965. Before they shot him, Aidit was almost certainly subjected to a perfunctory interrogation. Fragments of what he was supposed to have said found their way into the narratives of selected journalists and authors, and at least one British diplomat tells me he recalls seeing something of it.

A different and somewhat suspect account, attributed to a Colonel Yasir Hadibroto, was offered in October 1980 by a Jakarta weekly, *Kompas Minggu*. According to this account a double agent was used to track Aidit to his hiding place at kampong Sambeng. After his capture Aidit abstained from making a written statement, but things allegedly said by him were written down by his captors and an amateur snapshot shows him signing what could be that document. After that there seems to have been a disagreement between Yasir and a military police officer who appeared on the scene. Yasir avoided handing over either Aidit or the signed document, managed to separate himself from the military police officer and had Aidit shot before the other officer caught up with them. When Yasir reported to Suharto and asked whether he had done right, the general smiled – but said nothing.

Although the slaughter went on for many more months, it was at its height in October and November 1965. Accounts of it have tended to focus on Central and East Java and Bali. But the military campaign and the killing were nationwide.

The army's rôle was two-fold: to handle the surgical elimination of the PKI's leadership structure and to muster, train, arm and transport civilian squads to penetrate and kill the grass-roots of the communist movement. The gangs were made up almost entirely of Muslim and nationalist youth. The motivation behind the strategy, aside from its logistical convenience, was icily calculated. A campaign carried out exclusively by the army could have provoked a counter-reaction and might well have increased rather than diminished support for the PKI. It was necessary to make it appear that the purge was a spontaneous act of the people. Wherever possible popular fury was turned against the usual target of the Chinese minority to reinforce the fiction that they were at the core of communist membership. Religious fervour was another ready resource, as were disgruntled landholders dispossessed as a consequence of positive PKI action to get land redistributed.

By the beginning of 1966 Ambassador Gilchrist put the slaughter toll at 400,000. The figure was challenged by his Swedish colleague, who called it 'quite incredible' and returned from a probing tour of East and Central Java in February to describe it as 'a very serious under-estimate'.[22]

Half way through 1966, the army employed more than a hundred graduate researchers from the universities of Jakarta and Bandung to describe and quantify the extermination campaign nationwide. After two months of investigation on the ground – and with the slaughter far from over – they returned a tally of nearly a million killed. Central and East Java were the worst with 800,000 between them; next Bali with more than 100,000; Sulawesi and the lesser Sundas (including West Timor) 10,000 each; Aceh 6,000, and so on down to South Kalimantan with fewer than one thousand. It was noted with regret that one in every five murders had probably been committed in error on non-communists.

The picture they painted in a report not destined for publication was a blood-chilling collage of youngsters amok on the sheer pleasure of beheading people and the quiet orderliness of victims compliantly digging their own mass graves. Where firearms were not provided or ammunition ran out the preferred weapons were clubs and axes and machetes and wooden spears. Group executions, on the other hand, were generally done by soldiers using automatic guns. Usually the killing was done by night at some distance from the villages with military vehicles used to convey the victims to their death. Bodies not put in graves were disposed of inches deep in paddy fields, sometimes hung in trees and burned or in many cases thrown into rivers. Along the coast of Aceh and North Sumatra bodies were cast into the sea to be found by fishermen.

The British line, in both Jakarta and Singapore, was ignorance of the scale of the operation and endorsement of the Suharto group's depiction of events. Allowing the possibility of a measure of ignorance, however, it is not to be construed as indifference. The then Counsellor at the British Embassy, (now Sir) James Murray, recalls how during a spell of acting as Chargé d'Affaires he was authorised to tell Suharto that in the event of Indonesian troops being transferred from the confrontation area on the Sarawak border to help deal with the situation in East Java, British forces would not take military advantage. Access to Suharto by British and kindred diplomats was not easy since he was anxious not to be branded as an 'imperialist lackey', so Murray was obliged to find an opportune moment to communicate his assurance during a Japanese reception.[23]

In addition to those killed, up to 200,000 had been arrested by the time of the 1966 survey. Tens of thousands more were to suffer that fate; for many it spelt death by starvation, torture or disease.

It took a long time for the scale and extent of the slaughter to emerge. Travelling the full length of Java early in 1967 I discovered a people loath to speak of it, either traumatised or terrorised into silence or unimaginably indifferent to what had happened. Similarly in Bali, in the course of a conversation lasting several hours with a celebrated local artist surrounded by friends, I extracted not a single word in acknowledgment of the killings.

More forthcoming was Made Mantik, chairman of the Bali branch of the nationalist PNI since shortly after the putsch, hence by definition in good standing with the Suharto régime. He did not believe many killed as communists had in fact been PKI members; but neither did he accept the high figures being bandied about; 'a few thousand' was his estimate.

A quarter of a century later the author Norman Lewis persuaded a Balinese tourist guide to reminisce about the 1965 massacre:

> I was in the school when the *kelian* who is head of the *banjar* (village council) sent someone to beat on the *kulkul* to call the men to the square where we saw the soldiers and the Javanese men they brought with them waiting.
>
> All work had stopped in the padis, animals allowed to stray. People had no idea what communism was. All loved Sukarno; many thought he was a communist. Some Christians thought PKI stood for Partai Kristen Indonesia and therefore joined it. There was no way to escape; the only thing was to stay put and hope the priest would say you went to the temple everyday. The *kelian* told all women and children to stay at home, then a Javanese who was with the officer read names from a list – communists, atheists and people not certified in the *banjar* as members of any religion. The *kelian* called these people out and the Javanese men who were with the officers roped them in lines. The officer said 'these are your enemies. I call on you to fight for your religion'. The officer got angry because no-one wanted to have anything to do with killing these men. He asked the *kelian* for lists of Hindus and Buddhists. These were exempt because they're not allowed to take life. All the others were given pangahs or clubs and told to kill the communists.[24]

Now that two of the coup's three strands had been dealt with General Suharto could turn his full attention to the third, the question of the presidency. He had a problem. Handling the first two strands, the putsch and the extermination of communists, he had needed and unhesitatingly called for the nation's loyalty to President Sukarno. Intelligence reports were telling him that that loyalty remained strong, especially in Java where the culture had invested Sukarno with a monarchical status. Likewise a large part of the officer corps was devoted to Sukarno both as revolutionary nationalist and innovative political thinker. It was even suggested by earlier commentators that Suharto himself experienced pangs of conscience about undermining an almost godlike Javanese hero.

Andrew Gilchrist, the British Ambassador in Jakarta, reflected a prevalent sentiment when he told me in November 1965 that the preferred solution was to keep an emasculated Sukarno in office provided his would-be successor, Dr Subandrio, could be eliminated. Probably he was relaying the view of Dr Adam Malik, the civilian politician Suharto was to appoint as his foreign minister.

Whether Suharto beguiled Sukarno into a sense of security or Sukarno, the master tactician, made his own appraisal of the power equation must remain a matter of speculation. Only a fortnight after the putsch he appointed Suharto commander-in-chief of the armed forces, thus acknowledging the realities of the moment. It was the first step along the way that ultimately led Suharto to supreme power.

Suharto forthwith set the Paras (RPKAD) under Colonel (later Brigadier-General) Sarwo Edhie to work on their bloody mission in Central and East Java. Sukarno was appalled by the carnage; tyrannical he may have been at times, but not bloodthirsty. Moreover, the assault on the PKI spelt the undoing of the power balance that he saw as offering the only prospect of national reconciliation and unity. He went on speaking out against it.

Meanwhile, a well-organized youth movement hit the streets in Jakarta. There too it was observed that they were often transported to the sites of their demonstrations in military vehicles and were working from typed address lists. In Singapore Norman Reddaway, presiding over the British propaganda programme, was in no doubt: the youth movements were organized by the army, he confided to me. Their demands were explicit: crush the PKI and do something about the cost of living. At first they did not pick on Sukarno himself, but that was to change in response to accumulating evidence of his recalcitrance.

In February 1966 amid mounting tension he defiantly – but ineffectually – banned the main youth movement KAMI (Students' Action Command) and sought to rally support among loyal military officers and political leaders. Provocatively he recast the cabinet, dropping General Nasution as armed forces minister, but retaining Subandrio and the handful of communist ministers.

The youth demonstrations merely intensified and there were confrontations between Sarwo Edhie's Paras and the palace guard, until on 11 March another crunch day occurred. Gilchrist recorded in a diary item what apparently happened:

Sukarno had bidden all military and civilian commanders to a meeting in Jakarta and yesterday they began arriving. Sukarno was then at the Palace having a meeting of his cabinet. As the military commanders arrived they were approached by Suharto's people to find out if they would be loyal to him and the Army, to stage a showdown with the President. It appeared they were and the Proclamation giving power to Suharto was accordingly drafted. Sukarno got wind of the ultimatum and left the cabinet meeting, flying off to Bogor with Subandrio and Chaerul Saleh. When he got there he found Bogor surrounded by armed units of the Siliwangi. Three generals followed him there and presented the ultimatum. It was eventually signed at midnight. This morning the same three generals fetched Sukarno back to Jakarta . . .[25]

So Suharto had taken another stride on the path towards the presidency. What Sukarno had signed in Bogor authorised him to take 'all necessary steps to guarantee security and calm and the stable conduct of government and the course of the Revolution'. The generals for their part undertook to ensure Sukarno's personal safety.

The first step that Suharto deemed necessary was to issue a presidential decree banning the Communist Party (PKI). Within a week he ordered the arrest of fifteen cabinet ministers, foremost among them the serpentine first deputy premier and foreign minister, Dr Subandrio. Also arrested was Chaerul Saleh, a respected non-party politician of the 1945 generation, ardent supporter of Sukarno and a likely contender for the presidential succession.

Most of the USA's political objectives in Indonesia had now been achieved; the possibility of a communist take-over was eliminated; Sukarno was politically undermined without being totally humiliated; government was in the hands of a dependent soldier who could be relied upon to tune the economy to capitalist requirements. Before the month was out the cabinet was reshuffled yet again, enshrining the triumvirate which many hoped would lead Indonesia on the long journey towards prosperity and some sort of moderate, non-militaristic government: the urbane Sultan Hamengku Buwono of Yogyakarta, establishment figure *par excellence* and guarantor of Suharto's Javanese legitimacy; the left-wing (but non-communist) Sumatran intellectual, Adam Malik, and Suharto himself.

But Sukarno, still titular president and acknowledged 'great leader of the revolution', declined to enter into the spirit of the new régime. Despite a modulated campaign of denigration – IRD, for instance, was assiduous in assembling and disseminating details of his financial manipulations – he continued to command major support in Java and elsewhere. On the military front the police and naval commanders stayed loyal to the president, as did the marine corps (KKO). Generals were divided, and not all who sided with Suharto could vouch for the allegiance of middle-ranking officers. Actual physical clashes and confrontations were occurring sporadically in Java and civil war was a serious possibility.

For this reason the managers of the transition publicly stressed the importance of constitutionality; parliament came suddenly into unaccustomed favour. The People's Consultative Congress stripped Sukarno of his title of 'president for life' and called for elections within two years – which in fact never eventuated. Rumours began to circulate that Sukarno had had foreknowledge of and was even involved in the '30th September' putsch. Invariably, the political misdeeds attributed to him were cited side by side with the economic privations of city dwellers.

Speaking to the People's Consultative Congress (MPRS) in July 1966 Sukarno repeated that the putsch had been a complete surprise to him. But none of his disclaimers was going to be of any avail, and perhaps he had some premonition of the end one day in December 1966 when he emerged from a back door of the palace wearing shorts and a T-shirt and began distributing dozens of his old neck-ties to members of the press corps. Sukarno did consent to speak once more, and in January 1967 we were all summoned to hear him broadcast a statement concocted after more than a week of haggling with the Suharto group.

He walked briskly into the ballroom of the Merdeka (independence) Palace, sat down facing us across a table with a microphone, put on his glasses, took out his script and began to read with sarcastic emphasis. He said he was under no obligation to account for his activities, and if things had gone wrong why should he alone be held responsible? What about the former minister of defence? – and he departed from his script to name him, General Nasution. When he had finished he peeled off his spectacles, got up and was walking out when an American correspondent went up to him: 'You seem to be angry, Mr President'. Sukarno punched him on the arm. 'I am angry', he retorted. He would have been more so had he known that Indonesian Radio was about to broadcast not his recorded voice, but an actor reading the script, so that even by that means he would not be able to convey his feelings to his listeners.

Determined that Sukarno's displacement should be perceived as an act of parliament rather than the armed forces, Suharto set up an ad hoc committee to investigate the question of his complicity in the putsch. Adam Malik was known to be urging Sukarno to step down. In February the House of Representatives (DPR) called for a special session of the MPRS to remove Sukarno from the presidency and appoint an acting successor.

On 20 February Indonesia's first president and greatest modern leader bowed to the inevitable, signing over his remaining powers to General Suharto during a three hour meeting at his palace in Bogor. The situation was formalized by the MPRS following a closed session on 12 March, a year after the first delegation of partial powers to Suharto.

Once more, on a drab and sunless Sunday afternoon, correspondents foregathered in the presidential palace. At the appointed hour General Suharto stepped forward into the television lights to be sworn in, followed one step behind by a military minion bearing a silver tray. Nonchalantly he turned, took first his spectacles from the tray and put them on, then the script from which he was to read: the performance of a born tyrant.

After the passage of yet another year the MPRS removed the word acting from Suharto's presidential title. The coup was over.

## Notes

1  Interview with author, 8 February 2000.
2  Peter Dale Scott in an article entitled 'The United States and the Overthrow of Sukarno', 1965–1967 in the Summer 1985 edition of *Pacific Affairs* supports the thesis that Nasution's stock with the Americans had fallen. Quoting from a CIA memorandum of 22 March 1961 by Richard M. Bissell, he attributes CIA disillusionment with him to his consistent record of yielding to Sukarno on several major counts and adds that by 1965 it was deepened by Nasution's opposition to the American involvement in Vietnam.
3  Personal letter dated 11 April 1968 from K.C.O. Shann, Department of External Affairs, Canberra to Sir Andrew Gilchrist, British Ambassador, Dublin. Churchill Archives Centre, Churchill College, Cambridge, GILC 962 13 K (ii).
4  *Literaturnaya Gazeta* Number 13, 1968.
5  Anderson, Benedict and Ruth McVey 'A Preliminary Analysis of the October 1, 1965 Coup in Indonesia', Cornell Modern Indonesia Project, Ithaca N.Y. 1971.
6  Public Record Office FO 1110.
7  Churchill Archives Centre, Cambridge GILC/13/B iv.
8  CIA memorandum cited in *The Times* 8th August 1986.
9  Blum, William *The CIA: A Forgotten History*, Zed Books 1986.
10 Public Record Office FO 800/897, letter dated January 18, 1963.
11 Churchill Archives Centre, Cambridge GILC/13/A iv.
12 Public Record Office PREM 13 428 T21/65.
13 Lee Kuan Yew *The Singapore Story*, Singapore, Prentice Hall, 1998.

14 Public Record Office Annex to JPS. 1114/25/6/63 in DO 169/221.

15 Norman Reddaway was sent to the Imperial Defence College holding the unusually junior rank of first secretary, suggesting he may have been singled out for his future specialism in clandestine matters.

16 Letter to author, 12 May 2000.

17 Lashmar, Paul and Oliver James, *Britain's Secret Propaganda War*, Stroud, Sutton 1998.

18 Letter to author dated 27 May 2000.

19 Churchill Archives Centre, Churchill College Cambridge GILC 13K iii.

20 Details of this part of the CIA's multi-faceted involvement in the Suharto coup were first exposed in the *Washington Post* of 21 May 1990.

21 Soebekti, *Hari-Hari Terachir Aidit*, Yogyakarta, B.P. Kedaulatan Rakyat 1966.

22 Churchill Archives Centre, Cambridge, confidential letter from A.G. Gilchrist in Jakarta, dated 23 February 1966, GILC 962/13Dii.

23 Interview with author June 2000. Evidence that Britain was even better than its word turned up in a Jakarta weekly. According to the 5 October 1980 edition of *Kompas Minggu*, on hearing of the Gestapu killings in Jakarta the colonel commanding an infantry brigade on confrontation duty at Kisaran near the north-east coast of Sumatra, found a ship to transport his troops back to Jakarta. Flying the Panamanian flag, she sailed safely down the heavily patrolled Malacca Strait – escorted by two British warships. The colonel in question, named as Yasir Hadibroto, was the same who, according to the article, claimed responsibility for the subsequent arrest and murder of Aidit. An English translation of the *Kompas Minggu* article was published by *TAPOL Bulletin*, No. 41–2 in November 1980.

24 Lewis, Norman, *An Empire of the East*, London, Jonathan Cape, 1993.

25 Churchill Archives Centre, Cambridge GILC/13/A Diary, 12 March 1966.

# PART TWO

## The Suharto Era

# SIX

## *Army Rules*

The coterie headed by Suharto was now ready with plans for what he would call the 'new order'. Setting aside the imposition of economic disciplines adequate to mollify the international financial community, and the murder of hundreds of thousands of communists and others, the next three decades would reveal remarkable similarities between the new order and the old. But it would take time for that underlying reality to emerge, and in the post-coup months the generals' advent to power gave rise to euphoric hopes, both at home and abroad, which, with hindsight, were never to be justified. As with so much of the history of these islands, the shadow seemed for a time brighter than the reality.

Resolved from the outset to have no further truck with the tangled skein of political parties, the generals brought into alliance two civilians whose appointment bore heavy symbolism: the Sumatran Adam Malik as foreign minister and Sultan Hamengku Buwono of Yogyakarta, the acme of Javanese élitism, in charge of the economy. The agenda was fourfold: to consolidate the army as the absolute effective authority in every aspect of the nation's life; to enlarge the middle class as a consumption-oriented force; to re-establish Indonesia's good standing with the capitalist West; to put the nation's finances in order.

It was an integrated programme which had to move forward simultaneously on all fronts; but the highest priority, born at that time of sheer urgency, though later of expediency, was given to economic and financial reform. Such was the vigour of its prosecution that the criteria by which Indonesia is measured remained for many years primarily economic. Name one 'emerging nation' and Indonesia immediately springs to mind.

Although the army was clear-minded about the use of physical force for political ends, it was intellectually un-equipped – and its American mentors knew it – for the economic and financial exercises upon which its ultimate success would depend. It would have to rely on civilian experts, and a team was already to hand. Throughout the thirty-two years of Suharto's autocracy the men chosen for the task would enjoy a degree of independence in their speech and actions which, though not absolute, was unique.

Because several of them had gained their doctorates at the University of California, in Berkeley USA, they were dubbed the Berkeley Mafia. Chairman of Suharto's economic advisory group was Widjoyo Nitisastro, former dean of economics at the University of Indonesia. Also from Berkeley were the former associate dean, Ali Wardhana, and Emil Salim. One who had not been to Berkeley was nevertheless the begetter of the mafia to which its name adhered; this was the Dutch-educated Sumitro Djoyohadikusumo, who founded the economics faculty at the University of Indonesia and, in response to a request by the Ford Foundation, had recommended some of his brighter students for scholarships at Berkeley. Widjoyo and Ali Wardhana had been lecturers at SESKOAD, the military staff academy in Bandung, and were on hand as Suharto advisers from the moment he took over. Sumitro (not to be confused with the general of that name) joined the group a year late, having first to arrange his return from the exile into which he had fled following the Sumatra revolt, in which he was a prominent player. The relative freedom of action the Berkeley Mafia were given was, in the phrase of one Western diplomat at the time, part of the deal.

There were, broadly speaking, two possible ways of describing the economic priorities confronting Indonesia. One related to what could be termed the formal economy, the economy of Jakarta-based bureaucrats and bankers. The other had more to do with the fundamentals of what some called the real economy. They should have been inseparable but were not.

The fundamentals had not changed much since the termination of Dutch rule. Seen from an earth satellite most of the country was still a jungle-clad wilderness. Apart from Java, Bali and to a lesser extent Sumatra, most was only sparsely populated or even unpopulated. Java, by contrast, was critically over-populated, unable to provide anything better than subsistence for most of its people, dependent in consequence on wealth generated in Sumatra. No significant effort had been made to limit population growth, which continued at a national average rate of about two and half percent every year. The production of food and other goods needed to sustain the growing population was not keeping up.

In some of its aspects this fundamental economy could not be regarded as national at all. Much economic activity was arranged locally. Both the collection of taxes and the application of centrally allocated funds were ineffectual and vulnerable to subversion by people with powers of local coercion, especially the military. More than half the inter-island trade with non-Indonesian territories – Singapore, Malaysia, the Philippines, Burma, Thailand – evaded central government regulation and, although often elaborately organized locally, was therefore categorised as smuggling. The problems of land-use policy cried out for rational control; in its absence, land could be, and was, seized by any who had the power to get away with it. Crowded Java in particular went on suffering from the fragmentation of land-holdings as a consequence of traditional inheritance rules.

In essence Indonesia still had a colonial economy, organized to satisfy the demands of foreign trade and foreign investors. To become a truly independent nation it needed wholesale mobilization of its resources to meet the requirements of its own populace. That would mean investment in education and the creation out of almost nothing of diversified manufacturing and service industries.

This picture of the real economy and its needs was fully understood by the architects of the new order and was indeed fulsomely acknowledged at the level of public rhetoric. As it turned out, three decades of Suharto's rule saw change and improvement to some aspects of the fundamental economy. But events were to show that it was not what motivated their highest priorities.

The overriding orientation of new order economic management was towards restoring the confidence of Japanese, American and West European investors and trading partners. Indonesia had to be slotted back into the international capitalist framework from which President Sukarno had done much to remove it. Some months before the GESTAPU affair he had decreed the government take-over of all foreign businesses, thus making comprehensive what had already gone far with the expropriation of Dutch and British enterprises. Just six weeks before the counter-coups Indonesia had withdrawn from the World Bank and the International Monetary Fund, both reasonably viewed as instruments of American economic manipulation. Reversing these acts was a matter of urgency if the new order was to reestablish the collapsing network of foreign creditors and investors.

The new order technocrats had few choices. The nation was bankrupt. Acknowledged exports, dislocated by the confrontation of Malaysia, were in decline. Overseas debt reached two thousand million US dollars and export income was no longer sufficient to pay even the interest on it; with loan repayments in default, Japan and others refused to extend new credit. Imports – notably of Chinese clothing and textiles – had declined to the point where they no longer met immediate demand; spare parts for industrial machinery were in short supply; inflation consequently soared to around 650 percent and the currency became almost worthless. One of the only manufacturing activities in full production was the printing of bank notes as money supply much more than doubled year by year. There would be a succession of rupiah devaluations.

Towards the end of 1967 there was a major rice shortage. In a country where nearly three-quarters of the active population were farmers or forestry workers it was always the city-dwellers who were going to be worst hit by shortfalls in food production. To what extent the supply of rice was curtailed by the ruinous condition of the road system and to what extent by the phenomenon of farmland left unworked by victims of the anti-communist slaughter is open to conjecture, but certainly the shortage at that crucial time contributed to the frenzy of the young city action groups who were being whipped into anti-Sukarno demonstrations by certain members of Suharto's military coterie. Meanwhile the USA, Britain and others organized a big food-aid programme

Whichever way they turned, the Berkeley technocrats were going to have to rely on foreigners for the achievement of their goals. Sukarno's self-reliance strategy was not working. Abandoning it in the short term was an imperative. Abandoning it as a long-term objective was a quite different proposition and remained for many years an object of dispute. The history of economic management under Suharto is by no means a story of wholly unfettered market forces. In the longer perspective it did not mark an unambiguous break with the economic thinking of the Sukarno era. Many of the changes were forced on the régime by external pressures mediated through the Berkeley Mafia.

Suharto's team turned immediately to the spurned International Monetary Fund and World Bank, whose advisers quickly reappeared in the capital. They ordained a programme in three parts: stabilization, rehabilitation and increased production; the third, they warned, could not realistically be expected in less than three years.

Urban consumers were the first to feel the pain of their prescriptions; on their advice measures were taken to restore order in the price structure; these were not often popular among shoppers who on the one hand had been enjoying petroleum prices lower than the cost of water and on the other were having to live with the soaring prices caused by inflation. All the same they did, as time went on, begin to reap the benefits of less regulated imports which brought more goods on to the market.

On IMF advice, too, a 1965 decree placing the major oil companies, Caltex, Stanvac and Shell, under supervision, was rescinded. As under Sukarno, Indonesia was heavily dependent on oil revenue for foreign exchange earnings – all the more so until foreign creditors could be re-enlisted. To do that the government was willing to swallow the bitterest pills. It was placed on notice that the luxury of multifarious and competing bilateral credit arrangements was a thing of the past; it would have to meet all its capitalist creditors at the same time and accept their concerted assessment of Indonesian needs.

Difficult decisions were demanded on both sides. Aware that they could easily become victims of total default, the creditor nations first agreed to a three-year postponement of all interest followed by repayment in full within eight years. By 1968, realizing even that ambition was hopeless, they adopted a German proposal – and executed a revolution in international finance – by accepting payment within thirty years with all interest waived.

In December 1965, facing its creditors at the first of what became an annual event, a statement by the Indonesian government seemed to concede on all points:

A fundamental aspect of the new Indonesian order is the recognition that market forces have a vital role to play in the rehabilitation and growth of our economy . . . first by putting the many State economic enterprises on a competitive footing with the private sector. Their [the State enterprises'] easy access to ample and cheap bank credit and to especially favourable exchange rates and allocations has been removed. They are now on the same footing as private enterprise in regard to bank credit and the exchange system.

At the same time nearly all State enterprises have been freed from arbitrarily determined and often artificially low prices for their goods and services. As a result they can now charge realistic prices and are being forced by competition toward efficiency and reduced costs . . . Only a few enterprises are now receiving subsidies.

The private sector has been given the opportunity to work toward a fuller utilization of productive capacity by the removal of import licensing restrictions on raw materials, equipment for maintenance and other essential commodities. It has also been encouraged to undertake investment in a wide variety of fields by a new investment law, which provides tax and other incentives to both domestic and foreign capital.

Even with all the past tenses turned into futures it was make-believe – the same siren calls would be solicited and rehearsed many times during the following decades – but as a contrast with the rhetoric of the fast-fading Sukarno era it was the desired signal that Indonesia recognised where its future lay.

Nevertheless, although the government statement was premature in announcing them, two seminal investment laws were being readied for enactment. That covering foreign investment, introduced in 1967, was radical and far-reaching. Previous governments, the direct heirs of the independence struggle, had effectively closed the country to foreign investment and made a determined although not altogether successful attempt to promote indigenous businesses. Now the doors were opened.

It took time to persuade foreign entrepreneurs that their ventures would be rewarded, yet by the time Suharto fell from power three decades later nearly four and a half thousand enterprises financed with foreign money – and more than five and a half thousand financed under the terms of a parallel law on domestic investment – had seen the light of day, with mining, metals, chemicals, construction, public utilities, tourism, estate crops, forestry and paper prominent in the listings. In other words, this law began the vital task of building up the non-oil sector in the nation's exchange-earning economy.

Even this 'private' sector was enfolded in government relationships most analysts consider corruptive, with the result that big enterprises handling large resources forged ahead while badly needed smaller ones lagged behind. Meanwhile major areas like transport and high technology were retained in the public sector, evincing precautionary instincts redolent of Sukarno's guided economy.

Like Sukarno, Suharto initiated a national plan. Ironically, one of the planners, the Berkeley mafioso Professor Widjoyo, had also been one of the progenitors of Sukarno's unrealized monster. The new five-year plan concentrated on food, agriculture and the labour intensive textile industry and was launched in 1969. Despite achieving most of its rather modest targets, it failed to bring the prices of land and consumer goods down, did little for the non-Javanese provinces and nothing for the masses of the very poor. In 1974 half the population were worse off than they had been at the beginning of the plan.

Far greater, and more characteristic of the new order, was the impact of a pioneering innovation in the oil industry which had its roots in the Sukarno era. Production sharing had long been familiar in agriculture: the tenant farmer surrendered a share of his crop to the landlord. Indonesia under Sukarno began to introduce it into the petroleum extracting industry in the late 1950s.

Production sharing has more than sentimental value. Unlike the joint venture or the previous system of work contracts based on the division of operating profits, it treats the foreign contractor as merely the provider of a service paid for with a proportion of the oil produced. For Indonesia, as well as leaving the government in control of its petroleum resources, it had the advantages of flexibility and yielding higher income. For foreign companies which had not yet made inroads into Indonesian oilfields – especially Japanese companies and offshore oilfields – it opened the gate into an area formerly dominated by two major American corporations, Caltex and Stanvac.

Suharto's men, keen to master and maximise what was by far their biggest foreign revenue earner, enthusiastically embraced this legacy of the Sukarno era. From 1968 on, when the energy industry was formally consolidated into the single state-owned Pertamina, virtually all new mineral-extracting ventures involving foreign capital used the production sharing system, and Indonesia had the satisfaction of watching it spread to many other parts of the world.

Seen through military eyes, the revamped petroleum industry was too valuable to be entrusted to any but the army. For that purpose Suharto shifted his close personal colleague Ibnu Sutowo from his position as minister of mines, oil and gas into the executive directorship of Pertamina. Sutowo, who liked to be addressed as doctor, was more importantly a lieutenant-general. One of his early deeds, heralded as a triumph of pragmatism, was to exempt the two American giants from production sharing and allow them to continue under the old system which they preferred. Relations between Pertamina and the Americans grew so close as to lead a British diplomat in Jakarta to the view that the position of a US embassy official who acted as a kind of oil attaché was in reality funded by Pertamina.

No less close was the relationship with Japan, whose petroleum interest was twofold. Being so near geographically, it was much the biggest buyer of Indonesian oil (and indeed of Indonesian exports over-all), taking never less than half and more often around seventy per cent. Dependent nonetheless on Middle East oil, Japan also had an anxious interest in the reliability of west-east shipping lanes through Indonesian waters.

One of Sutowo's earliest experiences of petroleum diplomacy had been with the Japanese in the late 1950s when, as the army's representative, he negotiated his first production sharing agreement in the north Sumatran oilfields seized from Royal Dutch Shell. It was then also that he received his first rebuke for corrupt practice from the defence minister, General Nasution. In October 1965, within two weeks of the counter-coups, Suharto despatched him to Tokyo ostensibly to warn pro-Sukarno embassy staff of the way things were going back home, but doubtless also to give reassurances to the Japanese government.

Within less than ten years of 'new order' government the volume of oil production grew threefold and stayed high. Combined with the global oil price boom triggered by OPEC in 1973–4 (average price per barrel went from $2.93 in June 1973 to $12.60 in August 1974) it presented the country with a glut of money, unprecedented opportunity – and a lot of trouble.

Under Sutowo and with Suharto's vigorous endorsement Pertamina cultivated a hot-house economy of its own. Its accounting practices were found to be scandalous, and there is no doubt that the huge oil revenues which it controlled could have made a significant difference had they been properly and honestly used as part of the national development programme. Instead, Sutowo turned it into an investment corporation with seven wholly owned subsidiaries, majority interests in a dozen joint ventures and minority interests in another nine. Their scope lay far beyond oil, in construction, civil aviation, steel, tourism, rice production, insurance and others. In all of them he carefully nurtured his own financial interests as well as those of the army and the family and friends of General Suharto. There were estimates that as much as forty per cent of the armed forces' annual income was being provided informally by Pertamina.

It was in the climate of public and international indignation over this burgeoning scandal that the Japanese Prime Minister, Kakuei Tanaka, paid an official visit in January 1974.

It was and is still an easy matter to steer the xenophobia of the Javanese and Sumatrans against east Asians, be they the ethnic Chinese in their midst or the Japanese who had tried to colonise them. Throughout the thirty-two years of Suharto's autocratic rule it was standard practice for the political police and the army to deflect anti-régime resentment in that way.

The Japanese, whose knowledge of the Indonesian scene was second to none, knew of growing public anger about the régime's misuse and abuse of the nation's wealth. Yet the manifestations that greeted Tanaka clearly took them by surprise. The Indonesian security forces cracked down hard but did not restore order before many had been killed, dozens of shops looted and up to six hundred cars, most of them Japanese, destroyed. It culminated in Tanaka having to be taken by helicopter from the presidential palace to the airport. A dozen newspapers were shut down for reporting the disturbances. Several universities, where protégés of the Berkeley Mafia were understood to have given lectures on the evils of the alternative economy, were closed. Some eight hundred people were arrested; six months later when forty-two of them were sent for trial the government still judged it necessary to warn against further rioting.

It was the biggest and most violent outbreak of public disorder in the capital since the army-sponsored anti-Sukarno demonstrations of 1966. For Suharto, a conceited man with a powerful sense of Javanese superiority, it was a high-profile humiliation in full view of the Asian government with which he had always been careful to maintain a valuable relationship, and the way he fought back only added to its political significance. Choosing to disregard the essentially economic motives that stirred the demonstrators, he hit out in all directions: it was alleged that the banned Masjumi and socialist parties had been planning an insurrection; two 1965 communist 'plotters' were taken out of store and put on trial; in August another was executed.

Everyone else, it seemed, was to blame but Suharto. To press the point home, amid rumours of a bid for power by military rivals, he removed two of his closest military-political aides from KOPKAMTIB (the political police) and took it over himself. One of them was his expert on the political parties, Ali Murtopo, widely resented as a middle-man for Japanese business; the other was the deputy armed forces chief, General Sumitro, who had advised dialogue with the rioters and was thought by some to have incited them.

After nearly eight years of the 'new order' it was no longer possible to pretend that there was an impermeable border between the economic and the political. Whether or not incitement contributed to the disturbances, the demonstrators were unanimous in their discontents: wealth was not being fairly distributed; the president was guilty of nepotism; his wife, children and a group of mainly Chinese friends were corrupt; the gap between the well-off and the poor was widening; three out of every four school-age children in Jakarta could not go to school, either for want of teachers or because their parents could not afford the minimal costs; only one in every five buildings was a permanent structure; many were still using Jakarta's canals both as sewers and their only source of water. The economic activity brought by Japan, Indonesia's most prominent trade and investment partner, was felt to be benefiting only the armed forces and a small section of the middle class. There were also specific grievances about Japanese fishing in Indonesian waters and the environmental impact of Japan's mounting participation in the logging industry.

These events in the first half of 1974 alarmed the Western powers. Contrary to assurances by the 'oil attaché' in the US Embassy that all was well with Pertamina, the IMF had spotted the flaws in its operation. While money flooded in thanks to oil sales and buoyant exports of other raw materials like tin, timber and rubber, much of it was being misapplied at home or pouring into private bank accounts in Singapore, Hong Kong, the USA and Switzerland. Astonishingly, not content with Pertamina's oil income, Sutowo was raising lavish loans from Indonesian and foreign banks, offering nothing better than government paper and sovereign risk as security. Only when Professor Widjoyo, the chief Berkeley mafioso, urged upon Suharto that no government paper must be issued without the approval of the Bank of Indonesia was the scandal exposed.

It emerged in 1975 that Sutowo had run Pertamina into a debt of more than three billion US dollars in revenue dues and foreign loans, and by 1976 its total debt was officially put at ten billion dollars – more than double the aid the Paris club of western creditors gave Indonesia in any one year and five times the national debt President Sukarno was castigated for leaving behind him. The range of Pertamina's activities was cut back severely and Ibnu Sutowo forced to resign and take long leave in the USA, though only with the utmost reluctance on the part of General Suharto whose interests had benefited so massively from the Pertamina spree.

The opportunity afforded by soaring oil income – to create the infrastructure of an economy that would not be oil-dependent – had been squandered. Indonesia was more oil-dependent than ever. The only people who could derive any consolation from the affair were the Berkeley Mafia and their foreign mentors. They were now relied upon to retrieve the situation.

Not that the armed forces and the Chinese entrepreneurs upon whom they largely depended ceased their exploitative behaviour – Suharto would not have wanted that – but for a few years discretion became the better part of greed, enabling the technocrats to focus more effectively on developmental priorities. Suharto began to recognise the virtue of representing himself as the father of the nation's development. With an adroitness worthy of his predecessor, he played off the economic actors against one another and brought back the strings of decision-making to himself. Privilege now consisted of a presidential decree granting monopolistic control of some part of what the technocrats said was necessary in the national interest, typically the importation of raw materials.

Events chimed with the more sober mood. Oil prices faltered in the mid-1970s. Timber exports, which had grown dramatically, fell in response to a worldwide dip in building construction. The second five-year plan got under way on a set of discouraging indicators. Unemployment was still around thirty-five percent and gross productivity per head was the lowest in South-East Asia. Looking back over the eight years since Sukarno's final departure, analysts questioned the government's will to deal with crucial basic problems.

Yet international media comment, fed with interpretations offered by the US Embassy in Jakarta, persistently depicted Indonesia's economic situation in glowing terms. This could be done by alluding only to the formal statistics of foreign trade, aid and investment – and above all to the fast-evolving relationship with Japan. By 1980 Japan was not only Indonesia's most important foreign customer but also its biggest overseas investor. In the years following Kakuei Tanaka's turbulent visit, Japanese money deluged into joint ventures covering activities as various as aluminium smelting in Sumatra, petroleum exploration, trains and tuna fishing. Indonesia ended the decade as Japan's third most important trading partner and would progress further.

A ground-swell of unease built up over Japanese economic domination and overdependence on foreigners in general. A major factor was vulnerability to the vagaries of the global oil market; whereas prices rose to another peak at the beginning of the 1980s, actual production had to be reduced in compliance with OPEC agreements. There were more specific grievances close to home as well, like Singapore's near monopoly of the domestic market in refined oil products; that was exacerbated by the amount of crude oil smuggled – by the army – into Singapore. Consequently protectionist sentiment took hold. On the positive side, this could have beneficial effects like the decision to stop exporting timber to Taiwan and Korea, where it was processed into plywood, and to develop an indigenous plywood industry instead; inevitably it put more money into the pockets of the Suharto family and their cronies, but it also created workers' jobs and helped the balance of payments.

At one stage, in the early 1980s, seeing the balance of payments moving into deficit, the government experimented with a policy requiring foreign suppliers to buy offsetting quantities of Indonesian produce, a kind of high-level barter. It might have suited Japanese trading houses, but it suited no-one else; the Americans objected and the policy was dropped.

From 1982 onwards the price of oil began to slip and in 1987 it plunged, marking the middle of that decade as an economic turning point. It ended a period in which the characteristics of Suharto's management style were established and tested.

Statistically, there were good things to report. Although grass-roots agriculture was still in a bad way, government-sponsored schemes and subsidised fertilizers had combined to make the country self-sufficient in rice, with some to spare for export. Employment opportunities were multiplying and, although many were in the grossly bloated public services, many were also in the manufacturing sector. There was relative fiscal discipline. The tax take was rising. On paper at least there was a broadly-based infrastructure for basic education. National income, as measured by gross domestic product, was growing at around seven per cent every year. Average annual income per head which was US$260 in 1970 had doubled, admittedly a misleading figure because of the widened gap between rich and poor concealed within the average; incontrovertibly, the middle class was growing.

In spite of difficulties posed by the presidential régime the Berkeley Mafia could claim progress.

DOWN WITH THE PEOPLE

On the political plane, as on the economic, the military group that had come to power devoted its primary attentions to what it considered urgent, which was the imposition and consolidation of its authority throughout the Republic. This it did predominantly by the threat and exercise of physical strength. The army was put in charge and was to remain the leading force in Indonesian politics until the end of the Suharto dictatorship three decades later.

The accomplishment of a political and institutional régime that was both viable and controllable would take time and was regarded as less urgent, although it was the main long-term objective. Markedly more pressing was the need to stabilize relations with near neighbours – Malaysia, the

Philippines, Singapore and Australasia – and with the USA and Japan, the great powers in whose orbit Indonesia was now destined to live.

The military confrontation of Malaysia was terminated in an almost summary fashion. Once he had the necessary presidential powers Suharto dissolved the operational command set up by Sukarno to prosecute it. Amicable talks in Bangkok opened on the presumption of friendship and military collaboration between the two countries and dealt mainly with the formation of a new inclusive regional grouping to be known as the Association of South-East Asian Nations (ASEAN) – the brainchild not, as was sometimes claimed, of the Indonesian government, but of far-sighted Foreign Office officials in London.

By the middle of 1967 General Suharto felt strong enough to change gear. The youngsters of the 1966 generation whose energy and idealism he had skilfully orchestrated against Sukarno soon learned that his famous smile was little more than a Javanese mannerism. Playing the anti-communist card for all it was worth, he intensified the military complexion of the régime. A significant pointer to the real focus of power was a conference in Yogyakarta of territorial army commanders from the whole of Java – but nowhere else in Indonesia – together with the commanders of the Army Strategic Command (Suharto's old bailiwick) and the special para brigade. A public declaration afterwards spoke of efforts to organize a communist come-back and threatened 'stern measures against anybody and any group who wants to rehabilitate the power of the leader of the Old Order, Dr Engineer Sukarno'.

Public attention was directed to a reinterpretation of the security situation in the border area between West Kalimantan and the Malaysian state of Sarawak. What Sukarno had represented as an area of confrontation with neo-colonialism was now characterised as an assembly area for communist elements trickling in from elsewhere in Indonesia. No sooner was the anti-Malaysia operational command abolished than a unified service command was set up in the self-same military headquarters in the West Kalimantan capital Pontianak to resist what Beijing Radio obligingly described as armed counter-revolution. Three fresh battalions were assigned to West Kalimantan. Malaysia provided logistical support and the two governments came to a speedy agreement on hot pursuit.

In Jakarta on the second anniversary of the 1965 coup a gang of students made a business-like job of sacking the Chinese embassy. A few days later on Armed Forces Day, General Suharto's order of the day instructed the services to wipe out the communist guerrilla army in the Kalimantan-Sarawak border area.

The usually taciturn soldier had relatively little to say about political evolution at the level of ordinary people. Indeed he had already hinted that general elections promised for July 1968 would be postponed, as they were, for a further three years. The real burden of one speech after another was what he, the chieftain of a military oligarchy, deemed 'necessary'. There was the necessity of demonstrating legitimacy under the 1945 constitution; there was the economic emergency; and, as always, he stressed the unremitting threat of communism.

Unmistakable in an address in 1967 to Indonesia's ambassadors in Australasia and South-East Asia were the attitudes of one who has succeeded in overthrowing an old order, rather than one who has resisted a take-over:

To understand the present political development and our future course we must understand the essence of our present struggle; that is, to struggle to build a new order, based on the genuine implementation of Pancasila and the 1945 constitution. The new order is nothing other than an order that makes corrections and was born as the result of corrections and introspection – in principle and in general – on policies or practices which were not founded on the genuine implementation of Pancasila or the 1945 constitution by the preceding order, that is the old order.

Only days later, he ordered a long-awaited cabinet reconstruction, abolishing the unconstitutional praesidium, or inner cabinet, that had been running things since the GESTAPU affair. Suharto assumed the style of prime-minister in addition to his existing posts as defence minister and acting president. Most of the old Sukarno appointees were flushed out. Armed forces commanders lost their ministerial rank and military representation was reduced overall, but in reality the change consolidated military rule insofar as it freed Suharto to use a pared-down personal staff of about a dozen senior officers for policy formation – what came to be known as the 'green wall'.

By contrast, Suharto's cabinet reconstruction began a slow decline in the influence of the foreign minister, Adam Malik. A civilian from northern Sumatra and a notable Marxist leader in the early years of independence, he was a necessary member of the trio publicly fronting the new order and was strongly supported by the Western powers upon whose grace and favour Suharto was relying. The abolition of the cabinet praesidium swept away Malik's special position as overseer of political affairs. Thereafter that function was left to a general in Suharto's personal staff. General Soegiharto, a member of the army's political advisory body and attorney-general in the new cabinet, wished to assure me at the time that the foreign minister was still highly respected and would remain an important figure in an unofficial inner cabinet. Yet fewer than three months passed before Malik, sensitive to the misgivings of many foreign observers, was uttering barely disguised warnings. In a guest article in *Foreign Affairs*, the journal of the US Council on Foreign Relations, he wrote:

> Indonesia's problems will not be solved by making scapegoats of opponents. In most countries when the military takes over the running of the government its first act is to abolish or distort the Constitution. . . . In our case, the armed forces have committed themselves to restore a constitutional government and to revive the democratic spirit. General Suharto and the armed forces have assumed the solemn duty of fulfilling this. I am convinced that General Suharto wishes to do so, as do also, I hope, all the top military leaders.[1]

So Suharto's long rule began as he and his personal staff of military decision-makers clearly intended it to continue, a military dictatorship.

Like Sukarno before him, from whom he learned many lessons, he fashioned a parliamentary system with, it turned out, few effective powers beyond endorsing his decrees and decisions and re-electing the president every five years. Under the 1945 constitution restored in Sukarno's time Indonesia has two parliamentary bodies. The lower (the DPR) is a House of Representatives. It approves draft legislation submitted by the government and has the right to initiate legislation on its own account. As a matter of record, the Houses of Representatives formed after five general elections between 1971 and 1992 initiated not a single item of legislation. It has the right, equally theoretical during the whole Suharto period, to control the budget. In certain circumstances the House of Representatives can convene the larger upper house of which it is a component, the Peoples' Consultative Congress (MPR).

Technically, the MPR is the supreme organ of state: it could propose amendments of the constitution, elect the president and periodically adopted a document called the Broad Outline of State Policy. It is obliged to gather at least once every five years to elect the president but can, and in the late 1960s did, meet more often.

The House and Congress inherited by the Suharto régime, while it was fairly representative, excluded Muslim and socialist tendencies which had been involved in the 1958 Sumatra rebellion. Suharto drew them in but, in his turn, excluded his special enemies, principally members and supporters of the communist party.

At its session in 1966 the Consultative Congress had ordained general elections by 1968. But democratic institutions had no priority on the generals' agenda. As the time approached the Congress dutifully agreed to putting them off until 1971. The respite was used to refashion the parliamentary institutions, in the provinces as well as the capital, and to commence a radical reformation of the party political structure.

It was laid down that a hundred members of the 460-strong House of Representatives, and one in three of the 920-strong Consultative Congress, would be appointed by the government, meaning the president. Most of the appointees would be military. Political party reform produced further effects which virtually ensured a military majority whenever either body voted.

The new rulers faced the quandary which Sukarno had sought to resolve with his theory of guided democracy: how to give a meaningful but not disruptive voice to the many elements of a fragmented society. Warmly supported by General Nasution, he had come up with the idea of functional groups which, among other things, would give the army a legitimate and assured role in the body politic. In 1964 – during the run-in to the 1965 coup attempts – the army had created an anti-communist group which it called Golkar, the short-form of a phrase meaning 'functional groups'.

Suharto vigorously expanded Sukarno's original scheme. Golkar was now built into a substantial political organization, in effect a government party, although never styled as such, representing the interests of the armed forces, the civil service, organized labour, farmers and so on. It had a central leadership council the members of which were chosen by a council of founders. Cabinet ministers were automatically members of the council of founders presided over by the President of Indonesia.

Side by side with the forced growth of Golkar, steps were taken to constrain the scope of the other political parties. Suharto delegated this work to an old friend in his personal staff, Brigadier-General Ali Murtopo, a Javanese and a veteran intelligence practitioner. An almost totally disempowered party political structure was beginning to take shape.

The PKI was already out of the way, most of its leaders and members having been killed. Other parties presented different problems and needed delicate handling. The socialists of the PSI, for instance, were in good standing with the USA. Briefly at first there were thoughts of resurrecting some kind of non-virulent socialist force; Murba seemed on the verge of a come-back; it was, after all, Adam Malik's own 'Marxist' party and had even at one stage received furtive American encouragement as a counter-attraction to the PKI. But in the climate of fear generated by the military rulers few apart from a handful of intellectuals wanted to risk that stigma. Marxism was banned by decree and I recall Malik's hopeless, wordless shrug when I asked him how it would be possible to cultivate a healthy political discourse without admitting a Marxist element into the debate.

The huge nationalist PNI was having a similar problem. Even under new leadership engineered by Murtopo, it was accused of acquiescing in infiltration by communist supporters seeking cover from the great slaughter. Interviewed in Bandung early in 1967, the PNI secretary-general Usep Ranawidjaya conceded there had been some infiltration but told me with some force 'the new executive leadership of the party have already issued new regulations to prevent the recruitment of any communists in the body of the Nationalist Party; we have had bitter experience of such infiltration and do not wish to repeat it'. He added archly: 'In the event of such tendencies existing in the Nationalist Party, they would be brought to our attention by the government so that we could take action'.

Suharto's close Javanese advisers, aware of the need to accommodate nationalist, anti-foreign sentiment, were not overtly hostile towards the PNI. The problem for Murtopo, however, was that the PNI meant different things in different parts of the country. In the Indonesian heartland of Central and East Java it was, in the wake of the PKI, the pre-eminent political force and staunchly Sukarnoist. During the much publicised youth action manifestations against Sukarno in Jakarta, PNI youth activists in the heartland had been every bit as ardent in their under-reported demonstrations in favour of Sukarno. The party was suspended altogether in Sumatra, and in Sulawesi, Kalimantan, Bali and elsewhere local military commanders compelled it to purge itself, to such effect that in Jakarta and West Java groups of intellectuals, correctly anticipating its ultimate demise, embarked on a doomed bid to enfold the military régime in a modernising and mildly socialistic movement.

The displacement of Sukarno in fact plunged all the political parties into a renewed though temporary ferment, to which the generals themselves contributed; and nowhere more strenuously than in the intricate realm of Islam. Despite a general ban on new parties, they set about encouraging the formation of a new Muslim party embracing all the major tendencies. In the Javanese heartland where the Religious Scholars League (NU) had support second only to the PNI, the nationalists viewed this as a cynical attempt to enlist Muslim sentiment against them.

It all took time and was further complicated by the absence of an up-to-date law on political parties. Consequently it was still incomplete in 1971 when, despite misgivings among some of the military (but to the plaudits of the Western world), Indonesia experienced its first general election for seventeen years. The number of parties permitted to take part was reduced from twenty to nine. Thanks to the régime's success in imposing its own preferred leaders on those nine and promoting Golkar as a contender, Golkar swept home, winning 336 of the 460 seats in the House of Representatives; of the remaining 124, another hundred went to appointed delegates of the armed forces.

PARTY TIME

The régime's mastery of the 1971 elections opened wider the window of opportunity for Suharto. The 1945 constitution, already in force but only on the basis of President Sukarno's disputed 1959 decree, was proclaimed with parliamentary sanction. Within two years, to complete the restructuring of the political parties, the Peoples' Consultative Congress rubber-stamped their distillation into only two – plus, of course, Golkar.

Into one of them went the PNI, its divisions still unresolved, together with the two main Christian parties, Murba and a few others. It was dubbed the Indonesian Democratic Party (PDI). The other was an attempt to reconcile the various parties of Islam: the heavyweight NU (Religious Scholars' League), PARMUSI – which Murtopo had cobbled together from the remains of the once-powerful Masjumi banned by Sukarno in 1960 – and some smaller groups. Conspicuously excluding the word Muslim, Suharto gave his consent to it being called the National Development Party (PPP in Indonesian). The two major tendencies, nationalism and Islam, were thus wrapped up in separate packages. As in most matters under the new order, the approval of party leaders was General Suharto's prerogative.

Here indeed was Sukarno's guided democracy, refined to a perfection at which he was never allowed to arrive.

With that, although party politicking did not stop, it was effectively divorced from the processes of government for twenty years or more. The parties, but not Golkar, were forbidden even to have branch offices or organize activities below the administrative levels of district capital and municipality; they could not therefore operate in the tens of thousands of villages where the army permeated the socio-political fabric, as the PKI had formerly done in Java. The justification offered was the stability necessary for economic development. A different view might speak of public order and the conditions required to enrich the armed forces, an autocratic presidency and overseas trade and investment partners who benefited vastly from the country's relatively disciplined conditions. The underlying instability inherent in the system, and how much better a properly functioning democracy might have done, was acknowledged only at the very end of the régime.

Suharto's military and other political advisers doubtless hoped that by exterminating the communists and circumscribing the nationalist PNI they would have calmed and propitiated Muslim sentiment. Diverse though its faces and degrees of intensity are, Islam is an integral part of the social and spiritual consciousness of nine Indonesians in every ten. Being more than a merely political phenomenon, it is for that reason of particular importance politically. It is the engine of the moral imperative which drove many Muslims into physical conflict with the communists and also fuelled indignation over the military régime's abuse of the nation's resources. At the time of its merger into Murtopo's new PPP the powerful NU alone was reckoned to have thirty million followers – ten times more than the PKI at its zenith. The next largest component of the PPP, Muhammadiyah, also counted its nationwide following in tens of millions.

Some Muslim leaders may have believed the help they gave the armed forces in purging communists would earn them a privileged status in the new order, perhaps even progress towards the Islamic state desired by the more zealous. Such expectations were quickly dispelled. In this again Suharto acted as Sukarno had. He laid heavy stress on Pancasila (the five principles) – including belief in one God – as the state and constitutional philosophy. And, as had been the case in 1945 when Sukarno propounded the doctrine, the intention behind the religious principle was to accommodate religious pluralism and thwart the minority of Muslim fundamentalists (a term not then in vogue) who wanted an Islamic state founded on Muslim law. Muslim unrest, often involving confrontation with communities regarded as outsiders such as Christians and Chinese, had never been wholly subdued under Sukarno and was not now.

Suharto's troubles with his new public enemy number one began in 1967 on the west coast of Aceh, the northernmost and also the most militantly Islamic province of Sumatra. A mob of hundreds burned down a couple of Christian churches. Far away in Makassar, the provincial capital of South Sulawesi, Muslims used a perceived slight by a Christian teacher as the pretext for a chapter of attacks on schools and churches. Clashes like those, suppressed by police or troops, typified the rash of Muslim unrest that spread through the nation into the 1970s. Firm media censorship ensured that few of them were reported at the time.

The trouble-makers were not all fundamentalists, or 'extremists' as they were called. Neither were their targets invariably the real cause of their anger. Poverty, flagrant nepotism in the capital and the unremitting corruption of the military, grievances for which there was no available redress, were at the root of the unrest. The depoliticising of the Muslim parties merely compounded their resentments.

The outlook soon became so serious that Suharto demanded and got from his obedient House of Representatives a mandate to take whatever measures he chose to deal with threats of subversion. Communists were the ostensible target, and always a useful cover for the military régime's measures against the more difficult problem of political Islam.

By the mid-1970s Suharto's militaristic management of Muslim discontent, combined with the violent suppression of communist remnants, anti-corruption riots and rural protest against land appropriation, had bred a climate of fear. At the northern tip of Sumatra, where Acehnese nationalism and Muslim fervour were inseparable, the Free Aceh Movement came into being.

The official response took several forms. One was an attempt to loosen the ties between Islam and the people in the Javanese heartland by adding the body of traditional Javanese beliefs known as *kebatinan* to the list of religions which citizens were legally permitted to profess; the others were Buddhism, Christianity, Hinduism and Islam. Another was the government's decision to take control of the teaching curriculum at the Muslim boarding schools where millions of children received a blend of religious and secular education – a move that provoked deep suspicion.

When the time came for another general election, in 1979, the government's standing was not high. The Pertamina oil company scandal of 1975–6 was still reverberating; it was public knowledge that the Suharto family enjoyed privileged access to major business opportunities; people saw, too, how media manipulation and the administration of justice were being used to shield the presidential circle. International concern over the neglected human rights of political detainees was staining Indonesia's reputation; even in the army there had been rumours of plots to overthrow Suharto.

It was principally the Muslim PPP that made parliamentary gains in the shadow of public discontent. Despite Golkar's sturdiest efforts, and although inevitably it still won a large majority, it saw the Muslim party making significant inroads – the PPP now had ninety-nine seats – and suffered the humiliation of losing control in Jakarta.

Although the physiognomy of Islam in South-East Asia differs from that in the Arab and Persian world, Indonesia could not be altogether isolated from the then prevalent atmosphere of Islamic revival. Travellers of the period noticed, for example, that photographs of the Iranian cleric, Ayatollah Khomeiny, were for sale on market stalls in Aceh, and the famous name was several times linked with terrorist acts. Even if Suharto believed the influence of Arab-style Islam could be offset by encouraging Indonesia's own religious traditions, he could not ignore the obsessive American hostility towards Islam that would have been a permanent consideration in the close army circle where policy was really made.

In its public rhetoric the régime went on sounding the alarm about communism. At fairly regular intervals another convict from the time of the counter-coups in 1965 would be brought out and shot, or someone else would be put on trial following the unceasing activities of the intelligence community. There was an inexhaustible supply of human fodder for this purpose. In answers given to *The Times* in 1973 Suharto admitted to 2,457 detainees described as known communists implicated in the Gestapu affair, 26,650 suspected of involvement but against whom no legal guilt could be established, and many thousands merely suspected of harbouring communist sympathies. It was what the Americans wanted to hear and it played well with Muslim sentiment. But as Indonesia entered the 1980s it was plain that the rising global power of Islam was the régime's greatest anxiety.

So began a phase of re-indoctrination. Civil servants were sent on refresher courses on the principles of Pancasila. The messages of the unified nation, of the duty to improve the people's lot and of the impracticability of the Islamic state were driven home. By a presidential order, departmental heads (not military) were to read out lists of corrupt offences within their remit on the 17th of every month. Presented as the defender of the social order, the army likewise came in for doctrinal refreshers. There was talk of bringing on young blood in the officer corps. Suharto delivered a lecture in Bandung re-asserting the army's dual function, which analysts interpreted as a rebuff to Nasution. The original author of the concept was now a member of a new group of intellectuals calling publicly for more democracy. And in case anyone questioned whether soldiering remained part of it, troops were deployed to suppress Muslims attacking Chinese in many parts of the country throughout 1980–1981. In October 1981, the army launched a major operation against guerrillas fighting for independence in Christian East Timor.

None of it had any effect on the steady growth of Muslim discontent. The régime's remedies were viewed as essentially repressive, while its gestures against fundamental ills came across as either ineffectual or merely cosmetic.

## Note

1  Malik, Adam in *Foreign Affairs*, January 1968, Council on Foreign Affairs Inc, New York. Reprinted in the *Straits Times*, 26 March 1968.

# SEVEN

## *Suharto's Javanese Empire*

Nearly all the religious problems of the first twenty years of the Suharto era were seated in what the Javanese refer to as the 'outer islands.' It is a phrase loaded with assumptions of Javanese cultural superiority. While the Muslim communities in what – for convenience rather than strict accuracy – I prefer to call the outer regions have a doctrinal affinity with worldwide Islam that distinguishes them from the diluted Islam of the Javanese heartland, they are also different from one another. Those differences go some way towards explaining why Islam in Indonesia has never consolidated itself into the force that its size might suggest.

Not all the outer regions are coterminous with islands. West Java, Aceh, South Sulawesi are examples of well-defined, disparate entities on large islands where there are other quasi-political regions as well. West Java, the province surrounding Jakarta, has little in common with the Javanese heartland in the central and eastern reaches of the island. Its population is Sundanese, not Javanese. By establishing a great entrepôt harbour on the lip of the strategic Sunda Strait the Dutch turned it into the fulcrum between the maritime trade routes to the west and the rice-bowl of central Java. Thanks to the incessant traffic of European, Arab and Indian traders it was well-placed for the proselytising activities of Darul Islam and the disruptive activities of Dutch elements trying to prevent Indonesia's progress to independence as a unified state. Their advocacy of an Islamic state was still detectable in 1967 when the military régime preferred to write them off as communist agitators.

All of this would have been in Suharto's mind as his security forces grappled with rural and labour unrest in West Java in the later 1970s and in 1981 when separatists staged an aircraft hijack in Bangkok. And again in 1984, when what was to become one of the most notorious incidents occurred at Tanjung Priok, Jakarta's dockland. Carefully deployed troops trapped more than a thousand demonstrating Muslim activists in a pincer movement then opened fire, killing dozens and injuring hundreds. The armed forces chief, General Benny Murdani, compounded the outrage with the lie that only nine had lost their lives. Another sixteen years were to pass before the role of the security forces at Tanjong Priok could be subjected to anything like an independent investigation.

Quite different was the picture in Aceh, the northern Sumatran province which in 1967 was granted the status of special territory in acknowledgement of some local prerogatives extracted from the Jakarta government in matters of education, religion and culture. To the people of Aceh, it was a totally inadequate reflection of a sense of autonomy going back more than five centuries. Commanding the northern end of the busy Malacca Strait, it was where Islam made its first Indonesian landfall and was a powerful trading centre rivalling Malacca on the Malaysian side of the Strait and extending its influence far into eastern Indonesia.

Even with the gradual attrition of its power in the face of Dutch, Portuguese and finally British penetration, Aceh managed to preserve its independence until the end of the seventeenth century. A final gasp was made possible by a secret treaty with Britain which breathed its last when the British ended their resistance to the Dutch occupying Aceh. The Dutch, despite a long and bloody war, were never wholly able to secure their claim against vigorous Acehnese resistance. The Japanese occupation during the Second World War was at first welcomed but then ran into nationalist opposition. Indonesia's post-independence government tried to contain it by incorporating Aceh into the province of Northern Sumatra, only to be rebuffed in 1952 by the proclamation of an Islamic Republic of Aceh. That lasted less than ten years until, under pressure from the army, Aceh became once more a separate province and, after a few more years, was conceded its special territory status.

There is, then, a deep-seated nationalism in Aceh's persistent demands for recognition of its autonomy. It is reinforced by resentment at seeing its rich economic resources – petroleum, timber – exploited by foreigners and soldiers under the aegis of the central government with scant benefit to its own people.

The fact that rigorous adherence to a pure form of Islam is part of Aceh's historical identity need not have led to blaming its separatist sentiments on religion. That this did happen is attributable largely to attitudes adopted by the army and the Javanese establishment in Jakarta in the mid-1970s, when the formation of the Free Aceh Movement GAM coincided with the rising tide of Muslim revivalism. From that time on, Suharto's military régime, under the banner of national unity, imposed a reign of terror and waged a brutal war against the Acehnese independence movement. Only fitfully reported and therefore impossible to document accurately, it resulted in tens of thousands of deaths, held down substantial military forces and was still blazing in 1998 when General Suharto finally relinquished the presidency.

A flight of some 1,500 miles east-south-east from Aceh, beyond the Malay Peninsula, beyond the huge island of Kalimantan (to which we shall return), brings us to an island that looks on the map rather like a contorted glove, Sulawesi, once known as the Celebes. A luxuriant territory with some unique fauna, its fractured topography and poor communications have endowed it with ethnic problems and a fragmented history. Each of its main fingers has its own characteristics and its own story.

To the north, Chinese influence is evident in the faces you see and in the designs of the local batik prints. Many of the people there, the Minahasans, are Christian. Manado, the city at the northernmost tip, is closer to the Philippines than it is to Java or even the southern end of Sulawesi itself. That explains why one of the rebel leaders in the American-inspired 1958 rebellion had his headquarters there and why the Indonesian air force bombed its radio station.

The southwest finger is famous for its coffee-trading port long known as Ujung Pandang, but now rejoicing again in its earlier name, Makassar. It appealed to the Dutch as one of the many places in the archipelago that overlook busy sea-lanes and was a useful entrepôt for the spice trade. It always was, and is, ideal territory for pirates, small-time buccaneers and armed outlaws; home also to the rough-cut Bugis, whose high-masted sailing vessels are a familiar sight in harbours throughout the area. Here Islam is firmly entrenched; during the 1958 rebellion rebel elements signed a charter of collaboration with Darul Islam forces operating in Sumatra and West Java.

More recently, improving communications brought Sulawesi's various communities into closer contact and quite often into conflict. Remnants of separatist groups encouraged at one time and another by the Dutch, the British and the Americans lingered on and engaged the vigilance of the armed forces all through Suharto's rule. In the era of the 1965 coups, for instance, when the USA and Britain were conniving to destabilize Sukarno's Indonesia, Royal Navy submarines provided transport for dissidents coming and going from Sulawesi and its neighbouring islands.

Further east still and you are in a vast stretch of sea dotted with something like a thousand islands popularly known by the products which first attracted European traders centuries ago – the Spice Islands. The Moluccas, to use the European version of their proper name (Maluku), show a mixture of the Polynesian features found in their easterly neighbours and have a definite air of separate ethnic identity. Their history, which includes resistance to Dutch rule and a shadowy secessionist movement in the post-independence years, revolves around just a few of the larger islands: Ambon, Buru, Seram and Halmahera, with its two clove-producing island satellites of Tidore and Ternate.

The capital, Kota Ambon, lies on an islet, and has a long history; for it was the focal point of an unusually benign Dutch presence. Christianity is strong there, with a tradition going back to the sixteenth century when Francis Xavier, the Apostle of the Indies and co-founder of the Jesuits, arrived in the Spice Islands from Malacca. Pro-Dutch sentiment and the prevalence of Christianity both had political significance in the 1950s when the Dutch were trying to impose a federal structure on Indonesia, and in the first half of the Suharto era when it became apparent that widespread poverty was getting worse.

The relative harmony of Muslim-Christian coexistence was to change during the last years of the Suharto era, in a manner that dramatised both the fragility and the political exploitability of inter-religious relations in Indonesia. A volcano on the tiny island of Makian off the west coast of Halmahera erupted, driving thousands of its Muslim inhabitants to northern Halmahera, where the population was predominantly Christian. To make matters worse, an administrative adjustment resulted in a gold mine that had been in a Christian area finding itself in a new Muslim sub-district. Hostility flared between the two religious communities and was blatantly exacerbated after Suharto's departure, when military elements close to the fallen dictator set out to show that only the army could prevent the nation collapsing into anarchy. Violent clashes between Muslims and Christians continued, sometimes with army and police units taking opposite sides in inter-communal incidents.

But the Moluccan island that achieved the greatest notoriety in the 'new order' was Buru. Noted for its crocodile-infested malarial swamps, it among Indonesia's more than thirteen thousand islands was chosen in 1969 as the site of a concentration camp for detainees believed to be communists but against whom no case could be proved. Up to ten thousand men were sent into the so-called Buru Resettlement Project, a designation which, as we shall see, fitted it conveniently into the government's transmigration programme. The army presence grew, numbers of people arrived from Java; and, several decades later, when inter-communal riots erupted, the tidings from Buru were of local people fleeing for their lives into the hills.

If ethnography were the only criterion, Maluku would mark the eastern limit of Indonesia's outer regions and of their simmering discontents. But the next island along, New Guinea, is unambiguously part of Melanesia. It is the second biggest island in the world. Although more than half of it is under Indonesian sovereignty, for the sole reason that it was formerly under Dutch colonial rule, its people are quite distinct, physically, linguistically and in every other cultural sense, from the Malay peoples in the Indonesian archipelago.

West Papua, as it has been called since President Abdurrahman Wahid adopted a more emollient attitude towards its sensibilities, figured prominently on the new order agenda as West Irian. For General Suharto it was unfinished business in a personal sense. Following Indonesia's failure in 1957 to secure a favourable United Nations vote on its motion calling for the speeding up of negotiations on the transfer of sovereignty over West Irian, President Sukarno launched an escalating campaign of harassment against Dutch interests in the Republic. This culminated in 1962 in appointing Suharto, then a brigadier-general, to a special area command committed to settling the dispute by force. A few army units landed, routinely looted and then retired, having had seemingly little effect. In fact the military gesture was collateral to a vigorous diplomatic offensive successfully conducted by the foreign minister, Dr Subandrio. Before the year was out, the USA, alarmed that West Irian could become a trump in the Soviet hand, raised the pressure on the Netherlands, forcing them to cave in.

When Suharto took over from President Sukarno the United Nations and Indonesian flags were flying side by side in West Irian; administration was effectively in Indonesian hands and it only remained for the people of the territory to decide, by an 'Act of Free Choice' before the end of 1969, whether they wanted independence or integration into Indonesia.

Another pivotal, but unseen, development was also motivating all the players. As early as 1936 a Dutchman called Jean Dozy had discovered a massive gold and copper deposit beneath a 15,000-foot peak in the mountain chain that runs west to east through the territory and on into neighbouring Papua New Guinea. Preparations for its exploitation, which must have taken years, went ahead in utmost secrecy and only surfaced in 1967 with the signature by an American company, Freeport Sulphur, of the first-ever contract under Indonesia's new foreign investment law. The resulting company, Freeport-McMoRan Copper and Gold, joined much later by the British company RTZ, lost no time in deploying mining machinery described as the biggest ever invented by mankind. With it they extracted ore valued in tens of billions of dollars, leaving great holes where once were high mountains, levelling valleys with the spoil and negotiating fresh concessions which will bring riches to the owners of the Freeport mine until at least the middle of the twenty-first century. The territory once known as the land of unlimited impossibilities was suddenly producing wealth that could have made almost anything possible.

Almost none of it went to the Papuans. The Indonesian authorities probably reckoned that a million and a quarter tribesmen armed with spears and bows and arrows could cause them no real trouble. Freeport, which had to depend on the armed forces for its security, was, to say the least, recalcitrant in offering relief and compensation to the people it was displacing and unenthusiastic about recruiting them into that part of the workforce (15,000 strong by the mid-1990s) which was locally employed.

There was trouble from the outset. Soon after Indonesia's 1963 administrative take-over, the Free Papua Movement (OPM in Indonesian) started developing a guerrilla army which, as time went on, seriously embarrassed both the Indonesian security forces and the Freeport mine. United Nations observers returning in 1964 were shocked at the régime that was being inflicted on the Papuans by their new rulers. The logging industry was beginning to make inroads, some clearly in preparation for the forthcoming mining operation; the labourers were Papuans accustomed to winning their subsistence from the forest, now forced to work in conditions akin to slavery. Settlers of non-Papuan stock were arriving from Java under the government's transmigration programme and were placed on poorly managed areas of crudely cleared land near the coast; later many of them would be employed at the mine, but at first they were left to deal with unfamiliar farming conditions and communicate as best they could with the local populace. A start was made on shifting Papuan hill people from their settlements, destroying their longhouses, requiring them to live in camps, and forcing them to abandon their near-nakedness for western clothing.

There was a temporary respite in the months prior to the Act of Free Choice, the referendum held in 1969. For several weeks the shops in the more urbanised areas filled miraculously with consumer goods calculated to please the Papuans. There were reports of prime livestock flown in as gifts for village elders. The government faced a genuine problem in deciding how to conduct the promised consultation in such a large and undeveloped land. Conventional balloting was impracticable. Instead, they opted for a series of local consultations at village level. Thereafter, headmen and other elders were delegated to speak for their communities. Properly overseen and honestly conducted, it could have yielded a reasonably credible result. Observers, including those of the United Nations, were however kept at bay during much of the consultation.

Interested nations had reasons of their own not to impede a final solution of the long-running West Irian affair. The USA, with its strategic interest in Indonesian raw materials, was staunchly behind the Suharto régime. Australia too, following the American lead, was setting its hopes on the new order; it too hoped for profitable investment opportunities. Indonesia is its nearest neighbour; at that time, because the other half of New Guinea was still under Australian administration, it actually shared a land frontier with Indonesia. In a report written in April 1968 and unearthed by a scholar at the University of Hull, a British diplomat delivered his opinion that they (the Indonesians) must know that, even if there are protests about the way they go through the motions of consultation, no other power is likely to conceive it as being in their interests to intervene. 'There will be protests from the Papuan exiles in Holland, Japan and at the United Nations. . . . But I cannot imagine the US, Japanese, Dutch or Australian governments putting at risk their economic and political relations with Indonesia on a matter of principle involving a relatively small number of very primitive people'.[1]

No-one in the international community brought any rigour to oversight of the Act of Free Choice. When the day came the onus of decision was placed on a thousand and twenty-five community leaders chosen by the Jakarta government. Brought together to say on behalf of the indigenous people whether they wished to be independent or part of the Indonesian Republic, they stood surrounded by armed members of the security forces. Each individual was asked to speak his verdict. West Irian chose thus to stay inside Indonesia.

Many of its people thought otherwise. Resistance to the régime grew and was met with armed brutality. The army behaved in the fashion that was customary in the outer regions: the soldiery with lethal savagery, the officers turning human and other resources to their own enrichment. While thousands of native people were either driven from their land or saw it polluted into uselessness by the activities of the Freeport mine and the

logging companies, the continued influx of non-Papuans led to accusations
of racial dilution – an official policy of eradicating the indigenous people.

In 1977 the Free Papua Organization staged a substantial insurrection.
Dani tribesmen, wielding only their traditional weapons, planted stakes
across Wamena airfield and captured several Indonesian soldiers. With
explosives stolen from the mine they blew up a section of the landline that
conveyed ore in the form of slurry from the mine down to the company
port of Amamapare for shipment to Japan. Swift retribution included
strafing by aircraft. By then Papua New Guinea had gained its
independence; the frontier now became a gateway to refuge for active
members of the highly mobile Free Papua Movement. Across that border
following an even more serious, but abortive, uprising in 1984, more than
ten thousand Papuans fled to safe havens in Papua New Guinea
constituting a problem for both governments.

On paper it was beginning to look as if the territory was prospering on
the back of all the new economic activity. Its average GDP per head rose in
the 1980s to be the sixth highest of Indonesia's twenty-seven provinces.
But, as so often in Indonesia, the average concealed gross inequality. The
extent of rural poverty was the worst in the Republic; average life
expectancy was forty-eight years; infant mortality was almost double the
national average. And as the first twenty years of Suharto's military
dictatorship ended, Indonesia's easternmost province was in a state of
escalating civil war in which many thousands had already died.

Looking back no further than the damage done by blatant American
incitement of the Sumatran and Sulawesi rebels in 1958 and by the British
and Malaysian encouragement of separatists in Sulawesi and Sumatra in
the mid-1960s one might have expected the Jakarta régime to treat the
outer regions, out of sheer prudence, with care and sensitivity. But Javanese
attitudes towards outsiders, which, in this context, includes the ubiquitous
and industrious Chinese, were essentially colonial. Post-independence
Indonesia became another Javanese empire and Suharto, even more than
Sukarno, ruled his 'colonies' as crudely and violently and greedily as had
the Dutch before independence.

It would have been possible to return to the Sumatran provinces,
including Aceh, a fairer proportion of government revenues derived from
Sumatran oil and timber, and to make greater efforts to guarantee that
what central funding there was was honestly spent. In Sulawesi and
Maluku it would have been possible to enforce proper discipline on logging

projects and follow through – as was done in Malaysia – with decently administered land settlement projects affording better lives to displaced people. In West Papua it would have been easy to provide proper and prompt compensation to the native people dispossessed of their customary land rights by the Freeport mine and to introduce amenities that would have made them pleased to be Indonesians. In all the outer regions it would have been possible to require civilized behaviour on the part of the armed forces and to allow provincial administrations the uninhibited exercise of their prerogatives. But the régime feared devolution – except within its own strictly military parameters – and showed an unbending obsession with security. Often that meant brutal repression.

Up until the 1960s the outer region where serious trouble might least have been expected was Kalimantan (Borneo). It was, to be sure, an anthropologist's paradise, and still is. Not wonderfully hospitable, on account of its high mountains, dense jungle and swampy coastline, its interior life was compounded of a multiplicity of indigenous, non-Muslim peoples dwelling in isolated longhouse communities and subsisting off shifting cultivation and jungle produce; coastal settlements were typically occupied by Muslim Malays, some owing tenuous allegiance to crumbling sultanates.

Everywhere, but especially in the coastal cities – Pontianak, Singkawang, Banjarmasin, Balikpapan – there were Chinese, relatively numerous by comparison with other parts of Indonesia, engaged in their customary pursuits of growing food-crops and acting as commercial middlemen. Writing of them shortly after the Second World War, when he got to know West Kalimantan and Sarawak well, Tom Harrisson said: 'In most of Borneo the future internal politics of China, whatever they may be, will not have to be considered and worked out locally against an embittered and blood-stained pattern of racial or group conflict on the spot. In Borneo, broadly speaking, the Chinese, in common with other races, lived together through the war and live now in reasonable harmony and kindliness'.[2]

Because it was sparsely populated Kalimantan absorbed change relatively easily. Oil was being extracted on the east coast early in the twentieth century. Under Dutch rule immigrants arrived from Sulawesi and from the impoverished Javanese island of Madura and from the latter kept on coming as part of the post-independence transmigration programmes.

The proviso for Harrisson's optimistic prognosis was that nothing abrupt happened to upset the benign rhythm. But by the time the Suharto régime took over it had been severely and intentionally disrupted by a number of agents: by President Sukarno's 'Crush Malaysia' campaign, by the Chinese Communist Party's proselytising in neighbouring Sarawak and by British rummaging in the detritus of local history.

The nub of the Indonesian-Malaysian confrontation was at the western end of West Kalimantan's frontier with Sarawak, in the area between Pontianak and Kuching. The local sultan, Hamid the second of Pontianak, believed Sukarno had promised in 1945 that Kalimantan would enjoy autonomy after independence. When, in 1949, Sukarno reneged by opting for a unitary republic the sultan entered into league with the Dutch military adventurer Turko Westerling and, after trying to enlist help from Queen Juliana of the Netherlands, was deposed and gaoled.

Hamid was still in prison in 1965, but followers went on supporting his cause. Thanks to a British connection I met one of them, Zainal Abidin bin Mohammed Shah, in Singapore in January of that year. He was, he said, secretary-general of a newly declared Provisional Government of the West Kalimantan Sultanate. With financial aid from Malaysia and also, he hoped, from Britain, West Germany and the USA, he and his colleagues sought to separate a free West Kalimantan from the rest of Indonesia, reinstate the sultan, denounce communism and open the way for the sultan to join SEATO if he so chose. He wished me to believe there was an army of up to three thousand men lying low in Kalimantan, mostly Bugis, which they aimed to concentrate into the western tip of Sarawak. Given appropriate cover, they were hoping for simultaneous uprisings in Kalimantan, Sulawesi and Sumatra.

I judged it to be a planted story – albeit containing truthful elements – and chose not to file it. Nevertheless, it highlighted the vulnerability of Indonesia's outer regions to dissidence fomented by its foes. If any part of Zainal's army actually existed, it was one more factor in the situation Generals Suharto and Nasution had to deal with in West Kalimantan when they reversed President Sukarno's confrontation policy.

In fact they had worse problems. Some of the army units committed to the campaign against the northern Borneo states – 'Subandrio's army' as propagandists called it – were ardent Sukarno supporters. They did not join in the general damping-down of the military confrontation; they withdrew into the hills and made contact with PKI elements fleeing from the slaughter in other parts of Indonesia. They were joined by mostly Chinese sympathisers, some from China itself, others from Sarawak. The official assessment, described to me in 1968 by the then Indonesian ambassador to

Megawati Sukarnoputri, Indonesia's vice-president and prospective President, with her father, Ahmed Sukarno, the nation's first President, December 1949. (*Associated Press/ Topham*)

(*Below*) Abdul Haris Nasution, father of the Indonesian army and author of its dual military-political role, visiting London in 1961. His forces suppressed the US-inspired rebellion in Sumatra and Sulawesi in 1958. Long regarded as a possible successor to President Sukarno, General Nasution was encouraged by the USA in 1960 to stage a show down, but later fell from American favour. (*Associated Press/Topham*)

The brilliant young Communist Party (PKI) leader D.N. Aidit was among those hunted down and summarily executed by the army in the 1965 purges. In what is believed to be the last known photograph of him, he is seen apparently signing a paper which may have been his written confession, shortly before he was shot. (*TAPOL*)

September 1963, as the anti-British 'Crush Malaysia' campaign gathered momentum, a well-organised band of young men described as 'students' attacked the British Embassy in Jakarta. They replaced the Union Jack with the Indonesian red and white, set fire to the chancery building, then sacked and looted the homes of embassy staff. (*Associated Press/Topham*)

Norman Reddaway, the Foreign Office propaganda specialist sent in 1965 to the headquarters of Britain's Far East Command in Singapore to support the Anglo-American policy of toppling Sukarno and helping to instal General Suharto in his place. (*Jean Reddaway*)

A 'black propaganda' campaign orchestrated between Jakarta and British Intelligence units in Singapore helped to conceal the true origins and extent of the 1965 counter-coups which led to the massacre of almost a million suspected communists and sympathisers and, ultimately, Sukarno's downfall. Ambassador in Jakarta at the time was Sir Andrew Gilchrist, seen here in retirement at his home in Scotland, shortly before his death in 1993. (*Jeremy Gilchrist*)

Sukarno, Indonesia's first President, was manoeuvred out of office and replaced in 1967 by another Javanese, Major-General Suharto, right, who became a military dictator but seldom wore military uniform thereafter. (*Associated Press/Topham*)

The Sultan of Yogyakarta, acme of the Javanese establishment, with The Kian Sang, a Chinese entrepreneur better known as 'Bob' Hasan, right, Suharto's golfing partner and financial mentor. Hasan became Indonesia's plywood king and, briefly, minister of trade before being imprisoned for embezzlement after Suharto's fall. (*TAPOL*)

Some of the most massive machinery ever built was used to turn a jungle-clad 15,000 ft high mountain in West Papua into the Freeport gold and copper mine – a source of wealth no Indonesian government could afford to surrender. (*Survival International*)

General Wiranto, left, was for a time the running mate of President B.J. Habibie, seen with him here at an Armed Forces Day parade, 5 October 1999. Associated with the Suharto clan, Habibie's star was already on the wane and Wiranto, sponsor of the 1999 military repression in East Timor, sought solace instead in a new career as a pop singer, dedicating the profits from his first CD to aiding refugees. (*Associated Press AP*)

With the ailing President Wahid (left) under fire for his involvement in two financial scandals, the political focus in 2001 has shifted to his vice-president, the popular leader of the PDI-P, Megawati Sukarnoputri. The late President Sukarno's daughter, she is increasingly gaining the support both of the army and of the Muslim political leadership, although whether she will be able to control the many factions jostling for power in Indonesia is the unanswerable question. (*Associated Press AP*)

Malaysia, Colonel Benny Murdani, was that the PKI planned to build Kalimantan into its long-term base for operations throughout the Republic. Soon, soldiers of the old order were fighting those of the new. Playing that aspect down, the régime chose rather to stress the communist threat and, as Indonesians often do, made scapegoats of the Chinese.

Of fewer than a thousand Sarawak Chinese who crossed into West Kalimantan to fight against the creation of Malaysia, between five and six hundred were left when confrontation was officially halted in August 1966. They were incorporated into a communist body called the Sarawak People's Guerrilla Force under the command of the former military governor of East Kalimantan, a pro-Sukarnoist, Brigadier-General Suharjo. Their new task was to muster support among the resident Chinese farmers in the inland reaches of West Kalimantan. An American missionary working there, Bob Peterson, told me they offered a 'heaven on earth', independence from Java and complete control of their own province. He said they had been planning a general uprising. But, forearmed no doubt with information supplied by field missionaries and others, the military authorities struck first.

In an astonishingly candid and self-congratulatory interview I had with him in Pontianak, the military commander of West Kalimantan, Brigadier-General Witono, a specialist in Chinese affairs, told me how he did it. The specialist knowledge he employed was not of the Chinese but of the indigenous hill people, loosely referred to as Dayaks – the people whom the British anthropologist Tom Harrisson had used during the Second World War to oppose the Japanese occupying forces and again, in 1962, to put the Brunei rebels to flight.

Witono recounted how in November 1966 his men triggered a 'soldier-hero' movement among the Dayaks, harking back to half-forgotten tribal tradition. More than a dozen villages in guerrilla-infested areas were persuaded to revive an old oath-taking (*mapang*) ceremony; cups of blood were passed round in token of imminent danger; Dayaks and their Chinese neighbours pledged solidarity against strangers and specifically against the guerrillas.

It was only a matter of time before the trap was sprung. Chinese communist guerrillas allegedly killed a Dayak headman; the army captured and killed a number of guerrillas who were said to have taken part in the oath-taking. Evidence was produced that other Chinese were supporting the guerrillas with food. Acting on their oath, the Dayaks thereupon unleashed their fury against the Chinese. It began with looting. If that did not drive them out they dressed themselves in red, denoting heroism, and burned their houses and crops. Finally, if any yet remained, they decked themselves in green and killed them – more than two thousand, according to informants and witnesses I spoke to in Pontianak.

There were several consequences. It contributed handsomely to Witono's policy of bringing the inland Chinese to the coast and regrouping them near towns where an eye could be kept on them. It removed them as a potentially supportive element from remote areas where armed PKI subversives would linger for many more years. But it also did economic damage. Most of the pillaged Chinese farms reverted to jungle; there was a rice shortage; rubber trees were not tapped; pepper groves were abandoned. And it inflamed the worst sort of racism. In Pontianak I saw that nearly all the doctors and nurses treating the sick and wounded, many of them young children, were Chinese. The hospital where they worked close to a river bank outside the city consisted of makeshift tents in which the patients lay uncovered on the ground waiting for medical supplies which would never arrive because, despite the best efforts of the Red Cross, they had been stolen.

Some of the fleeing Chinese made their way into Sarawak where Malaysian and British personnel were shocked to learn that they had been harrassed not only by their Dayak neighbours but by Indonesian soldiers as well.

Nevertheless the delicate task of turning a hostile relationship into one of collaboration between Indonesian and Malaysian security forces was, despite occasional differences of opinion about the scale of the threat, efficiently accomplished and sustained. Regular military liaison meetings were instituted in Pontianak and Kuching. Chinese officers from the Malaysian police crossed frequently into Kalimantan to interrogate Chinese prisoners captured by the Indonesian army. There was a slight resurgence of communist activity in the mid-1970s following the communist victory in Vietnam, but as the decade ended the PKI force in Kalimantan was much diminished, and towards the end of 1982 the Indonesian Defence Minister, General Muhammad Yusuf, declared the Sarawak border area clear.

In at least one respect, however, the province had suffered long-term damage. The Dayaks, having tasted blood, wanted more and turned their attention to the continuing inflow of transmigrants shipped across from Madura. As the skies in 1982–3 filled with smoke from the burning-off of huge timber-logging concessions, it began to look as if the racial harmony Sukarno had striven to promote had gone for ever from Kalimantan, and by 2001 Madurese transmigrants were fleeing in thousands before the onslaught of enraged Dayaks.

The excoriation Indonesia drew upon itself in West Kalimantan was lessened by the tact of its Malaysian neighbour and the internationally-attuned prudence shown by Generals Nasution and Suharto in the early days of the new order. No such saving graces came to its rescue in East Timor, where the brutality, the greed and the incompetence of Suharto's military dictatorship would finally be exposed.

Lying in the extreme south of the archipelago, Timor is the largest of the island group known as the Lesser Sundas, but differs from the others by virtue of its rugged hills and mountains. Sweet-scented sandalwood used to grow there in some profusion, attracting first Chinese, Javanese and Malay exploiters then, in the sixteenth century, Portuguese who had sailed eastward from their colony in Malacca. Over the next three centuries the traders from Portugal stripped the island almost bare of sandal but injected Christianity, their language and a mixed-race progeny. Their rule was at best nonchalant. When in the eighteenth century the Dutch arrived, established a port at Kupang and began competing for the sandalwood trade, the Portuguese drew back into eastern Timor. The result was a virtual partition of the island which was incorporated into formal agreements between the two colonial powers at the turn of the nineteenth and twentieth centuries.

So were established West Timor, part of the Netherlands East Indies, and East Timor, a colony of the Portuguese empire. By definition the one, as a former Dutch territory, became part of independent Indonesia; the other, being Portuguese, did not.

The people of East Timor, fewer than a million in number, never took to their immigrant rulers. They had chieftains and strong men of their own under whose leadership they not infrequently rebelled against the colonial administration until, early in the twentieth century, they were bloodily pacified and thousands died.

Next to terrorise them was a force of more than twenty thousand Japanese troops landed during the Second World War, to hold the territory as a possible stepping stone on the way to Australia. Many East Timorese gave their support to a few hundred Australian soldiers sent to resist the invader. Farmsteads and entire villages were destroyed in reprisal. An estimated fifteen hundred Japanese were killed, and fifty thousand Timorese.

In the post-war years the Portuguese returned to carry out some rehabilitation, most of it at the expense of virtual slave labour brutally exacted from the islanders. Coffee cultivation was given a fillip to occupy part of the gap left by the run-down sandalwood industry. But the developments that changed East Timor for ever were Indonesian independence and, in 1974, the military coup d'état in Portugal, following which East Timor was simply abandoned.

Poorly resourced, under-developed, under-populated, by any rational standard East Timor lacked the potential to be an independent nation-state. The map argues that at the very least the two halves of Timor should make a single unit. And, like it or not, every detail of its political, economic and cultural life is inextricably entwined in that of the archipelago we know as Indonesia. The case for incorporating East Timor seemed unanswerable.

First into the vacuum left by Portugal were the East Timorese themselves. Several political parties were born, the most important of which, Fretilin (an acronym for the Revolutionary Front for an Independent East Timor), was to form the hard core of the resistance movement. Another group, funded from Jakarta, spoke up for integration into Indonesia; it won little support but was a useful pawn for Major-General Ali Murtopo, the soldier who had emasculated the mainstream Indonesian political parties for Suharto; this group was used as a mouthpiece for the unwarranted allegation that Fretilin was pro-communist.

Aware that neither the USA nor Indonesia would stomach a left-wing administration – but still perhaps hoping against hope that independence was achievable – a number of political elements combined to propose the election of an assembly to devise a constitutional solution. Suharto stifled that with his peremptory public verdict that independence was not a viable option for East Timor. A few weeks later yet another political group attempted a coup, set itself against Fretilin and spoke of expelling communists. In the ensuing confusion, although Fretilin fighters gained the upper hand, Indonesian units were infiltrated and enabled the régime to make political capital out of what was represented as a civil war. Several thousand Timorese lives were lost.

For a few brief months Fretilin more or less ruled in East Timor with, as its foreign minister, a man whose name was to become a legend, Jose Ramos Horta, destined to spend many years exiled in Australia.

The Jakarta régime exchanged some fruitless courtesies with Portugal but planned an invasion. Before going ahead they took the precaution of checking what the American and Australian reaction would be. President Gerald Ford of the USA and his Secretary of State Henry Kissinger, still painfully digesting their country's recent defeat by the communists in Vietnam, not surprisingly consented. Ford paid a state visit to Jakarta in December 1975 and gave Suharto the USA's explicit go-ahead to the bloody invasion that was about to occur. In Canberra, when asked what he might do if Indonesia invaded East Timor, Australian Prime Minister, Malcolm Fraser, reportedly replied 'absolutely nothing'.

Emboldened by what came to be known as the 'big wink', Suharto launched his invasion while Ford was still airborne on his way home from Indonesia. The invaders employed naval bombardment, amphibious landings and parachute drops. Considering the disparity between the forces engaged, the Indonesian army came impressively close to making a complete botch of the operation. Fretilin was ready for them and took a substantial toll. Only in their specialism of unbridled brutality against unarmed civilians did the new invaders show their customary flair.

In Dili, the capital of East Timor, it was reckoned they shot three-quarters of the male population and the entire community of ethnic Chinese. Those who were not mowed down randomly or herded into buildings to be incinerated alive were dealt with more systematically by the sea-front, where the victims were lined up on the pier so as to tumble into the sea as they were murdered. Onlookers were ordered to count.

That massacre, the first of many, was only the beginning of the cleansing which went on until Suharto in July 1976, making out he had acted in support of a majority who wanted integration into Indonesia, announced the annexation of East Timor. In spite of frantic American efforts to prevent it, the United Nations duly passed the first of several resolutions ordering the Indonesians to withdraw. Suharto ignored them.

The 'cleansing' developed into a secret war against the East Timorese, hidden from all who did not have the benefit of satellite surveillance systems. Outsiders were barred. Untold thousands of families fled into the hills but were still not immune from harassment. The army's unambiguous policy was to stamp out both the Fretilin guerrillas and those who supported or concealed them. A target area, once identified, would be subjected to long periods of intense aerial bombardment and strafing followed by attacks on the ground. The mere evacuation of a village would be taken as evidence of hostility and punished by the destruction of homesteads, crops and livestock. Food became scarce and the management of that scarcity became another weapon in the hands of the occupying army.

In his book, aptly entitled *An Empire of the East*, Norman Lewis records that in one eight-week period in 1978 the Indonesian air force was dropping up to eight hundred bombs every day as its contribution to the cleansing of East Timor – using military aircraft and weapons obtained from the West. Interviewed by John Pilger in 1998 for a Carlton Television documentary, a CIA officer, C. Philip Liechty, admitted: 'We were providing most of the weaponry, helicopters, logistical support, food, uniforms, all the expendables the Indonesians needed to conduct this war'.

Using such means Suharto's advisers evidently judged that by 1979 they had East Timorese resistance under control. Gingerly they allowed the International Committee of the Red Cross and the Catholic Relief Services to send representatives in. Budget allocations rose, doubling to US$100 million in 1981. The build-up of Javanese administrative personnel began. Transmigrants were shipped in. Money was channelled into basic social amenities.

But the Indonesians misjudged the people they were colonising. In spite of ferocious repression, which included widespread use of torture, the East Timorese fought on.

In 1980, ahead of another major army offensive in East Timor the following year, the International Committee of the Red Cross and the Catholic Relief Services were ordered out. A technique favoured during the operation that ensued, timed to prevent the planting of new food crops, was the 'fence of legs'. Practised earlier in Java, it was now given a distinctive local twist. It consisted of encirclement by a cordon of slowly advancing troops who would tighten the noose round a selected area, driving unarmed islanders ahead of them as a human shield. At that time it was estimated that a third of East Timor's population – more than two hundred thousand – had been killed or died of starvation during the first six years of Indonesian occupation. The Italian-based human rights organization Permanent Tribunal of the People accused the Indonesian régime of genocide. In that same period Indonesian army officers and civil servants applied themselves to acquiring land and building themselves high quality houses; plans were elaborated for the de-monopolization of the coffee industry, making way for private entrepreneurs, among whom were members of General Suharto's family.

Knowledge of what was happening in East Timor was more than sufficient to have justified firm diplomatic and economic reprisals by any government that cared, but none did. Not until 1983 did the United Nations Human Rights Commission express its 'deep concern' over the continuing violation of human rights, and almost immediately there was another round of military atrocities. Again in 1985 the conflict flared as Fretilin inflicted more casualties on the security forces and the Indonesian occupiers executed people accused of communing with guerrillas. The German Society for Endangered Peoples drew attention to the use of the transmigration programme to import Indonesians from other areas in an attempt to dilute the East Timorese. Only weeks later the Australian Prime Minister, Bob Hawke, announced his government's recognition of Indonesian sovereignty over the annexed territory. Few doubted that it was an opportunistic manoeuvre in preparation for the impending Australian-Indonesian treaty on mineral and petroleum rights on the sea-bed between Timor and Northern Australia. Portugal, by then as guilt-ridden about the fate of the East Timorese as previously it had been indifferent, withdrew its ambassador from Canberra in protest.

Hawke's diplomatic blunder marked the end of a phase. In East Timor, as in other Indonesian affairs, the later 1980s saw a sea-change. Recognising the unsustainability of a purely military resistance, Fretilin under its leader Xanana Gusmao added a political string to its bow. A new generation of young resisters learned how to press their case by non-violent means. With Gusmao at home and Ramos Horta abroad, plus significant public sympathy in Jakarta, Fretilin's voice could no longer be ignored. International indignation began to stir. Whereas previously the United Nations had neither recognised nor objected to the annexation, the Secretary General suggested in 1987 that Indonesia and Portugal should work out a compromise on the question of East Timor's future status.

Accustomed to disregarding international opinion – except when the pressures came from the USA or Japan – the Suharto régime either wrongly assessed the changing climate or resolved to tough it out or, which seems the most likely, was beginning to be divided within itself. There were generals blustering about crushing anything that threatened the unity of the nation, while others were beginning to perceive at least the expediency of winning East Timor's hearts and minds. Concurrently, Indonesia's unfortunate foreign minister, Ali Alatas, was having to instruct Suharto about the damage being done to the national reputation by the accelerating wave of international disapproval. Not only was the behaviour of the occupying army making a mockery of the dialogue he was trying to develop with Portugal, but Suharto's personal ambition of chairing the Non-Aligned Movement conference due in 1992 was looking problematical.

So, with the aim of persuading the world that all was well in East Timor, the territory was declared open late in 1989, open to Indonesians seeking jobs on their own initiative, open to tourists and journalists, open, as Ali Alatas planned, to a delegation of Portuguese parliamentarians who would be able to judge matters for themselves.

The Portuguese visit never happened. It was cancelled in the midst of a sudden heightening of tension among proponents and opponents of integration, generally thought to have been fomented by a branch of the security services. Fifteen days later there occurred the notorious Dili massacre in which more than two hundred mourners at a funeral were killed and dozens more wounded by Indonesian soldiers. In a pre-planned manifestation that was meant to be peaceful several thousand mourners processed to the Santa Cruz cemetery to lay flowers at the grave of an anti-integrationist killed in the trouble a fortnight earlier. Their plan was to move on and see through the anti-integration demonstration they had been preparing for the Portuguese parliamentarians. They were given a rough passage by security forces and were finally caught – and filmed – between two columns of troops one of which opened indiscriminate fire on sight; witnesses believed the security action was pre-planned.

The reverberations of those gunshots spread far and lasted many months. In an attempted cover-up which merely exposed how badly out of touch it was the army made out that no more than first eighteen, then fifty Timorese had been shot. It was seen to be lying but did not care. The American government, after initially describing the 'official enquiry' that produced those crass misrepresentations as serious and responsible, suspended its US International Military Education Training programme and did not reinstate it until five years later. The Netherlands, joined by Denmark and Canada, suspended their programmes of economic aid to Indonesia. Testily Indonesia responded by dissolving the Intergovernmental (aid) Group on Indonesia over which the Netherlands had presided. Not that it signified much; within months the USA had seen to it that the management of the aid consortium passed into the hands of the World Bank, and aid to the tune of five billion dollars annually was soon back on stream.

Nevertheless, the East Timor issue had burst irrevocably out of the confines of Indonesian domestic affairs and started processes that would strike at the very heart of General Suharto's military régime.

GOING UP IN SMOKE

The irony of the abuse inflicted on the outer regions is that they are potentially the fount of Indonesia's wealth and power. Even after the economic miracle said to have occurred during three decades of rule by a predominantly Javanese military régime, Java was still the headquarters of

Indonesian poverty. Constituting only seven per cent of the nation's land-surface, Java carries sixty per cent of its people. Its population nearly trebled between 1900 and 2000, giving it twice the density of Britain and Japan. Up to half of Javanese farm families are landless and of those with land forty per cent have less than two-thirds of an acre to work on.

Although land quality varies enormously among the outer regions, in terms of natural resources, space and revenue-earning capacity their collective carrying – hence political – potential vastly outstrips Java's. In only one major resource are they wanting: people. Without sufficient labour they cannot unlock their potential. President Sukarno favoured a laisser-faire approach to population management; in a unified nation, he argued, people would respond to economic opportunity and find their own way into available space. His policy, or lack of it, made no reckoning of the investment and complex organization needed to effect large-scale demographic shifts and never showed any sign of succeeding.

The Dutch, by contrast, had made a start on the redistribution of labour to reinforce their plantation industries early in the twentieth century. By 1940 when the Japanese drove them out they were transferring some forty thousand people a year from Java to Sumatra. In the 1950s the number rose to nearly 300,000 annually, but another million were being born. The numbers were small in comparison with what was attempted during Suharto's presidency.

To have any chance of lasting impact transmigration had to be integrated into several other policy programmes, not least the limitation of birthrate. General Suharto won public approval by taking a personal interest. 'Two children are enough' became a popular slogan under a family planning programme launched with his close involvement in 1970. Over the years thousands of advice centres were created. They did not, as some feared, encounter strong cultural resistance. They did make a difference to birthrate statistics, notably and interestingly in the most impoverished rural areas; yet Java's population went on growing at a rate which more than outstripped the benefits of the government's parallel transmigration programme.

The issue figured from 1969 onwards, and with mounting salience, in all the five-year plans of the new order régime. The sums of money allocated to it and the scale of policy aspirations rose sharply. Upward of three million had been transferred by 1984 and there was extravagant talk of shifting sixty-five million in a quarter of a century. As well as Java and its northern offshore island of Madura a regular stream of transmigrants was also leaving Bali and Flores for destinations as various as Sulawesi, Kalimantan, Sumatra, Maluku and West Papua.

Even so, it began to be obvious halfway through the Suharto era that as a means of constricting the population of Java transmigration was having little effect. The numbers were not sufficient, administrative and other limitations precluded further increase and birthrates rose to fill the gaps left by departing migrants. Viewed, however, as a contribution to the development of the outer regions, it could have been a great success. Assisted financially and in the design process by such agencies as the UN Development Programme, the World Bank, the Asian Development Bank and the World Food Programme, and with the nearby example of Malaysia's highly successful land development projects, the theoretical design of Indonesia's transmigration programme left little to be desired.

The scheme was meant to be voluntary. Applicants were supposed to be under forty, married and in good health. In their new location they were given a habitable hutment and two hectares of cleared land, at least half of which was intended to be cultivated so that they would become self-sufficient. To achieve that they were meant to receive a year's supply of food and enough seed, fertilizer and pesticide to enable them to establish their crops by the end of that year.

Where the settlements succeeded these conditions were broadly satisfied. The soil was good, there was access to markets where they could sell their produce and services such as health and education were provided. But many failed, for reasons that left both transmigrants and the host communities victims of corruption and abuse of their human rights.

Many transmigrants were only in theory voluntary. Arriving on site to find the land unprepared, hutments not built, access-roads incomplete, fertilizers and other essential provisions arriving too late or not at all because officials or the military had stolen them; the settlers frequently encountered hostility on the part of locals whose farms were rendered non-viable by the newcomers.

The shortcomings of the transmigration programme were in part attributable to stupidity as well as to the admitted complexities of establishing public services in a vast and diverse country. They could have been overcome, however, if the programme had been kept in focus, with its objectives held uncompromisingly to the fore and its authentic architects allowed to keep it on track. Unhappily Suharto's régime used it increasingly as a tool for the pursuit of activities which were not fully consonant with its social aims.

It was, for instance, unquestionably used as a means of modifying the ethnic profile of East Timor and bringing troublesome tribal communities such as those in Kalimantan and West Papua to heel. By planting Muslim Madurese on the non-Muslim peoples of West Kalimantan or the Melanesians of Papua the government provoked continual conflict, which did nothing for the ostensible goals of transmigration. Such schemes were, on the other hand, very favourable to the business interests of key components of the régime – the Chinese towkays who were Suharto's favoured associates, the officer corps of the armed forces and compliant civil servants.

Nowhere was this more apparent than in the explosive growth of the timber industry. The change of régime from Sukarno to Suharto happened at a time of vigorous industrial expansion globally and especially, under the stimulus of the Vietnam war, in East and South-East Asia. The demand for tropical timber and its by-products soared. British, Japanese, American and overseas Chinese entrepreneurs streamed into the Philippines, Malaysia and, from 1967 on, Indonesia to garner this prodigal harvest that could yield quick and great wealth in return for little investment.

The real power to sanction the exploitation of great tracts of rain-forest lay with the president, Suharto, at the centre and with military governors in the outer regions. The speed at which the bonanza developed was reflected in the growth of timber exports from barely a million and a half dollars in 1961 to nearly a hundred and seventy million ten years later. In roughly the same decade the proportion of Java covered by forest fell from twenty-three to fifteen per cent. As the devastation spread through the outer regions the annual cut nationwide rose to a million and a half hectares on an available base of a hundred and twenty million hectares.

Sometimes the timber concessions were allied to other developmental operations, as in Sumatra where deforestation was often scheduled as the prelude to palm oil, rubber and coffee plantations – schedules that were not invariably carried through. In West Papua the preliminaries to the establishment and progressive extension of the Freeport mine involved large-scale deforestion of native areas, earning big profits for the timber companies but only derisory compensation for the Papuans driven out of the forest areas which had provided their subsistence.

In another part of West Papua, Asmat, on its swampy south coast, Indonesian newspapers in the 1970s exposed the employment of forced native labour for logging of timberwood trees destined for Japan. Payment was piffling and often withheld. Labourers who resisted were beaten and subjected to other physical punishments inflicted by Indonesian military and civil personnel who were rewarded by the Jakarta-based concessionaires.

As the timber-stripping frenzy grew, integration into the broader process of planned development deteriorated and often ceased. Not only was forest regeneration neglected, but ever more extraction, countenanced by local military commanders and bureaucrats, happened without any licence at all. Indonesia was soon the world's biggest exporter of hardwood logs.

Data collected by the European Union at the end of the last century indicated that the illicit timber harvest was even greater than permitted under the licensing régime; extraction was double the sustainable rate. The government did institute interest-free loans for the development of forest plantations where extraction and replacement could be held in balance but, characteristically, only a quarter of the plantation areas for which funds were allocated saw any planting.

The biggest timber exploiters were military holding companies, commonly connected with members of the Suharto family. The army's timber interests in Kalimantan came to be reckoned as its most remunerative source of non-budgetary funding, and a significant but incalculable proportion of that income was spent on armaments additional to those purchased through regular inter-governmental channels.

Merely in terms of resource conservation the management of the nation's forests under the Suharto régime was a disaster. But it was disastrous in other ways too. The tax take from the prodigious turnovers achieved should have been a major contribution to the national development of which Suharto proclaimed himself the father; but an economist at the University of Washington, David Brown, calculated that between the early 1970s and the end of Suharto's reign in 1998 the government failed to collect more than fourteen billion timber dollars that were due to it – equivalent to three years of financial assistance by the Western aid donors club.

Most of the people whose homes were destroyed by unbridled forest depletion were not treated as Indonesian citizens in need of sympathetic assistance, but as a nuisance impeding business enterprise. They might be offered a few rupiahs if there were useful tasks to be done – like rekindling fires that had been extinguished in tracts cleared of timber – but it was just as likely that they would be left to drift away or actually forced away by troops bearing arms, their fate not very different from that of threatened wild-life species, such as orang-utan, which were also deprived of habitat and driven away by fire. Even the government's own transmigrants were not immune from the rapacity of the loggers; in Sumatra there were cases of settlers from Bali who had made good on coffee cultivation, only to be told that they had to make way for logging companies and had their houses burnt down when they refused. Anxiety about the ecological harm being done in the world's second largest rain-forest area spread far and wide, even to Japan, a principal beneficiary of the rape that was being committed. As international protest by reputable environmental groups rose in the mid-1970s, construction activity declined in the advanced industrial nations, precipitating a slump in the demand for timber. It was a dangerous time for the Indonesian economy because oil prices also fell.

But it was also in a sense providential. With the greed of timber exploiters unfed by market demand, government planners were able to push through a scheme that would create employment and generate more value from timber inside Indonesia. It would also, incidentally, create a big new investment opportunity for Suharto's closest Chinese and military associates. It was decided to curtail exports of raw timber to Japan, Korea and Taiwan, where it was the feedstock of plywood industries, and to promote the manufacture of plywood in Indonesia instead.

Timber from the outer regions had become the next biggest export revenue earner after petroleum and textiles. Inevitably the curtailment of exports caused a sharp but temporary revenue fall, but within a few years the move was an acknowledged success. Indonesia became and remained the world's foremost plywood exporter and was second only to Malaysia as an exporter of sawn timber.

The international market for raw timber nonetheless revived and illicit logging in the remoter parts of eastern Indonesia went on so vigorously that, in Maluku for example, workers were brought in illegally from the Philippines. In 1994–5 the forestry ministry in Jakarta started trying to remedy the problem by stricter enforcement of the licensing system, but the timber lobby was powerful, with its roots in the highest places in the land. The abuse went on, despite repeated World Bank warnings. Much later, after Suharto's retreat from the presidency, the aid donors consortium, spurred by European Union research, threatened to reduce the annual aid package if nothing was done about it.

It was too late. As they spoke the atmosphere over much of Sumatra, the Malacca Strait and the Malay Peninsula was thick with smoke from fires lit in central Sumatra to clear the land on vast areas denuded of what had been primal jungle. The Malaysian tourist industry in 1997–9 was all-but wiped out by atmospheric pollution such as had never been seen in the world before. Airlines, shipping and road transport were disrupted in daytime visibility sometimes as low as a hundred metres. Less remarked because it skirts no major shipping or air lanes, Kalimantan was in the same predicament. In a single day, it was reported, meteorological satellites had monitored two hundred and eighty separate conflagrations there; some may have been slow-burning fires endemic in the coal-mining area on the west coast; most were forest fires.

And so Indonesia's timber scandal went on after Suharto's departure, through the Habibie interim and into the Wahid presidency. Early signs are that the granting of timber concessions as a sop to politically potent military men is being extended now to benefit politically potent Muslim leaders. Under a scheme launched in 1999 a number of religious boarding schools in Java were granted concessions for forestry exploitation. Whatever its merits as a way of distributing some of the wealth to non-military bodies, seen through non-Javanese eyes it looks like the old story of Java plundering the outer regions for the gain of a few well-heeled individuals.

*Notes*

1   John Saltford, PhD student at Hull University.
2   Harrisson, Tom 'The Chinese in Borneo 1942–6' in *International Affairs* Vol XXVI, No 3, July 1950.

# EIGHT

## *Human Rights (and Wrongs)*

The transition from Sukarno to Suharto in 1965–6 marked a sea-change in the attitude of Indonesia's rulers to blood-letting. President Sukarno strove always to prevent the loss of his people's lives. Death sentences were rare during his presidency. During the Suharto dictatorship judicial executions were relatively common, and to these must be added hundreds of thousands – possibly millions – of Indonesian citizens who were slaughtered, most of them outside the law, most never to be recorded, without significant discouragement by the USA which helped to place and sustain him in power. Similar numbers must be supposed to have been beaten, tortured or otherwise injured. Yet another half million were arrested following the 1965 coup and in many cases detained without trial for years or decades. Similar arrests and detentions continued throughout Suharto's time in power.

If the purge of communist supporters in 1965–6 remains the most notorious atrocity on Suharto's record, it needs to be remembered that the most numerous victims of his bloodthirsty rule were in the outer regions. When the mass murder began to slow down towards the end of the 1960s, army brutality in other contexts continued in West Papua, Sumatra and, in due course, East Timor.

With so many political prisoners on its hands, the régime had a problem beyond its ability to cope. It sorted them into crude categories: into category A, according to Suharto in answers he gave to *The Times* in 1973, went 2,457 known communists said to be implicated in the abortive 1965 'coup'; category B prisoners, numbering 26,650 at that time, were suspected of taking part in the alleged coup attempt but no solid basis of legal guilt could be established against them; in category C were many thousands merely suspected of harbouring communist sympathies, most only after they had suffered years of unwarranted imprisonment. During the first two decades of Suharto rule Indonesia had more political prisoners than any other country in the world.

Worst off were the category B prisoners, since their chances of having their cases brought to any kind of trial were negligible. Indeed an Amnesty

International report in 1996, probably more reliable than anything ever likely to issue from an official Indonesian source, estimated that of the hundreds of thousands of people arrested in all categories only about a thousand were ever brought to trial, often years after their supposed offences. Not only were the security forces incapable of marshalling appropriate evidence, they were unable to provide suitable accommodation and care for prisoners. Four hundred concentration camps were set up in various outer regions.

The bulk of category B prisoners, approximately ten thousand, were despatched to the best known of these, an enclosed and tightly guarded area described as a 'resettlement project' on Buru island in Maluku. Among these supposedly 'known communists' were Pramudya Ananta Toer, Indonesia's most eminent twentieth century novelist, Dr Suprapto, a noted law professor, Bakasi Effendi, an internationally successful film director and at least one child who was twelve when arrested. More than half were practising Muslims and the rest practising Buddhists, Christians or Hindus, a notable tally in a community of alleged communists.

Conditions were hard, sometimes harsh. Prisoners had to grow their own food; many died. Unlike those committed to prisons close to their homes, they received no regular food supplements from friends or relatives outside. Medical attention was inadequate; under a régime that was enriching itself on oil, timber and tin dollars there were not enough simple medicaments like quinine, vitamin tablets and antibiotics for the unindicted inmates of the Buru Resettlement Project. As to the category A detainees, the great majority of the thousand who were put on trial were condemned to death, life imprisonment or lesser – but still long – prison sentences. Tendentious accounts of the many trials that were staged before military tribunals, frequently relying on the written evidence of witnesses who were described as unable to appear in court, gave rise from the outset to serious doubts about their fairness.

The execution of death sentences was unpredictable. On the one hand, decades could pass while enigmatic appeal procedures worked their way through the military, civil and presidential networks. On the other hand, Suharto used them as political pawns, bringing a few out to face firing squads from time to time when it suited him politically to do so. Six condemned prisoners, for instance, were shot in the space of a few weeks a quarter of a century after the 1965 putsch in which they were said to have been complicit. And as Suharto approached his own political demise in the mid-1990s there were still five 1965 prisoners living under sentence of death.

The same callousness with which Suharto worsted the communist party and its suspected sympathisers was applied to all who dissented from the nature and methods of his régime. Abuse of human rights was standard practice. Once parliament, the political parties and the judiciary had been emasculated, and the armed forces empowered to terrorise with impunity, there was nothing to prevent it.

The entire bureaucracy right down through district to village level was locked up in obligatory membership of the pseudo-party Golkar which, far from representing the people, was an instrument for controlling them. It was the mechanism through which its officers and functionaries, no matter how lowly, were enabled to share the benefits of power. They had their hands on the levers of corruption and the processes of development. Among the latter were the powers to offer employment and sell and requisition land – the most contentious and fraught of all issues. The appropriation of large tracts of land, much of it already in use, for plantation and other development by big businesses was probably the most acute single cause of grievance against the régime.

But there were other causes too: licensing of the press, limited right of assembly and association, movement control, trades union limitations, marked identity cards and denial of voting rights for former detainees, to mention only the more obvious. Inevitably, therefore, Indonesia during the Suharto years rode on an undercurrent of dissent.

Of course, there was a law against dissent. Originally decreed by President Sukarno in 1963 in the context of the confrontation against Malaysia, the Anti-Subversion Law was a candidate for annulment on the ground of unconstitutionality during the first two years of the new order. However, it was re-adopted and in 1969 was incorporated into law. This law, said Amnesty International in a 1997 report, has been employed extensively by the Indonesian government to silence dissent by detaining without trial hundreds of thousands of alleged political opponents since 1965. Hundreds of others charged with subversion have been put through unfair trials and sentenced to long terms of imprisonment or even put to death.[1]

The burden of proof under the Anti-Subversion Law was less rigorous than in the Indonesian code of criminal procedure. It did not provide detainees with the standard safeguards against being held incommunicado and without charge, nor against torture and disappearance. Under it, all those abuses were frequent in Suharto's Indonesia. Another important feature was the prerogative it gave to the military prosecutor of ordering the detention of civilians without trial for up to a year, renewable indefinitely.

Subversion included 'spreading feelings of hostility or creating hostility, dissension, conflict, chaos, instability or restlessness among the population or society in general . . .' So vague and sweeping were the law's prescriptions that anyone whose actions or words could be represented as disruptive of public order or criticising the government and its institutions, the president, government policy or the state philosophy of Pancasila could be prosecuted. Later, even after international pressure had brought about less frequent use of it in Java, it was commonly used in the quasi-civil war conditions of Aceh and East Timor. Under its cover it was estimated that some two thousand civilians were unlawfully killed by the military in Aceh between 1989–93, and the number had certainly risen far higher by the turn of the century.

What can never be known is how many of the military régime's victims were tortured. It is only certain that thousands were. The UN Economic and Social Council, the UN Commission for Human Rights, Amnesty International, Asia Watch, Survival International and other bodies concerned with human rights hold among them massive detailed evidence of the use of torture under Suharto – and since. Invariably it was denied.

An Acehnese journalist, however, gave personal testimony of torture at his trial in March 1991. His name was Adnan Beuransyah, and his testimony was published by Amnesty International:

My hair and my nose were burned with cigarette butts. I was given electric shocks on my feet, genitals and ears . . . I was ordered to sit on a long bench facing the interrogator. I was still blindfolded and the wires for electric shocks were still wound around my big toes. If I said anything they did not like they would turn on the current . . . I was tortured for about eight continuous hours . . . On the third night I was tortured again . . . My body was bruised and bloodied and I had been beaten and kicked so much that I coughed up blood and there was blood in my urine . . .[2]

In his book *An Empire of the East*, Norman Lewis quotes from an Indonesian military manual captured by Fretilin guerrillas in East Timor; it is entitled 'Established Procedure for Interrogation of Prisoners':

Hopefully, interrogation accompanied by the use of violence will not take place except in certain circumstances when the person being interrogated is having difficulty telling the truth. . . . If it proves necessary to use violence, make sure there are no people around . . . to see what is happening, so as not to arouse people's antipathy. Avoid taking photographs showing torture in progress (people being photographed at times when they are being subjected to electric current, when they have been stripped naked, etc.). It is better to make attractive photographs such as shots taken while eating together with the prisoner or shaking hands with those who have just come down from the bush. If necessary the interrogation should be repeated over and over again.[3]

The record of Indonesia under the military régime headed by General Suharto raises in an acute form the whole problem of how to define human rights. Gross physical and psychological assaults on the human person are generally acknowledged, even by those guilty of them as the Indonesian military régime clearly was, to be infringements of a basic human right. Equally, there is a fairly solid consensus for the view that every individual has the absolute right to food and shelter, while there are also the man-made political and civil rights many of us take for granted.

Suharto's régime failed on all counts, unless – and this is open to question – an exception be allowed for the nation's increased and somewhat better distributed wealth. The infringements for which it was criticised varied at different times during his rule. The first charge against him relates unambiguously to the murder of hundreds of thousands of alleged communist sympathisers in 1965–6 and several following years. As time went on, however, and international opinion became engaged in Australasia and western Europe, the primary concern of activists and monitors shifted to political and civil rights. A particular issue was the denial of voting rights to detainees. Partly in response to persistent criticism abroad, but also to thwart the possible recovery of the communist party, the right to vote was restored in 1981 to category C detainees, those held to be only indirectly involved in the 1965 putsch, most of whom were released over the years. An Interior Ministry official at the time let fall that there remained another million and a half for whom the right to vote could not be contemplated.

Given that the institutions involved had no representative legitimacy, almost no effective power and were only partially composed of 'elected' members, the right to vote for them might be thought to have been nugatory; nevertheless to be bereft of it was to be labelled. Real power lay with the armed forces, police included, who were the perpetrators of the great majority of human rights violations. The armed forces were above the law, accountable only to their own high commands, to General Suharto who as president was their supreme commander, and to their western arms suppliers, chiefly the USA.

As that reality grew more obvious people in Indonesia and abroad who were concerned with the deteriorating human rights situation focused increasingly on the abuse of law. In the early 1970s a group of prominent civilian lawyers in Jakarta, among them a former public prosecutor, founded the Legal Aid Institute which over many difficult years worked to raise people's consciousness of their legal rights. Working always within the constitution, it called for reform of the law and for stricter official adherence to the law. And in the face of official harassment and attempts to starve it of funds (largely from the Netherlands), it involved itself in what western lawyers call *pro bono publico* cases, cases that raised issues of general principle.

Among the institute's many achievements was to make nonsense of the contention advanced by military apologists that there was no culture or tradition of human rights in Indonesia. It was not an argument that could be sustained in the light of the independence struggle against the Dutch; neither was it consistent with the terms of the 1950 independence constitution or of the 1945 constitution that ultimately replaced it.

While the Legal Aid Institute and other groups raised the profile of human rights issues, they did not achieve any reduction in human rights abuses. On the contrary, these multiplied to a point where they were an embarrassment to the government in its international dealings. Already by the end of the 1980s the question of a successor to Suharto was beginning to exercise Indonesia's Western partners; they were anxious that human rights issues might symptomise destabilizing political discontent. Probably nudged by the USA, the foreign ministry began to argue that Indonesia should stop responding defensively to foreign critics and do something positive about its human rights image.

There were two reactions. One, succinctly expressed by General Try Sutrisno, a former armed forces chief who became vice-president, was that the advocates of human rights, civil liberties, environmental discipline and the like were a new generation of communists. The other was an officially declared period of openness, lasting on and off for four years in the late 1980s and early 1990s. A handful of playwrights, poets and journalists chanced their luck with social comment and were disappointed but unsurprised to discover that nothing much had changed; newspapers were closed and plays that would have been banned before were still banned; the Suharto family, military impunity and the state philosophy remained as ever out-of-bounds.

During that period Indonesia did, however, join the United Nations Commission on Human Rights. The move was aimed primarily at international critics, and Suharto must have been enraged to see his gesture spoilt soon after by the internationally censured shooting of dozens of mourners at the Santa Cruz cemetery on the outskirts of the East Timorese capital, Dili. In a bid to repair the situation he ordered an investigation by a commission headed by a supreme court judge who was also a retired major-general. The report came out with untypical despatch and wholly discredited General Sutrisno, who had lied about the numbers killed and backed the army action. Within two days of the report's calling for action against those responsible, Suharto dismissed the military commander in East Timor and set in train procedures that culminated in a court-martial.

By deft footwork, then, Suharto managed to preserve his standing as chairman of the Non-Aligned Movement conference in Jakarta in 1992, a position he duly used to rally opinion against western pressures on human rights issues. The cry was taken up at a gathering of Asian leaders when they met in Bangkok the following year to prepare their position ahead of the 1993 World Conference on Human Rights in Vienna. To that extent the reactionaries in Jakarta had won a tactical round, but the régime had been forced to take foreign opinion into account, and that pressure went on growing.

The UN Commission on Human Rights was vehement in its condemnation of Indonesia in 1992 and again the following year when it concentrated on East Timor. Heavy hints came from the European Community that the annual infusion of financial aid mediated through the inter-governmental donor group ought to be reviewed, which led Suharto, in a fit of pique redolent of President Sukarno's famous 'To hell with your aid!', to disband the group in 1992.

When it came to official American pressure, so long conspicuous by its absence, he behaved with greater circumspection. The first sign came in June of that same year when the US House of Representatives voted to stop funding military training for Indonesia, a small enough gesture within the totality of American military support and one that could easily be remedied. But there was more to come. In support of trade union rights, American human rights activists began targeting the duty exemptions that

Indonesia, as a third world country, was allowed to claim on certain goods exported to the USA. Threatened with the loss of its duty exemptions and pilloried for labour laws which even the USA could not stomach, in 1994 the Indonesian government rushed through legislation allowing some relaxation: company unions were to be permitted, the minimum wage in Jakarta was raised to the equivalent of US$1.20 per day and the army, subjected to the new experience of having its conduct determined under civil law, was forbidden, in theory at least, to intervene in strikes, which had become frequent.

At about the same time the régime set up Indonesia's own Human Rights Commission. None of the acknowledged leaders of the human rights movement in Indonesia was included, which led a lot of observers to assume that it was just another paper exercise designed to propitiate annoying but distant observers. In fact important and irreversible changes were occurring; the commission did better work than many feared and helped lay the foundation of a hope-raising human rights initiative launched almost immediately after Suharto's humiliating fall in 1998.

## THE STATE WITHIN THE STATE

The legacy of thirty-two years of military dictatorship under General Suharto was a record of continuous human rights abuse. While the misuse and neglect of civil law may be cited as the proximate cause in certain types of case, the reality is that in most cases the perpetrators were the armed forces. The contention that they were merely one functional group among coequals is disingenuous. In Suharto's version of guided democracy the power of ultimate decision in all areas came back to the presidency, and his principal coercive tool – aside from corruption – was the armed forces.

It is difficult to credit that the thousands of general staff officers who ended up flaunting arrays of campaign ribbons accumulated in operations against their own people were heirs to the same forces which had fought honorably for Indonesia's independence. As we have seen, the problems of corruption, impunity and the abuse of power which became the hallmarks of the military under Suharto were not new when he became president. Economically, the army was compelled to supplement its always inadequate budget by living off the territories it controlled. Sociologically, its mixed beginnings made it difficult to establish a unifying ethos composed as it was of disparate elements, each with its different political imperative.

Although the attainment of an apolitical military community under civilian political control would have been desirable as much in the interest of the armed services' own unity as that of the nation, President Sukarno had already discovered that the political system was not yet sufficiently mature to sustain that state of affairs. In the few years before his fall, much thought had gone into finding a realistic way to integrate the armed forces into the body politic. The most important theorist, as it then appeared, was General Nasution. His thesis was that, because the revolution and the attainment of independence had been the work of the entire people bearing arms, the supposed duality between the military and the political was illusory. The people's army was, as it were, just a slice out of society at large and, as such, entitled to play a full part in the political life of the nation. He advocated a middle way for the armed services in which they would have a civic mission as well as a military and that, indeed, was the doctrinal path along which first he and then Suharto led their forces.

The question was where the middle lay. Naturally everyone spoke up for partnership, only the nuances were different. Sukarno believed in balance. The communist leader, D.N. Aidit, lecturing in 1963 at SESKOAD (the Army Staff and Command School), declared: 'It is the duty of all members of the armed forces to struggle genuinely on the side of the people and oppose every attempt at counter-revolution. Another characteristic of the Indonesian armed forces is the unity and effective coordination of the four services, including the police . . . any attempt to emphasize one branch alone would not contribute to effective state power as required by the special conditions of the Indonesian island nation'. General Nasution too believed in the army and the people working closely together. Suharto and the American sociologists who were seldom far behind him spoke of 'partnership' and set up an elaborate décor to give it form, but over the years created a military oligarchy.

Already split over these issues, the armed forces emerged in even greater disarray from the 1965 season of coup and counter-coup. In their 1971 paper Anderson and McVey, still not quite ready to acknowledge the probability that a right-wing Council of Generals had indeed planned many of the events of October 1965, nevertheless described plausibly the dynamics of the issue confronting Generals Suharto and Nasution:

If military unity was to be restored following the coup, it could best be done through creating solidarity in a greater cause and through purges conducted under cover of larger events. If public attention was to be directed away from army fissures and from the counter-devil of the Generals' Council, the responsibility must be assigned somewhere else, namely – since the President is too sacrosanct to be directly charged – on the arch-enemy and major source of presidential power, the PKI. The choice for the army was between a major victory and a stunning blow to its morale and public position.[4]

Under cover of the high-profile purge of the PKI and a clamorous anti-communist propaganda campaign, Suharto conducted an internal purge within the armed forces. The two exercises did not always sit happily together, since different parts of the army were quite often set at one another's throats. Harmony was an ideal never wholly achieved; in fact a measure of disharmony served Suharto's divide and rule tactics.

His clear intention once he had secured presidential power and obtained the sanction of the People's Consultative Congress for the armed forces' civic mission was to insinuate military control into every level and cranny of government. Partnership, embodied in Golkar, was honoured more in the breach than the observance, and then only as a reluctant necessity. His newly-appointed attorney-general, General Soegiharto (one of several right-wing generals who had put out conciliatory feelers to Malaysia and Britain in 1964) complained to me rather wrily in 1967 that there were not enough generals to do all the jobs that had to be done. There were about 480 of them at the time.

Soegiharto's plaintive cry coincided with the publication of a book called *The Armed Forces/Army Civic Mission is no Militarism* by General Maraden Panggabean, a Christian who was to succeed Suharto as army chief. The armed forces, he wrote, were not only a defence and security agency but 'an instrument of the revolution which was a social force struggling in the political, economic, social and cultural fields as do the other functional groups and the political parties'. To demonstrate that they had striven to prepare themselves for this role he mentioned that even before the 1965 coups, all the cadres of the Armed Forces had been given lessons on their position in society. A rather convoluted passage skirts as closely as he dared, or perhaps was allowed, round the training of non-military groups (students, workers, militias and the like) to support the new order – 'Both the conventional way (ie the People's Consultative Congress) . . . and the unconventional one (granting facilities to mass-organizations which have joined the New Order) were applied by the civic mission workers of the Armed Forces'.

He described the main tasks of the army's civic mission as being to plan, to direct, to coordinate and to help in meeting the needs of and exercising control over army workers outside of the organization of the army itself.

No such tract – and one suspects Indonesia's military archives overflow with them – would have been complete without a disquisition on the theme of Pancasila. Panggabean's contribution was a caution against picking selectively among the five principles. For instance, 'sovereignty of the people alone will cause ultra-democracy or anarcho-democracy, ridden by individualism and liberalism so that the family principle and mutual cooperation according to Pantja Sila Democracy are eliminated'.

Audaciously, considering the events in which he had participated and the oligarchy he was helping to install, he contended that 'the social order of Indonesia does not know classes or class struggle, it does not know hegemony or domination of the one social collective over other social collectives . . . it does not know hegemony/domination of civilians over the military, or of the military over civilians'. Militarism? Certainly not, and if it sometimes seemed otherwise that was because 'research and development are far more advanced in the military sector than in other sectors, so that there is no harmony and balance between the civilian and military sectors of development'.[5]

If General Panggabean's theorising betrayed the quality of political thinking in a force that was planning the rigid control of the nation's political life, General Suharto's deeds left no doubt about his determination to succeed in that enterprise. In August 1967 he carried through a radical restructuring of the armed forces. The separate service ministries which had enabled Sukarno to promote inter-service rivalry were abolished. The four services were placed under a central joint command whose structure was replicated in six territorial commands. Their supervision was shared amongst the services, except the police, but notably the three key territories of Java, Sumatra and Sulawesi were reserved for the army.

The army itself retained its basic division into combat and territorial branches, and it was the latter which was infiltrated into the nation's fabric right down to the villages, every one of which was assigned a non-commissioned officer. With this structure, and alongside it the army-dominated functionaries of Golkar, bearing in mind the prohibition of party-political activity in the villages, General Suharto established nationwide a grass-roots grip far tighter than anything the communists had previously achieved.

So the army entered the 1970s more unified and with a more concerted sense of mission than ever before. Yet it was still an unruly institution, increasingly a nation within the nation, top-heavy with senior and middle-ranking officers and generally viewed as the preferred route into a secure and remunerative career. Once in, for all the talk of civic mission, a cosseted officer corps easily slipped into the habit of viewing the rest of the nation as something to be controlled and exploited. Moreover, it was plagued with internal rivalries. The so-called 1945 generation, the soldiers of independence, remained a significant element into the 1980s and kept alive the many doctrinal strands that had constituted the national political debate of the early years, including substantial Marxist sympathies. A number of army officers were arrested in 1972, charged with secret communist ties. The following year the army command in Central Java revealed a communist plot to kidnap military officers as part of a show of strength against the administration, and a former chief of police was condemned to death.

Loyalty to Suharto himself was far from unanimous. He had to move cautiously in the knowledge that many officers remained faithful in spirit to Sukarno's nationalism and Nasution's idealism. Rumours circulated of rivals waiting in the wings, and it was probably more than coincidence that the American army chief of staff, General William Westmoreland, paid a supportive and unprecedented visit to Jakarta in 1972. Nor was the propensity for warlordism dead. The implication of a former military governor of South Sumatra in a 1981 plan to set up a Muslim state drove home the prudence of never leaving a regional military commander or governor in post too long.

Suharto mastered the military factions by keeping personnel constantly on the move. At the beginning of 1974, for example, he temporarily assumed personal command of KOPKAMTIB, the political police, thus displacing two of his closest associates, Generals Ali Murtopo and Sumitro. To overcome the problem of ageing personnel thwarting the ambitions of impatient younger officers he initiated a long-running programme of regeneration. Those on the way out were propitiated with a variety of inducements, ranging from enhanced pensions paid for out of the business companies run by the military to salaried employment in such companies or in the state's civilian enterprises. Often retired officers were given first refusal on major government tenders and, even if they sold them on, would be able to pocket enough money to transform their retirement. For those of high rank grants of extensive timber and other extractive concessions spelled wealth far beyond the expectations of a standard military career. In one case a group of retiring officers was granted timber rights over a concession of 600,000 hectares – twelve times the size of Singapore.

Another frequent source of job satisfaction in a nation not militarily threatened was appointment to posts in the civil administration. Depicted as part of the armed forces' dual mission, it contributed to the totality of military control and, equally importantly, helped smother mutinous impulses within the military community. Coincidentally it broadened the scope for wholesale corruption. As the 1980s dawned, observers in Jakarta estimated that half the upper central bureaucracy were either military or former military personnel – servicemen being paid out of non-military budgets. Even so, the defence budget rose; in 1981, for instance, the year of a major offensive against Fretilin guerrillas in East Timor, it nearly doubled.

The presumption of military indispensability, superiority and impunity reached the point where participants in an army seminar in Bandung felt able to demand that all civilian posts should be filled by retired officers. Others, of a more modest or principled bent, older men loyal to the marginalized General Nasution, grew vocally alarmed at the direction the services were taking.

Suharto, no less adept than Sukarno at always locating himself in the middle, responded to both tendencies with an address at a military academy graduation strongly restating the army's dual function as guardian of the social order but also promising change. The change, when it came, was legislation entrenching the status quo; the armed forces' civic mission was written into law following an unpublicized debate in a special parliamentary commission. The garnish on what many saw as a cynical and in any case unnecessary manoeuvre was yet another reshuffle of senior posts. His veteran henchman, General Murtopo was removed from cabinet; and the powerful armed forces chief and defence minister General Muhammad Yusuf was replaced by another veteran, General Benny Murdani. Suharto faced an Armed Forces Day parade in 1984 with the assurance that the armed services would never impose a military dictatorship on Indonesia!

One of the things General Suharto's military régime could have done had it been so disposed was to regularize the provision of military finance. For such a vast and scattered country the four armed services were not large – usually around 530,000; during the first six years of the new order they enjoyed a generous quarter to a third of the state budget. However, even this was not enough.

In those early years of restoring economic and fiscal order Suharto and the Berkeley mafia could have imposed budgetary discipline on the military, but he chose not to do so. It would have meant exposing military finances to far greater public scrutiny and curtailing valuable business arrangements founded on smuggling and irregular trade, including military equipment. Such commerce enabled the military right down to district level to more than compensate for the shortcomings of the state budget. Within less than a decade of the new order, independent analysts were estimating that up to forty per cent of military expenditure was regularly covered by non-budgetary income. So it was with equanimity that the régime allowed the military share of the greatly increased national budget to slide from eighteen per cent in 1974 to only seven per cent twenty years later.

The system gave Suharto a power of patronage which went far to quell potential rivals in the military establishment and made it easy to sideline older, incapable and obstructive officers. His own family eagerly grasped the opportunities it offered them. By the middle of the 1980s each of the armed services and the major formations within them owned its own network of companies. Almost invariably there would be a link with the Suharto family plus business know-how contributed by members of the small, greatly resented but resourceful and energetic Chinese community.

The army, being the biggest service, had the biggest business empire. Its holding company, Tri Usaha Bakti, controlled dozens of enterprises with interests as various as engineering and construction, a charter airline, a multi-million dollar timber and plywood concern in East Kalimantan and quinine, tea and coffee export businesses in Sumatra. As in all business operations, everyone from the commander-in-chief (General Suharto) down to the lower ranks had an interest in tax avoidance. A frequent solution was to set up non-profit foundations (*yayasan* in Indonesian) – charitable trusts as they might be called in the English-speaking world – little smaller than the big holding companies and often sharing assets with them. They would, of course, have some quasi-charitable functions such as the funding of pensions or the provision of housing and educational amenities. It was a system dear to the heart of General Suharto who took a personal interest in a number of them.

The army was looking more like a business conglomerate than a professional military force. Taken together with the self-imposed obligations of its civic mission and the appointment of military men to more than three-quarters of the key directorates in the civil service, it resulted in an officer corps more attuned to commerce than to combat and a frankly incompetent armed service.

Another round of reform was plainly necessary, and in 1984 the new armed forces chief, Benny Murdani, set it in train. He was one of the Christian officers who were disproportionately represented in the upper échelons. This over-representation was regarded as part of a policy to curb ambitions for an Islamic state. Relations between political Islam and the army sank to their lowest level ever while Benny Murdani was armed forces chief, touching bottom with the army's suppression of the Muslim riots at Tanjung Priok in 1984. But Islamic sentiment was evolving; education was turning Islam into a more sophisticated political element in society, and that was being reflected within the armed services where a growing number of more than merely nominal Muslims were rising in the officer corps.

Another factor as Benny Murdani began his reorganization was unease in segments of the army about its automatic support of the government – or, in plainer words, of the Suharto presidency. It came principally from two inner constituencies: supporters of General Nasution, whom they still revered as father of the army, and the very different, better educated youngsters of the more recent officer generations. Pitted against proponents of maintaining the army's overwhelming dominance there were now a significant number of officers who wanted a more professional more tightly focused force. In this rather confused intellectual climate yet another issue came into prominence: after Suharto's election for a fourth presidential term in 1983, thoughts turned seriously to the question of the succession, prompted not least by his own misleading undertaking that it would be his last.

Broadly the Murdani reforms were in two parts. One set of measures strengthened the army politically at the expense of the other armed services. More political officers – somewhat analogous to political commissars in the old Soviet system – were injected at lower levels. The other main element of Murdani's measures was the revamping of the combat units. Two multi-battalion forces were consolidated on the principal islands of Java and Sumatra to complement the role of the 19,000-strong KOSTRAD, the trouble-shooting strategic command which Suharto himself had once commanded.

The period of Murdani's greatest military influence coincided with major purchases of war matériel from the Western powers. Britain, which had already sold three squadrons of Skyhawks to the airforce, refitted and sold three frigates, contracted to supply $120 million worth of Rapier missiles plus a training programme and entered into a co-production deal for six hundred Scorpion light tanks. West Germany and the Netherlands sold armaments to the navy. The USA, competing with France, sold eight F-16 fighters at the beginning of 1986 and within nine months Murdani confirmed a contract for four more.

The Murdani reforms undoubtedly reinvigorated the army, investing it, even amidst the confusion of its inner debates, with a renewed sense of its autonomy. Suharto quickly recognised the threat to his own position. Typically he struck out in opposite directions, in 1986 by bringing to trial a number of very senior officers who were critical of the handling of the Tanjung Priok disturbance, and in 1988 by replacing Benny Murdani as armed forces commander with a Muslim – General Try Sutrisno.

Not to be construed as a wholesale reversal of the army's attitude towards political Islam – it was still up to killing a hundred villagers wrongly stigmatised as Muslim extremists in the south Sumatran province of Lampung in 1989 – that appointment marked a fundamental turning point in Suharto's personal political strategy. For the first time he was acknowledging Islam as a potential power base and, to that extent, further widening the distance that Benny Murdani had opened between him and the armed forces.

MAKING UP WITH THE NEIGHBOURS

It was the behaviour of the military that pulled the last supporting prop from under Suharto's régime. American manipulation was the key to his ascent to power, and for three decades successive Washington administrations watched with relative unconcern as he cultivated his tyranny, making sure he was adequately supplied with the arms and military training he needed.

The USA and Australia resumed open military aid in 1970. Two years later Suharto toured Western Europe seeking credits in France, Germany and the Netherlands which, it was noted, would go essentially into arms purchases. In 1975 the US State Department recommended doubling military grants and credits. By 1980 Britain was delivering the first of the Hawk so-called trainers which were to become the backbone of Indonesian air defence. The repeat order for Hawks that followed a visit by the British Foreign Secretary, Douglas Hurd, in 1993 was described as BAC's biggest ever outside Saudi Arabia and was linked to a package of aid and soft loans.

The USA came in rather later on military aircraft sales, but from 1986 onward, coinciding with a new military onslaught in East Timor, caught up with a series of orders for F-16 fighters. France and the Netherlands also enjoyed a share of the arms trade, and none of them was deterred when, in 1987, the Indonesian government sought rescheduling of payments because of a severe drop in oil revenues.

For most of General Suharto's presidency the only real pressures exerted on him by the USA related to American economic and commercial interests in his country; to those – and to some extent Japan's – he invariably yielded. Where foreign policy was concerned, he needed little guidance beyond what he received from able civilian foreign ministers, notably Adam Malik and later Ali Alatas. Just as it had been President Sukarno's foreign policies – the spurning of US aid and the United Nations, the perceived drift towards the communist Chinese orbit and the confrontation of Malaysia – that had decided Washington to connive at his downfall, so now it was Suharto's reversal of all those policies that won him Washington's uncritical support. They wanted an anti-communist bastion and he was prepared to be it.

Dominating the international climate in South-East Asia in the first third of Suharto's rule was the American perception of an expansionist China bent on using communist ideology to topple successive post-colonial dominoes. After the partition of Korea and the conflict in Indochina the horror scenario envisioned a serial *dégringolade* progressing southwards through the Philippines, Cambodia, Laos, Thailand, Malaysia and Indonesia. Every counter-communist resource was marshalled to impede the anticipated wave: war in Vietnam, huge military bases in the Philippines, the Southeast Asia Treaty Organization (SEATO), British military bases in Singapore and – seldom mentioned but a crucial independent contribution to the nuclear deterrent against China – the Royal Air Force base in the Maldive island group in the Indian Ocean.[6] Suharto offered Indonesia unreservedly as a major item on the inventory.

At first there were differences between Britain and the USA on how to approach a fundamentally agreed agenda. Led by Eisenhower and the Dulles brothers, Washington was happier to resort to the gun and support frankly brutal, corrupt, military and only cosmetically democratic régimes. Britain was more inclined to a process of carefully planned withdrawal

leaving behind friendly, competent, stable – and therefore non-communist –
democracies. Where Malaysia embodied the British model in South-East
Asia, Suharto's Indonesia embodied the USA's.

Hence foreign policy was of more than average importance in Indonesia
in the last third of the twentieth century. The fact that it was seldom
particularly active merely demonstrates the mutual acquiescence that
characterised US–Indonesian relations until the very end of Suharto's
presidency. Domestic considerations such as economic justice, human rights
and the rule of law could be neglected in the knowledge that propitiation of
the American sponsor was sufficient in itself.

As well as Anglo-American differences over the most desirable formula
for the governance of ex-colonial nation states, there were competing views
about the most appropriate framework for regional stability. The real
problems posed by the colonial legacy had received little or no serious
attention. All the countries of South-East Asia were locked into mercantile
and legal systems that led back to metropolitan power centres on other
continents – the United States, Britain, France, the Netherlands – but
isolated them from one another and generated competition where the need
was for local collaboration.

Withdrawal from empire provided the impetus for a wave of regional
thinking. Since it involved the jealously nurtured economic interests of the
departing colonial powers – and of China and Japan which both reckoned
to benefit from their departure – non-regional powers played an active role
in the debate from the outset. Dean Rusk, the American Secretary of State
during most of the 1960s, recognised the sensitivity of the issue. In the
course of a conversation with the British foreign secretary, Lord Home, in
June 1962, a record now available in the Public Record Office notes:

Mr Rusk thought that, in addition to Malaysia, we should be looking at
the proposed organization of South-East Asian States. Some countries in
the area, who might be potential members of the organization, appeared
to be afraid that it was simply another US device to maintain political
control. It was therefore important that the Americans should remain as
much as possible in the background. He hoped that the UK would feel
able to use its influence to bring the organization into being . . .[7]

It was fully understood in the Foreign Office that Rusk's objective was
the realization of the 'island chain' concept and, in the longer term, phasing

out of SEATO. Britain's preference was for something more akin to the project advanced by the Malayan (later Malaysian) prime minister, Tunku Abdul Rahman. This had already surfaced in 1961 when Malaya as it then was, Thailand and the Philippines announced their intention to set up the Association of South-East Asia (ASA). Thanks in no small measure to sensitive, low-profile British diplomacy this was the trend that prevailed. Its great virtue, denounced by critics as a weakness, was the realism of its declared scope, being more concerned with consultation than with ambitious action programmes: technical cooperation, the promotion of regional trade and investment, fisheries, transport and communications making up the agenda. There was no talk of security.

Important elements were missing; Indonesia and Singapore were not included. All the same, the USA could feel some satisfaction. With the Philippines in, the island chain concept was not dead.

ASA, quietly devoting itself to what was possible, survived and finally won the day, though in a new form. Towards the end of 1965, when the displacement of President Sukarno was in progress, I began to pick up from British and Australian diplomatic contacts in several South-East Asian capitals rumours of work afoot to construct the cooperative regional framework into which a reconciled Indonesia and Malaysia could be brought together. Early the following year I was in possession of enough hard fact to write a story for the BBC foreseeing the creation of what came to be known as the Association of South-East Asian Nations (ASEAN). Soon after that the Indonesian–Malaysian negotiations that ended confrontation included agreement that the new association should be formed.

There was still some haggling over detail. Who would the members be? Burma, Ceylon (now Sri Lanka) and even India were talked about. The Indonesian foreign minister, Adam Malik, preferred to soft-pedal the truth that ASEAN was essentially an enlarged version of ASA with a similar range of committees and working parties and, with one exception, professing the same principles. The exception related to defence; it remained for some time an open question whether security matters could be brought within its orbit. Some right-wing generals in Jakarta urged that they should; and, possibly as a propitiatory gesture towards Suharto, the Malaysian deputy premier, Tun Abdul Razak, mused in public that defence arrangements might conceivably follow, 'once we have become good friends with a common interest and destiny'. The final compromise was incorporation into the inaugural declaration of a statement that foreign military bases should not remain indefinitely in member countries.

Aside from that, security did not figure in the ASEAN treaty. British caution had prevailed. In the words of Norman Reddaway, the Foreign Office official who ran Britain's propaganda programmme during the toppling of President Sukarno, the appropriate role for friendly non-regional powers was to 'put a little gravy on the ASEAN plate'. The wisdom of that hands-off stance was driven home by the New China News Agency the day after the conclusion of the Bangkok conference at which ASEAN was formed in August 1967: 'A new anti-China, anti-communist alliance was *knocked together* [my italics] on the orders of US imperialism in Bangkok yesterday'. The founding members were Indonesia, Malaysia, the Philippines, Thailand and Singapore. It was not quite the island chain the USA wanted and went on working for, but at least it had most of the right members.

ASEAN established its headquarters in Jakarta. It endured as a stabilizing factor in South-East Asia and a central plank of Indonesian foreign policy throughout and beyond the Suharto era, an incontestable success for British and Malaysian diplomacy. It served Indonesia particularly well in what Adam Malik called the repositioning of the country's international relations in the post-Sukarno period. Participation in ASEAN, he wrote, 'is neither against the non-aligned policy nor a deviation from the ten principles of Bandung'.[8]

Much was made of non-alignment, a Sukarnoist position from which Sukarno himself was held to have defected by allowing Indonesia to slip into China's orbit in the ideological conflict between Moscow and Peking. Suharto and Malik were able to argue that China's support of the PKI and its despatch of weaponry to arm a pro-communist fifth force had been infringements of the non-aligned principle, compounded after Sukarno's downfall by the infiltration of ethnic Chinese communist cadres into the border area between Kalimantan and Sarawak.

CHINESE CHEQUERS

Nineteen sixty-seven, the year in which ASEAN took shape, was a bad one for the Chinese minority in Indonesia. An inflamed and often provoked public turned readily on ethnic Chinese in a series of demonstrations and counter-demonstrations. There was a round of tit-for-tat expulsions of diplomats declared *personae non gratae*. In this disturbed situation the Indonesian government faced the delicate exercise of extending diplomatic recognition to

Singapore, regarded as a 'Chinese' state, as part of the post-confrontation settlement. At inter-governmental level the climate was favourable. ASEAN was in the making. I had myself conveyed a verbal message to Adam Malik from his Singapore counterpart S.J. Rajaratnam at the beginning of May 1966 – a sardonic, but nevertheless well received, assurance that Singapore was not on a mission to 'save Indonesia for democracy'.

The act of recognition came on 9 September 1967. Seven days later Malik ordered the withdrawal of Indonesian staff from the embassy in Beijing. It turned out to be part of a symmetrical deterioration ending with the suspension (but not the complete breach) of relations between the Chinese and Indonesian governments. By this means Malik contrived to cover the potentially unpopular establishment of relations with Singapore with a blow that placed Beijing at arm's length for many years. A fortnight later a mob was let loose on the Chinese consulate in Jakarta. I arrived there the next day to find it comprehensively sacked.

Thereafter there were periodical restatements of Jakarta's position that there could be no normalization with China until it stopped supporting communist insurgents. There were disadvantages. China had the potential to equal Japan as a trade partner, and the régime's hunger for revenue from that source was forever growing. In 1985, therefore, the thirtieth anniversary of the great Bandung Conference of the non-aligned movement was made the occasion for a slight warming towards China; formal commercial contacts were resumed, but it would still be some time before Jakarta would agree to restore diplomatic relations.

ASEAN FILE

Suharto's anxiety to secure the presidency of that 1985 conference, as Sukarno had thirty years earlier, surprised some of his close associates. So eager was he that he even permitted some cosmetic – and impermanent – concessions on human rights. Yet there was little surprising about it. Well advised by Malik, he had recognised from the start that the reality of his close alignment with the USA had for internal political reasons to be cloaked in a simulacrum of non-alignment. Unblushingly he told the Philippine parliament during a 1972 visit to Manila: 'Indonesia refuses to become aligned with the world's ideological blocs but supports cooperative endeavours for peace and progress. A strong and cohesive ASEAN can, I hope, become a nucleus for a wider regional organization which would encompass all nations of South-East Asia, irrespective of differences in political systems . . .'

A few weeks later, Malik delicately made the counterbalancing but not contradictory statement that 'there is no alternative for the moment but to accept that we need economic assistance from the West. But we are trying to convince the socialist countries that they ought to change their credit system, and there are indications that they may accept this position' – as indeed the Soviet Union did. Decoded, the two statements meant that Indonesia was not going to allow either alignment or non-alignment to prevent it on the one hand entering into bilateral security arrangements with the US-sponsored Philippines, and on the other maintaining a sound working relationship with Moscow at Peking's expense. It was, evidentially, a position that found general approval, since in 1972 Indonesia was asked and agreed to serve on the supervisory commission for the Vietnam ceasefire.

ASEAN furnished all its members with a supportive, credible and genuinely regional framework within which they could define and harmonise foreign policy objectives without unduly arousing the hostility that would have stemmed from a defence alliance. But security issues were frequently on the ASEAN leaders' minds. Hence their 1971 declaration of a Zone of Peace, Freedom and Neutrality (ZOPFAN) and subsequent initiatives that had significant security implications. Come the 1980s, with war still blazing in Indochina despite the US defeat and withdrawal from Vietnam in 1975, ASEAN and Indonesia in particular contributed vitally to informal meetings between Cambodian factions which led to the conclusive Paris peace conferences.

ASEAN had simultaneously sheltered its members from too much contamination by continuing great power rivalries and shown its value as a forum for defusing contentious regional issues. General Suharto especially benefited from it, gaining an international reputation for regional leadership and good neighbourliness in the mid-1980s which lasted for most of a decade and seemed to blind his admirers to the atrocities, injustices and corruption of his domestic régime.

*Notes*

1  'Indonesia – The Anti-Subversion Law: A Briefing'. London, Amnesty International, February 1997.
2  'Indonesia – Continuing Human Rights Violations in Aceh', London, Amnesty International 1991.

3   Lewis, Norman *An Empire of the East*, London, Jonathan Cape, 1993.
4   Anderson, Benedict and Ruth McVey, 'A Preliminary Analysis of the October 1, 1965 Coup in Indonesia', Cornell Modern Indonesia Project, Ithaca 1971.
5   Panggabean, M, *The Truth of Civic Mission as Carried out by Indonesia's Armed Forces is no Militarism*, Jakarta, Department of Information, 1967.
6   Dominions Office records in the Public Record Office, Annexe to JPS.1114/25/6/63 in DO 169/221, 25 June 1963.
7   Public Record Office DO 169/143. Record of conversation between the Foreign Secretary and Mr Dean Rusk on Monday 25 June 1962.
8   Malik, Adam 'Regional Cooperation – the Alternative for Asia', written for UPI and published in the *Bangkok Post*, 8 July 1968.

# NINE

## Suharto's Endgame

Something out of the ordinary happened in June 1986. The deputy chairman of the Golkar faction in the House of Representatives suggested establishing a mechanism for the presidential succession. General Suharto, coasting along in his fourth five-year term of office and then aged 65, ruled the idea out.

All the same it was a significant moment. Golkar was the pseudo-party designed to serve the interests of the military and their dominant role in the country's governance. With tentacles reaching into every cranny of the social fabric it was the institutional tool with which the army and Suharto ruled the Republic, a necessary factor in the formula of power. Other prime factors were the Chinese business class, the Berkeley economic mafia and the IMF (meaning in effect the USA). Any disharmony or dislocation would call in question the stability vaunted by Suharto and his mentors; and now here was a military fall-guy daring to give voice to the thought of life after Suharto – just as Suharto's early supporters had alerted the public to the idea of life after Sukarno.

The incident did not come out of a vacuum. For three years already the army had been engaged in a thorough structural reorganization. In charge of the exercise, was the indefatigable Lieutenant-General Benny Murdani. Among the last of the more idealistic 1945 generation who had fought for independence Murdani began as a Suharto favourite and ended in the early 1990s as a suspected rival for the presidency. The Golkar hint about succession mechanisms came when he was at the pinnacle of his influence. Under his aegis there had developed within the armed forces a sentiment that there should be distance between themselves and the president, and at the same time a perception that their ability to influence Suharto was declining.

From Suharto's perspective, the army was becoming menacingly independent. And, for reasons stemming from deep economic, social and political problems, the succession issue was not going to subside. Apart from his evident conviction of the rightness of his own indefinite tenure of the post, Suharto was probably justified in calculating that public discussion of how to manage the succession would inevitably result in a movement to bring it about. In any case, it was not as if there were no constitutional mechanism in place to handle the presidential succession, as was shown – albeit maladroitly – when Vice-President Habibie took over in 1998. The more practical problem was that Suharto's habit of shuffling leadership figures around prevented anyone emerging legitimately as a potential successor. Not until it was too late and he was an old man in his obvious dotage did he ever come close to grooming a candidate – and then his first impulse was to bring his daughter into the running.

In the course of Suharto's first twenty years in the presidential office, Indonesia had followed the general South-East Asian pattern by producing an enlarged middle class. This was attributable to a number of factors, only one of which was the country's unevenly distributed new wealth. No less important were the imperatives of social organization. An enlarged business class and a greatly inflated bureaucracy, in both of which the military were prominent, were torn between the benefits of the patronage system and their desire for a meaningful role in the decisions that governed the running of the country. Both in and out of the armed services many were finding it unacceptable that a closed group of senior officers in a corrupt and self-serving army should be the arbiter of the nation's affairs. The army itself was ridden with self-doubt and not favourably placed to confront Suharto as purported guardian of the national interest. There was, indeed, a widespread belief that the army's main interest in the succession was to ensure that the levers of power did not slip from its grasp.

But they were already slipping, and General Suharto was the architect of its decline. It was he who initiated legislation to reduce military representation in the (admittedly feeble) House of Representatives from a hundred to seventy. It was he who began to diminish the number of soldiers in the cabinet in the later 1980s. It was he who sanctioned the progressive fall in the share of the national budget allocated to the armed forces. Although it went on rising in real terms – and was consistently three times greater than the sums devoted to national development – in the context of a growing overall budget the military share fell from thirty per cent at the end of the 1960s to twelve per cent at the end of the 1970s and seven per cent at the end of the 1980s.

Indonesia's military establishment, it must be remembered, had been built up as a nation within the nation, better resourced over-all and better organized than the country it was supposed to serve. When any of its heavyweights spoke out their words were listened to. It was a matter of consequence, therefore, when a former commander of the internal security command (KOPKAMTIB) said shortly after Suharto had been re-elected yet again in 1988 that things must improve next time round. Come 1993, General Sumitro declared, the constitution should be properly implemented and there should be a fair and democratic presidential contest. He also called for presidential tenure to be limited to two five-year terms. His hopes were not to be realized, but his openly stated opinions were an indicator of the evolving political climate.

By 1995, with the succession issue intensifying and the army in disarray over its political role, Suharto commissioned a study on the subject by the National Institute of Sciences. Reporting back two years later the commission recommended that the armed forces' role in politics should be eliminated altogether by 2007.

Meanwhile, in a series of manoeuvres consistent with a presumed decline in military influence, Suharto embarked on an updated version of President Sukarno's old technique of balancing political forces against one another. With the communists out of the way, it was the ground-swell of Islamic sentiment that he deployed against the army. Previously he had been prepared to antagonize important sectors of Muslim opinion with brutal measures against groups calling for an Islamic state. Although its public rhetoric continued to demonize an almost non-existent communist movement, the régime had imprudently allowed Islam to become its main enemy. So there was some public surprise when it became known in 1990 that Suharto was encouraging the formation of a broadly-based Association of Indonesian Muslim Intellectuals (ICMI). His previous forte had been the frustration rather than the creation of large bodies, especially among civilians. Yet now he was seen to be urging, indeed pressing, the leaders of a wide variety of Muslim organizations to join up with this new interest group. To head ICMI he designated an old protégé, B.J. Habibie, a gifted German-educated civilian who had made his name as creator of the Indonesian aircraft manufacturing industry.

Everyone was immediately on the alert. The army was alarmed because it felt Habibie's industrial ambitions had requisitioned resources that could otherwise have been spent on the military. It also, rightly, saw Habibie as Suharto's puppet, a trammel to its own freedom to manage the succession. ICMI might even be a political rival to the army itself and to Golkar, its political front, which was undoubtedly what Suharto wanted them to fear.

The Javanese establishment too was worried, because Habibie was not one of them. His family roots and his wealth were in Sulawesi. The financial technocrats, heirs to the Berkeley Mafia who for years had been running the country's finances, were also worried, because they recognised in him a rival authority on financial matters, who had Suharto's ear.

Even the Chinese business community, makers and guarantors of the Suharto family fortunes, had cause for concern: Suharto's manoeuvres seldom came alone and in this case the setting up of ICMI coincided with an extraordinary presidential appeal – in effect a command – to big Chinese financiers to distribute a proportion of their assets among less endowed indigenous Indonesians. It was a gesture pleasing to many, and not least to those Muslims whose feelings towards the largely Buddhist or Christian Chinese tended to be hostile and envious.

In the resultant atmosphere of revived sectarian rivalries a major emerging figure, the Republic's future president, Abdurrahman Wahid, led a move in the opposite direction. Wahid, known popularly by his nickname Gus Dur, had astutely steered the thirty million strong NU (Religious Scholars League) out of the sanctioned political arena and thus cleansed it of the taint of submission to the régime. Wahid's was a voice of tolerance and multi-cultural harmony speaking from the heart of Islam. In March 1991, only months after the creation of ICMI, he presided over discussions that led to the setting up of a body called the Democracy Forum (Fordem). He and prominent intellectuals from other tendencies made it clear from the outset that they did not aspire to set up a rival ideological block but, on the contrary, to promote a more mature, tolerant and better informed atmosphere in which the nation might advance towards a juster and more democratic society.

Suharto may not have been displeased at the turn of events. Arguably, he through ICMI, and Wahid through Fordem, were in their different ways addressing the same dangerous problem of religious sectarianism, except that General Suharto was also sparring with the military.

He did his manipulating, it must be remembered, from within. In no sense was he ever a civilian outsider grappling with an alien military culture. His retirement from the army soon after he came to power was a smokescreen; his position as supreme commander of the armed forces was not. Twice in 1996, in what was widely considered a move to keep the armed services under his control as his career neared its end, he promoted his own son-in-law, Prabowo Subianto, to the rank of major-general and placed him in command of the special forces unit, KOPASSUS.

Throughout his presidential career he surrounded himself with military men, stuffed ministerial ranks with them, appointed them as provincial governors and put them in top business and civil service positions. The army was his main instrument of power and no-one knew better how to control it. No senior officer was either appointed or moved without at least his consent and more often his instigation.

The other potent form of coercion that he used to control the armed services – while serving the business interests of his family and close friends – was the black economy. One of the chief benefits of a territorial command was the so-called 'unrequited trade', in plainer terms smuggling. By the middle of the 1980s estimates of the contribution made to army income by its own commercial enterprise, not all of it black, varied between the equivalent of a third and a half of what it received from the national budget. It was no secret that some of it went into the more or less clandestine purchase of arms. Much also went into underpinning opulent military fiefdoms.

The story of how the corrupt application of financial and economic resources became the engine of Suharto's island empire deserves and will no doubt get a book to itself. The question of his personal corruption may revolve around definitions: whether the issue is the use of money to gain power, or of power to acquire wealth. As a cautious observer of legal and constitutional niceties, when he so chose, the final assessment could yet be that his own chief offence was nepotism and cronyism, and that he left more explicitly corrupt dealings to family, friends, bureaucrats, military officers, businessmen and foreign investors.

It was the scale and impunity of his financial manoeuvring which made Suharto unique, not that it was in itself alien to the post-colonial culture in which he was operating. In the neighbouring Philippines I once debated through a whole afternoon and evening with Benigno Aquino, the presidential hopeful who was later assassinated, about the propriety of official corruption; with a CIA officer nodding him enthusiastically on, he held that it was an acceptable, even desirable means of getting things done. It was and is a prevalent view – and not only in post-colonial societies.

Corruption in modern Indonesia had its roots in the Dutch colonial régime from which it broke free, and a sizeable proportion of the participants in corrupt practice are to this day Western businessmen and industrialists paying for the favours and 'services' that will enable them to secure a share of the country's wealth. Early in Suharto's presidency, for instance, it was alleged that even if no American government money reached him directly to facilitate defence contracts, the government-supported defence industry and probably others were generous in the deals they struck.

A striking feature of the huge investments of money and skills by major industrial corporations in Great Britain, France, Germany, the Netherlands, Canada, Japan and the USA is that they were obliged to work in tandem with Indonesian partners in which Suharto relatives and close associates had significant holdings. One of the justifications advanced was the constitutional provision that branches of production essential to the state and governing the life and living of the public shall be controlled by the state. From this stemmed an intricate web of financial and bureaucratic regulation. Attempts by foreign investors to dissipate it were among the earliest pressures the Suharto régime had to face, and were still an issue when he fell from power.

OILING THE WHEELS

In the years following the sharp fall in oil prices in the early 1980s a series of trade reforms were instituted in acknowledgment of the need to diversify the economy; in 1992 a directive permitted a hundred per cent foreign equity in new companies in Sumatra and Java. But even as deregulation progressed, new privileged monopolies were spawned. The most notorious example was the granting in 1991 of a monopoly in the trading of cloves to a conglomerate owned by Suharto's youngest son Hutomo – 'Tommy' as he liked his Western business chums to call him. Cloves are the distinctive ingredient in the *kretek* cigarettes manufactured by a major and profitable indigenous industry. Left to themselves the manufacturers might have been able to fight back, but as soon as they did so the government was instructed to bolster Hutomo's monopoly with a large state loan and raise the minimum prices of *kretek* cigarettes. Consumers suffered, the industry's workforce of several million had to be reduced, state revenue fell. Hutomo later lost the clove monopoly, but in the meantime he and the Suharto family were the sole beneficiaries.

General Suharto and his wife Tien (styled Mrs Tien Percent in acknowledgment of her business propensities) had six children, all of whom, thanks to presidential favours, often done in defiance of government advice, amassed fortunes. Characteristically, they would work closely with the ethnic Chinese businessman who became Suharto's investment adviser, troubleshooter and most frequent golfing partner, The Kian Sang. A Muslim convert who changed his name to Hasan – 'Bob' to his worldwide circle of friends – he nurtured a business empire comprising hundreds of companies and as many more shared stakes. Wherever the economy was growing Hasan, and by implication Suharto, were to be found: every sort of banking and insurance activity, mineral extraction, forestry and timber. Wherever new opportunity occurred, Hasan's Nusamba corporation was assured of privileged access and ready banking accommodation, to the point where it came to be seen as Suharto's investment vehicle.

Typically, it was Hasan who became the country's plywood king after the government had banned the export of raw timber to nurture an indigenous plywood industry. It was a master stroke which quickly turned Indonesia into the world's foremost exporter of plywood and sawn timber. Hasan, who was appointed head of the Plywood Association (AKPINDO), presided over a régime of fixed prices to prevent competitors undercutting AKPINDO, which some would have been able to do.

Hasan was not Suharto's only ethnic Chinese business adviser. Another prominent figure in the small Chinese élite which dominated the business, banking and investment scene under Suharto's tutelage was his stepbrother Liem Sioe Liong. Rated among the forty richest men in the world, Liem had supported the army financially during the independence struggle, later cornered virtual monopolies in the flour and cement trades and went on to develop his banking interests as far afield as Europe and the USA.

A study of the overseas Chinese financial network in South-East Asia, beyond the scope of this book, would show with what flexibility, speed and confidence the financiers and businessmen in that ethnic group are able to exploit opportunity even in well-regulated and disciplined environments, let alone the anarchy of an easy and corruptible prey such as Suharto allowed his country to be. Communicating rapidly from capital to capital – Singapore, Bangkok, Hongkong, Manila, Jakarta – Chinese big business under Suharto behaved as it always does in that region. Whenever the climate became menacingly unfavourable they fled the country for their alternative homes in neighbouring territories, leaving their less wealthy Chinese brethren to face the ire of indigenous Indonesians.

With the departing financiers would go their money, easily transferred under liberal foreign exchange regulations into Chinese and other banks abroad. Ever since the time of its independence Indonesia has been plagued by this phenomenon of large capital flights making matters worse at times of crisis; conversely much of the vaunted inflow of capital at economically buoyant times has consisted of old money returning.

The banking régime itself, under almost permanent political pressure, was used to provide lavish and unsecured funding for enterprises made possible by nepotistic favours for which there was always a price to pay. And, since a large proportion of bank liquidity was based on loans from foreign banks, that often meant that corrupt practice was being paid for from abroad. It was no less true in the 1970s, when the banks were largely state-controlled, than it was following the structural deregulation introduced in the later 1980s, the consequence of which was a spate of new Chinese-owned private banks.

The result was the same in both situations. In 1974 it had been the state-controlled sector that had accommodated the prodigal dealings of Pertamina, and had to sustain the crash. Eighteen years later, demonstrating that nothing had been learned or reformed, the state bank Bapindo extended a grossly excessive credit, amounting to billions of rupiahs, to a textile company which lost a lot of the money; the loan was written off.

In 1990 it was the turn of the country's second biggest private bank to sustain a huge default. The Bank Duta had furnished massive unsecured credit to a customer usually described as 'major' to speculate on the foreign exchange market. As nearly three-quarters of Bank Duta's stock was owned by charitable foundations controlled by General Suharto, it was known popularly as the president's bank. On this particular occasion the president's friend Liem Sioe Long joined an Indonesian member of the inner circle to bail the bank out with a gift of US$400 million. However ill-judged his speculation, Bank Duta's major client plainly did well from the deal.

Charitable foundations (*yayasan* in Indonesian) were among General Suharto's special interests. He inaugurated and controlled more than half a dozen. The institution, inherited from the Dutch, was not dissimilar from the British non-profit charitable trust or the German *Verein*. Its income was exempt from tax and its finances not liable to audit by the tax authorities. Importantly, it was able to invest assets in business and industrial enterprises. The first step was to muster assets.

Suharto had discovered the utility of the *yayasan* for that purpose in the 1950s when he was military commander in Central Java. Under his aegis a military aide set up two trusts, one of which was for the succour of retired army personnel. It solicited and, of course, received donations from businesses of every description: raw material producers, transport and communications operators, cooperatives, construction companies, etc. An officer sent from army headquarters to investigate concluded that the system was corrupt. On the strength of that General Nasution, who was Army Chief of Staff at the time, moved Suharto from his command and had him posted to SESKOAD, the military academy in Bandung where, as we have seen, he began to be imbued with American military values.

Later, in power, he and his wife Tien, probably the most assiduous fundraiser of her generation, remained devoted to the *yayasan* and its potentialities. As an example, among the many charities she headed was one whose outward purpose was the promotion of healthcare; contributions were exacted from businessmen who could not afford to refuse. Rumoured mismanagement in Mrs Suharto's charities was touched on fitfully in the press, but in general her trusts, and her husband's, were shielded by the régime's ferocious and unpredictable media controls. She died in 1996, three months after Suharto had set up what may have been his last trust. Called the Autonomous Prosperity Fund, with the purported mission of alleviating poverty, its treasurer was Suharto's second son, the multi-millionaire magnate Bambang Trihadmodjo. The presidential directive setting it up ordained that companies with after-tax income above a hundred million rupiahs, equal then to about US$30,000, must donate two per cent of their earnings to the trust; foreign companies, though not compelled, were invited to do likewise. Earlier, he had set up a non-profit foundation for the building of mosques which levied a small monthly contribution from the salary of every civil servant – exactions that were never audited.

Through a variety of channels, therefore, money to invest in the extraordinary opportunities offered by Indonesia's unbridled economy came easily to those with the right connections. During the ten or so years that ended with the Asian economic crisis in 1997 a whole new class of indigenously owned conglomerates and corporations was spawned; and it is on that basis that commentators spoke so long and so extravagantly of an economic miracle. Heading the list of indigenous Indonesians to whom the doors of opportunity were opened were the members of Suharto's own family and a relatively tight circle of personal friends.

With a cynicism that is one of the Indonesian saving graces, the family was dubbed the Cendana group, after the street where the Suhartos lived. Estimates of its wealth varied widely. In 1986 the *Sydney Morning Herald* got itself into trouble with the Indonesian authorities by putting it at US$2.3 billion. Three years later there was said to be a CIA estimate of US$30 billion, which fell to US$2 billion before rising again to US$16 billion in 1999.

An account based on solid and detailed research was compiled in 1999 by Didik Rachbini, director of the recently established Institute for the Development of Economics and Finance in Jakarta:

> Soeharto's second son, Bambang Trihadmodjo (estimated personal assets in 1993: US$220.2 million), was particularly successful and is the leading businessman among the children. His Bimantara Group had an estimated 134 subsidiaries. The eldest daughter, Siti Hardijanti Rukmana (known as Tutut, estimated personal assets in 1993 US$190.5 million), had built the Citra Lamtoro Gung Group which has some 62 subsidiaries.
>
> The president's other children were also involved in business. First son Sigit Harjojudanto (estimated personal assets: US$178.6 million) had the Arseto Group with about 15 subsidiaries. The youngest son, Hutomo Mandala Putra (Tommy, estimated personal assets: US$107 million), despite his youth managed within a single decade to build his Humpuss group into a significant business with some 69 subsidiaries. The president's other two daughters, Siti Herijada (Titiek) and Siti Hutami Endang Adyningsih (Mamiek), also own companies, and in the mid-1990s the first of the Soeharto grandchildren made a dramatic entry on the business scene.[1]

To that catalogue of directly controlled assets must be added countless minority stakes in companies owned or controlled mainly by Chinese businessmen plus a recorded *ten million acres* of land, nearly all acquired during Suharto's presidency.

Corruption cost Indonesia – and the foreign tax-payers whose money the IMF spent on supporting it – dear. A former chief of the National Audit Board, General Wirahadikusumah, guessed in 1986 that it accounted for more than a third of the state budget; that was on the strength of a system in which only one per cent of the population paid income tax and accountability mechanisms had totally collapsed.

Even the forgiving World Bank grew restive. In a barely veiled reference to the favouritism shown to the Cendana group, its 1995 report said the government must select the bidders who offered the highest payment or the lowest cost so as to 'reduce post-contract negotiations and charges of favouritism, and increase international interest; it would also yield direct benefits to the consumers and assure the international markets that borrowing was being used efficiently'. Three years on, and a leaked memorandum revealed the Bank's estimate that at least 20–30 per cent of the Indonesian government's budgeted development funds was diverted into informal payments to government employees and politicians.

Corrupt payments inflated all transaction costs; a presidential favour involving licences or the easing of a regulation or the raising of a protective barrier could cost up to a third of the money put into a project. The seven per cent on Japanese contracts that Norman Reddaway alleged President Sukarno took was a peccadillo in comparison.

That the economy was able to stand such waste, given always a reasonable oil price, was due to two principal factors; low wages and the annual aid subventions (usually around two and a half billion dollars in the 1980s) paid through the IMF. But for the rampant nepotism and corruption, there is widespread agreement that the annual aid payments would not have been needed and more could have been spent on rural development. In other words, the corruption of the Suharto régime was being subsidised by the industrialized West.

From being an issue that he dealt with almost flippantly – at one stage in 1985 he simply ordered General Murdani to put a stop to it where it was hurting the economy! – corruption grew into the salient issue sustaining the succession debate. Angered by criticism not only among the general public but in influential quarters, including sections of the armed services, Suharto began, with reason, to regard all criticism of corruption as criticism of his régime.

ENTER MEGAWATI

By accelerating degrees General Suharto was losing touch with the realities of his own country and of the international context that had helped to maintain him in power for so long. Born in 1921, as he stood yet again for re-election in 1993 his judgment was beginning to falter. He clearly believed he had a firm grip on the relatively minor political adjustments that he considered necessary to maintain order and had no sense at all that his position was threatened by advancing age. He had learned to take for granted both his capacity to weather and suppress opposition and the dictatorial powers which made that possible. The USA and its principal allies had acquiesced in all the fundamentals of his brutal and repressive régime; he had the annual subventions of the IMF to prove it. Weaponry of virtually any sort, short of nuclear, was not just available but positively thrust upon him. Nine tenths of Indonesia's arms came from the USA, but Britain, France, Germany and the Netherlands did well too.

Indonesia's foreign exchange and infrastructural needs attracted phenomenal inflows of capital. Investors in the industrialized world arrived in droves seeking Indonesian partners to bid for construction contracts in such areas as power generation. With the prospect of Indonesia turning into a net petroleum importer early this century and a persistently unfavourable trade balance there was a high premium on broadening the exploitation of the country's multifarious mineral resources. It looked indeed as if the economy was in almost miraculously good fettle.

In 1993 Suharto could boast that, since 1967, gross national product (GNP) per head had risen from the equivalent of US$70 to US$570; by 1997, the last full year before his fall, it would have risen to US$1300. What he would not say was that that average concealed widening inequality in the distribution of wealth, that the new middle class was enjoying a bonanza at the expense of the great majority of rural and urban working people. While the presidential family and the military élite were building themselves golf courses and luxurious country houses on land stripped of forest and transferring funds to safe accounts abroad, more than half the population were still without electricity. Fewer than half of all urban homes had adequate sanitation, and fewer than five per cent were served by central sewage systems. Seventy per cent of all Indonesia's rivers were polluted and ninety-seven per cent of Jakarta's wells were tainted with sea-water.

The point was driven home early in 1995 by the Minister of Defence and Security, General Edo Sudradjat. Taking issue with textile producers who had asked for exemption from an increase in the minimum wage, he pointed to the growing gap between rich and poor and warned that 'the exploitation of workers who are paid inhuman wages and the exploitation of poor farmers whose lands are procured for very small compensation' had been a source of conflict in the past and could be a threat to security in the future.

Suharto dealt impatiently with criticism of any aspect of the situation. In the area of media regulation, for instance, there were sporadic shows of relaxation but the daily reality of editors being briefed and coerced continued, the licensing system endured, the withdrawal of publishing licences was an ever-present threat, and insulting the president was still an indictable offence.

The countries whose investors were enjoying the boom might occasionally mumble about public opinion but, in those diplomatic and financial places where nods and nudges are initiated, the quarter century for which Suharto had so far wielded power was applauded for its stability. As the last decade of the century began, with the prospect of a general election in 1992 and a presidential re-election in 1993, the assumption in Western investment circles was that there were still a good few years of that stability to run.

At the end of 1991, however, just when it was looking as if the government might wish to take a more pliant attitude towards the political aspirations of the people in East Timor, the Dili massacre occurred. Police and KOPASSUS special forces opened fire in what witnesses said was a pre-planned operation on a peaceful but politically motivated funeral procession. Hundreds were killed and wounded. As we have seen, military accounts of the incident lied. International reaction was extremely adverse, at the United Nations, in the European Community, in North America and – especially significant – in South-East Asia itself where neighbours had cultivated a convention of not being hyper-critical about one another's internal affairs.

The Netherlands and Canada suspended economic aid. More disturbing for Suharto and the army was the suspension, which was to last for five years, of American International Military Education Training (IMET) – not for any effect it had, which was probably negligible, but as a token of changing American attitudes in the post cold war era. The communist bogey was fading fast.

Ironically, by adopting a holier-than-thou attitude towards the army's handling of the Dili outrage and exploiting chauvinistic resentment of the censorious international reaction, Suharto contrived to turn it to his political advantage. He was also helped by his success in securing the chairmanship of the 1992 conference of a hundred and eight non-aligned nations – a formidable achievement for the man who was arguably the USA's most loyal and compliant asset in the region.

Bearing in mind, however, the impossibility of any election result radically divergent from that required by the régime, it would be wrong to link his relatively successful manipulation of public opinion and Golkar's inevitable success in the 1992 election. Although the high-powered dissident group, Petition of 50, which included General Nasution among its number, proclaimed publicly that there was no point in voting, election returns suggested a turn-out in excess of ninety per cent. Golkar was credited with sixty-seven per cent of the votes cast.

More significant than the predictable election result were the issues stressed by opposition candidates. Top of the list, according to the chairman of the Indonesian Democratic Party (PDI), Suryadi, was 'corruption, not inflation'. Others were transparency and open government, human rights and democratisation.

The voice of the PDI, the secular party cobbled together in 1973 out of nationalist and Christian parties, was of special significance, since of the three formations allowed to put up electoral candidates it alone called for change. Both Golkar, the régime's political machine, and the PPP, supposedly representing the muffled voice of Islam, argued for the status quo. And although PDI was credited with only fifteen per cent of the votes in 1992 (an advance on the eleven per cent of five years earlier), events were to show that in fact it spoke for a vastly bigger segment of public opinion – far too big for the régime's comfort or acceptance.

It was within the PDI, if anywhere, that the flame of nationalism with which President Sukarno had led Indonesia in the first years of independence burned quietly on. After his fall in 1967 and death in 1970 Sukarno's name was seldom spoken in official circles. For many years the Sukarno family eschewed conspicuous participation in politics. Then in 1978 it was announced that the Great Leader would be given an elaborate tomb. Subsequently, in 1981, a statue was raised to him in Jakarta standing side by side with his former colleague and rival Muhammad Hatta.

In the early 1990s the name Sukarno was heard anew in the political arena. One of his sons, Guruh Sukarno Putra, let it be known that he was willing to let his name go forward as a candidate for the presidency. In a system devised with the express purpose of returning Suharto to office, he represented no immediate threat. It was, however, a signal that the Sukarno family was abandoning its low political profile, a message driven home three years later by events in the Indonesian Democratic Party (PDI).

Under the measures taken to emasculate the political parties in the 1970s, Suharto had the final say in selecting the leaders of the groups. In 1993, wielding that prerogative, the government rejected the PDI's unanimous decision to re-elect their chairman, Suryadi. At the extraordinary congress held subsequently to choose an alternative the party elected Sukarno's daughter, Megawati Sukarnoputri, in defiance of hectic spoiling tactics by the régime, which included locking the doors of meeting rooms.

One of the first things she did was to introduce a direct election system within the party, weakening the régime's control. In June 1996 the authorities hit back by engineering a party split, had her thrown out at an illegal extraordinary congress and, with 2,800 troops standing by, re-installed the deposed leader, Suryadi. In the ensuing days crowds of supporters converged on the PDI headquarters in central Jakarta, fed by arrivals from other parts of the country. It turned into an unprecedented month-long demonstration, with Megawati refusing at first to leave the banner-festooned bungalow. As the worst rioting for many years spread through Jakarta and other cities in an outpouring of public rage over this and other issues, including low pay, she appealed for calm and finally left the building rather than confront the security forces.

Confrontation was coming, however. As the seventy-five year-old Suharto prepared to leave for a nicely timed medical check-up in Germany, a gang of some two hundred thugs purporting to be civilians was let loose against the PDI headquarters on 26 July; while army officers stood watching, police joined in an assault that resulted in dozens of injuries and a disputed number of PDI supporters murdered by knifing.

Politically, Megawati benefited greatly from the régime's resort to these heavy-handed tactics. The régime, however, was determined not to yield to the reality that was growing ever more obvious. When Megawati filed a writ against her dismissal from the party leadership the judge (a presidential appointee) accepted the state's contention that the matter lay outside the court's jurisdiction.

It was during this period that Megawati formed a loose association with the leader of the Religious Scholars' League (NU), Abdurrahman Wahid, Indonesia's future president and Suharto's *bête noire*. At a time when inter-religious tensions were building in various parts of the country it was a potent alignment. Wahid's advice to Megawati was to keep a low profile and take things slowly, which she did. Four months after the régime's attack on the PDI headquarters the courts, clearly acting under revised instructions, ordered the release of the hundred and twenty-four Megawati supporters arrested during the disturbances.

Presidential advisers may well have felt that they had more than enough troubles to manage. The country was seething with discontents. Only weeks after a visit to East Timor during which Suharto ruled out any form of autonomy two of its principal leaders, Jose Ramos Horta and Bishop Carlos Felipe Ximenes Belo, received the Nobel Peace Prize. The leader of the illegal Indonesian Welfare Labour Union, Muchtar Pakpahan, another dissident with a high international profile, was committed to a farcical trial, charged with calling Suharto a dictator and threatening a people's power revolution. In West Java inflamed Muslims rampaging against Christian targets were put down by troops and police with dozens injured and arrested and, as usual, a disputed number killed. For Suharto, the year 1996 was not ending well.

FALL OF THE TIGERS

The following year held worse in store. For better and/or worse the Suharto régime was to be reminded of the global context in which it subsisted but which it could not control; this at the very moment when Suharto succumbed wholly to the last infirmity of ageing dictators: the fallacy that having got away with so much in the past they are capable of anything.

As the year began, yet another scandal involving special favours to the members of the presidential circle was maturing. A company had been formed to import Korean cars, give them an Indonesian name, the 'Timor', and pass them off as made in Indonesia. Once the deception was unmasked it was admitted that they were of foreign manufacture but claimed that Indonesian workers had built them. Because the car did not sell well, the government arranged a big loan for the company and granted import duty exemptions which were not available to competitors. The predictable protests by industry and government representatives in Japan and the USA were in one sense the lesser part of the harm that resulted; worse was the damage to sentiment ahead of the economic storm that was about to break over East and South-East Asia.

The East Asian economic crisis of 1997–8 had been brewing for some years and finally broke in Thailand in July 1997. In a kind of ecstasy investors and speculators, riding on the wave of prosperity that gathered pace after the Vietnam war, had become recklessly indebted. Property and construction were the core of the problem and Tokyo its epicentre. It had spread rapidly and for a time was regarded benignly as nothing worse than a sign of good times.

But debts have to be paid. The fundamental reckoning was in US dollars, and confidence depended on steady relationships between the dollar and local currencies. In July 1997 Thailand was forced to let its currency float, and it fell. South Korea was the next to go, then the Philippines, then

Indonesia which allowed the rupiah to float freely in August. Confidence collapsed throughout the region.

Rupiah devaluations were nothing new but the scale of the problem and the regional context were. The nation's public overseas debt was more than US$80 billion dollars. There was another US$50 billion of private overseas debt. The total exceeded 1998 gross domestic product by twenty per cent. Nearly half was attributable to a close circle – the Cendana group – of some fifty people. About a fifth of it was repayable within six months.

The rush of private companies to buy the dollars they needed to pay off debts accelerated the rupiah's fall. From 2,450 to the dollar in July 1997, it dropped to 11,000 in September 1998, having sunk even lower to nearly 17,000 in March of that year in response to local political factors. About two-thirds of the banking sector's loans became non-performing, that is they stopped earning interest. Suharto turned automatically to the financial technocrats – heirs to the Berkeley Mafia that had bolstered him since his earliest days in power – to see him through the crisis. They turned to the IMF, the World Bank and the Asian Development Bank.

The IMF responded with its usual formula, uncannily similar to that applied after the collapse of President Sukarno's régime three decades before: cutting subsidies on vital consumer commodities like rice, soya, electricity and petroleum products, deregulation of the economy, tighter fiscal discipline and higher interest rates to discourage the flight of money out of the country. In return for a rescue package totalling US$43 billion the IMF managers demanded the closure of sixteen private banks, all connected with the presidential circle, and the merger of several more.

Suharto signed up, but with tongue in cheek and fingers crossed. In less than a week two of the expunged banks with Suharto family connections were back in business. From here on his behaviour became erratic and increasingly irresponsible. He was not helped by suffering a mild stroke, after which he ceased to look far beyond the family circle for advice. He turned his back completely on the specialist advisers who had been his mainstay in financial affairs for so many years, even to the point of excluding his own finance minister from a critical face to face meeting with the IMF's deputy managing director.

Suharto was affronted by the severity of the conditions the IMF was imposing on him. In January 1998 he introduced a budget which left no doubt about his personal unwillingness to conform, and also signalled to the public in general how badly he was out of touch with reality. Panic buying spread nationwide with such speed that there were fears of repercussions throughout the region. Food prices soared. The rupiah lost half its value in less than a week.

President Clinton, giving a rare insight into whose voice really spoke when the IMF moved its lips, telephoned Suharto to make clear that the IMF package must be implemented if the proposed help was to be forthcoming. Germany and Japan added their voices in the same vein. This second attempt at an IMF agreement embodied minor concessions on fiscal matters in response to Indonesian criticisms but went further in prescribing structural reforms. These, in the words of the IMF's managing director, Michel Camdessus, were designed 'to dismantle an economic system based on conglomerates, the collusion between the state, banks and business, and restrictive markets'. Designed, in other words, to put an end to the workings of the Cendana group.

As Suharto signed the second letter of intent Camdessus was photographed standing over him with arms crossed in the manner of a champion wrestler. Newspapers, so often the victims of Suharto's manipulation and suppression, published the image many times, delivering its unmistakable message to the Indonesian people.

Suharto and his family were not ready to give in yet, though they must by then have realized that the USA saw in the evolving situation an opportunity to bring the régime to some sort of order if not to its close. Days after signing the second letter of intent he announced his 'willingness' to stand for a seventh term in the 1998 presidential election. His vice-presidential running partner would be his old friend B.J. Habibie, an economic nationalist, civilian and known critic of the policies wished on Indonesia by the post-Berkeley technocrats and their friends in the IMF. Also, he began to talk about Indonesia setting up a currency board to look after its own currency problems.

It was at this juncture that the rupiah plummeted to 17,000 to the dollar. Camdessus stated in public that the IMF package would be stopped if the currency board scheme went forward. Clinton was back on the 'phone twice in one week to add weight to a Treasury warning that it could be stopped if Habibie stood for vice-president; Vice-President Walter Mondale went to Jakarta to reinforce the message. In the event the USA climbed down over Habibie and Suharto abandoned his currency board idea. In March he was rubber-stamped into his seventh term with Habibie as vice.

He at once appointed an extraordinarily provocative cabinet. His personal financial adviser, the ethnic Chinese and plywood king 'Bob'

Hasan, was given the ministry of trade and industry. Suharto's eldest daughter Tutut got social affairs, and it was widely thought he saw this as a step towards having her succeed him in the presidency.

The combined effects of the currency tumble and Suharto's political sparring were commodity shortages, dramatic price rises and rapid unemployment. With no other avenue of protest available, people began demonstrating. At Gajah Mada University in Yogyakarta more than twenty thousand students marked General Suharto's swearing-in with a rally; they called for democratic reform and blamed the régime for the economic chaos which they attributed, not to the IMF, but to corruption, collusion and nepotism – the 'KKN' which quickly became the slogan of the time. Soon less orderly and less articulate unrest poured onto the streets, focusing on the usual scapegoats, the ethnic Chinese.

Suharto was persuaded to negotiate yet again. This time, in April 1998, the agreement included a precise timetable for the application of 117 measures. Again the Suharto family and its monopolies were the object of the onslaught; again there was a programme for reform of the banks. Overseas observers were delighted; the rupiah rose to 8,000 to the dollar. For ordinary Indonesians the picture was bleaker. At the beginning of May, in compliance with an IMF requirement, the government cut the subsidy on petrol. It could have been done in stages to alleviate the impact, but for whatever reason it was done at a single stroke and caused the price at the pumps to leap by seventy per cent.

Rioting redoubled. In the North Sumatran capital Medan, Indonesia's third largest city, the army was called out to suppress student disturbances amidst intimations of sympathy between some of the troops and the demonstrators. In Jakarta students returning to the private university of Trisakti from a street demonstration against the price rise were fired on with live ammunition and a number (between four and six) killed. There was talk of an army faction being responsible.

The next day in Jakarta was one of bloodshed and arson. The funeral procession for the dead Trisakti students degenerated into a riot that lasted several days. Thousands of shopping centres and houses were looted and destroyed; many hundreds of cars were set on fire, with the notorious Timor selected for particular attention. Other symbolic targets were the homes of Suharto's business colleague, Liem Sioe Liong, and the parliamentary speaker, Harmoko. As many as 150,000 ethnic Chinese and foreigners fled the country. When the spasm subsided more than a thousand were reckoned dead. Police records subsequently acknowledged three and a half thousand demonstrations nationwide during the period of unrest, unprecedented since the army-managed demonstrations which helped to bring Sukarno down thirty years before.

Harmoko, who as Speaker of the House of Representatives (the DPR) was by definition a Suharto puppet, now performed the penultimate act of the drama. On 18 May, implicitly delivering the verdict of even the closest loyalists, he gave General Suharto four days to resign the presidency or face impeachment. Student and other demonstrators flocked into the parliamentary building to support the ultimatum. Still Suharto tried to hold on, talking of forming a reform cabinet. On 20 May the American Secretary of State, Madeleine Albright, called on him to go, and a group of economic ministers he had in mind for his new cabinet wrote him a letter refusing to serve.

On Thursday 21 May, abandoned by the super-power that had sponsored his rise to power, General Suharto resigned, ending the thirty-two years of his bloody tyranny.

THE TIMORESE QUESTION

B.J. Habibie was bundled into the presidency in May 1998 under a constitutional provision that made him look like a temporary incumbent from the start. Only two days earlier Suharto, who had pleased no-one when he imposed the hapless Habibie as his preferred vice-presidential candidate, tried to shore up his own case for hanging on by insinuating that his old friend would hardly be a suitable president. Even so, Habibie carried into office the stigma of being Suharto's stooge.

Some therefore took hope from his firm handling of an army problem that confronted him on his first day in office. He confirmed a decision by the defence minister and armed forces chief, General Wiranto, to sideline Suharto's son-in-law General Prabowo Subianto. Commander of KOSTRAD (the army's strategic command) thanks to his father-in-law, Prabowo was angling for a re-disposition of senior posts that would take him a step nearer the top. Instead, Habibie endorsed Wiranto's decision to send him to a staff college post in Bandung. It was an important symbolic decision; he had not done what Suharto might have been thought to want.

Many hoped that the end of Suharto meant the end of the dual function which had enabled the army to play a major role in government as well as its conventional security role. It was the use the army had made of its dual function under Suharto that had provoked so much public anger. An ambitious but cautious man with barely concealed presidential aspirations, the wily Wiranto wanted to pare down its political functions.

Not himself a military man, Habibie was in theory well-placed to begin the long task of asserting civilian control over the armed services. It was high time. The army was in bad odour over the shooting of Trisakti students; details were circulating about the employment of army units to kidnap anti-régime activists in 1997–8; the long-running sore of army atrocities in East Timor, Aceh and Madura was exposed; the part played by the security forces in the sacking of the PDI headquarters rankled. And as recent scandals were aired, so others from the past were reopened, notably the 1983 shootings of Muslims at Tanjong Priok.

Having gratified General Wiranto by backing his action against Prabowo, Habibie next instructed him to carry out an internal reform of the armed forces. And, in the course of apologising for the human rights infringements of the Suharto régime in his first state address, he alluded specifically to the army's part in them, well knowing that Wiranto himself was not immune from criticism.

Habibie confronted the army, but he never brought himself to do anything about corruption and misapplication of resources during the Suharto presidency, partly out of loyalty to an old friend, and perhaps because there was some apprehension about business and financial interests shared between them in earlier years.

So, on the one hand Habibie came to office carrying too much of the wrong kind of baggage. His reform agenda – for there is no doubt he had reformist intentions – was Suharto's and he was working in Suharto's time-scale, which was too slow. The reforms he required of the armed forces were broadly in tune with Suharto's thinking. Precipitated prematurely into office as he was, his leadership of ICMI (the Indonesian Muslim Intellectuals Association), set up under Suharto's tutelage, had marked him with the undeserved image of sectarian conservatism.

On the other hand, the studies he had initiated within ICMI had produced clear thinking about necessary reform, and on that basis he was able in the early months of his administration to launch a reform agenda which, for the first time in decades, addressed the demands of urban Indonesia for the rule of law, transparency in business and the bureaucracy, and genuinely democratic institutions. It also envisaged legislation, which was subsequently enacted, preparing the legal ground for the democratically supported decentralization of the by-then highly centralized Republic.

Symbolically, one of his first acts was to visit the House of Representatives (DPR), something General Suharto would never have dreamed of doing. He announced that there would be a parliamentary election in June 1999 and set in train the legislation that made it the first free election since 1955. Instead of the three political parties that Suharto had permitted in his so-called 'festivals of democracy' there were forty-three in contention (and dozens more which did not compete). The counting of ballot papers was opened to public scrutiny.

He also agreed with the DPR leaders that the other house of parliament, the MPR (the People's Consultative Assembly which included the DPR), should convene before the end of 1999 to elect a president. It was a signal that he understood the moral impossibility of trying to hold on until the end of his full term in 2003.

A month after taking office, President Habibie's government instituted a five-year action programme on human rights which consisted primarily of commitments to ratifying the various United Nations conventions – including the vital Convention against Torture – and incorporating them into Indonesian law. As an earnest of what people hoped was a firm intention to give real substance to this agenda, restrictions on free association and assembly were lifted and the pernicious system of requiring publishers to apply for licences was dropped. Political prisoners were released on conditions that left only membership of the communist party as a possible reason for continued detention – though a number of PKI prisoners were in fact set free on humanitarian grounds. Many restrictions on the activities of trade unions were removed.

On the financial and economic front Habibie faced an urgent need to satisfy an international as well as his domestic constituency. Suharto's corruption and inept handling of relations with the IMF had brought about a contraction of his vaunted growth economy by an estimated fourteen per cent. During his last critical weeks the national currency had fallen by two-thirds against the American dollar. Inflation was at eighty per cent. The price of rice in urban shops had tripled. It was a situation reminiscent of that left behind in far more difficult circumstances by President Sukarno's last government.

Nothing was more urgent as Habibie entered the presidency than to mend relations with the IMF and World Bank. The remedies he accepted

from them likewise resembled those of the early post-Sukarno period: re-
establish fiscal discipline, reschedule foreign debt, attract new capital
investment from abroad, restock the shelves with essential foodstuffs and,
yet again, restructure the banking system. One element that was new –
testimony to three decades of neglect under Suharto – was acknowledgment
of the need to foster the real economy, that part of the nation's life that had
too often been overlooked in the financial preoccupations of the capital.

On paper, then, and at the level of public rhetoric – barring only his
refusal to bring his former master to justice – Habibie turned some
important corners and sought to demonstrate that he was his own man. But
two large hurdles loomed ahead of him.

Bringing sense and integrity to the private banks was a mammoth
undertaking. It had been recommended several times before only to be
confounded by the machinations of Suharto's Cendana group. This time,
determined not to be thwarted again, the IMF prevailed with its advice that
banks failing to meet minimal liquidity and capital adequacy criteria should
be taken over by a new institution called the Indonesian Bank
Restructuring Agency which, in the usual Indonesian way, was quickly
reduced to its acronym IBRA. Equally quickly, it became the country's most
powerful financial institution. It was good for creditors of the delinquent
banks because it gave them a government-backed guarantee of the return of
their loans. For the corrupt financiers of the Suharto era – including people
close to Habibie – it spelled the end of the non-accountable practices which
had made them rich and well-nigh bankrupted the nation.

Public attention now fastened on the case of Bank Bali. Anxious to
accumulate enough capital to avoid being taken over by IBRA, Bank Bali
was trying to call in debt from three other banks which had already been
taken over. The sum owed to it was astronomical. In what looked like a
desperate purchase of debt-collecting expertise, Bank Bali paid another
company a fee of more than half the sum owed for help in recovering it.
However, the company concerned turned out to be the creature of a close
Habibie associate who was also deputy treasurer of Golkar. It was alleged
that a large part of the so-called 'fee' was destined to be spent on buying
votes for Habibie in the December 1999 presidential election.

At IMF insistence Habibie agreed to an independent audit by the
international chartered accountancy firm – one of the biggest in the world
– PricewaterhouseCoopers. The outcome was a lengthy and compromising
report, implicating ministers, officials, Habibie associates and parlia-

mentarians in concealment, bribery, corruption and fraud. It alone was enough to tarnish the favourable image Habibie had striven to project of himself.

The Bank Bali scandal coincided with climactic developments in the annexed territory of East Timor. Insulated by the Suharto régime from the steady crescendo of international outrage, the virtually colonial fiefdom held by KOPASSUS special forces had been run rather like a huge plantation. Suharto, his family and some military colleagues had come into possession of large tracts of land and were enjoying the fruits of high-grade coffee cultivation. As 1998 came to a close two things were happening: coaxed by the United Nations, Indonesia and the former colonial power, Portugal, were edging towards a negotiated resolution of the East Timor question; simultaneously, the almost autonomous KOPASSUS gang running the territory was conducting another round of military operations against the Fretilin guerrillas. It was in this period that they also began mustering, training, arming and paying the notorious militias which were to be used in an attempt to obstruct political settlement.

In January 1999, conscious of the economic menace being mediated through the IMF and other western creditors, Habibie made the surprise announcement that the East Timorese would be allowed to opt in a referendum between full independence and wide-ranging autonomy within the Republic.

Given the isolation of the tiny, denuded territory in the gigantic Indonesian archipelago, if even minimal standards of civilized government had been maintained under Suharto's rule, the autonomy option would have deserved serious consideration. But the experience of distant Aceh and the familiar proclivities of the KOPASSUS occupiers allowed no doubt what autonomy would mean in reality.

The military, although divided on many issues, were enraged and embarrassed by Habibie's concession. Commanders both at the centre and in all the other regions where there were separatist leanings feared, with reason, that what East Timor was being granted others too would want.

As Indonesian–Portuguese negotiations progressed towards agreement in May, the occupying army in East Timor became hyperactive. Suharto's son-in-law, General Prabowo, was identified in April as one of a group of officers and intelligence men in effective control. In the same month one of the worst massacres of the entire occupation period was perpetrated in the town of Liquica, forty miles west of Dili, by militia who were fomenting bloody incidents all over the province. After killing five people and taking hostages at the home of the local Roman Catholic priest, they went on to storm the church at Liquica where some two thousand refugees were housed. They threw grenades and fired indiscriminately into the church, killing several dozen people and injuring many more.

The pro-independence leader, Xanana Gusmao, speaking from house arrest in Jakarta, called off the ceasefire intended to cover the peace talks, ordered his supporters to take up arms and called on the United Nations to establish a permanent presence.

Not the least to be embarrassed by the worsening state of anarchy in East Timor was the defence minister and armed forces chief, General Wiranto, whose inability to control the army elements – supposing he even wished to – was starkly exposed. The best he could manage at that juncture was an undertaking that his troops would remain neutral in fighting between independence guerrillas and the militias.

The Timor Accord, signed at United Nations headquarters a few weeks later by Indonesia and Portugal, spelled out the details and instrumentalities of the referendum. The United Nations was to supervise it, lay down a code of conduct and furnish the necessary resources. Supporters and opponents would have the same opportunities to spread their messages. Crucially and, as it turned out, tragically, the Indonesian authorities were entrusted with providing the necessary security for a free and just consultation process and guaranteeing the security of UN personnel. Everything was provided for and expressed as if all the parties concerned could be relied on to behave in a civilized and honorable fashion.

What followed was three months of organized terror, using techniques taught to Indonesian officers at American, Australian and British military training establishments. Wiranto's uniformed security forces did indeed remain neutral while the supposedly voluntary militias went about their work. Not only were the militias under the operational control of Indonesian field commanders, their bands often included regular soldiers who merely doffed their uniforms when they went out on sorties. Thousands of them had been recruited across the border in West Timor. They routinely returned to military encampments for food and shelter and, as one officer disclosed, to play billiards.

During the run-up to the East Timor referendum the rest of Indonesia went to the polls in July to elect a new House of Representatives (DPR). It was the first free election for nearly half a century. Habibie's Golkar formerly the automatic winner of all elections, gained only a fifth of the votes cast. The biggest vote, a third of the total, went to Megawati Sukarnoputri's Indonesian Democratic Party (formerly the PDI but now called the PDI-P to denote the struggle she had endured at Suharto's hands). Third on the list with thirteen per cent of the vote was a moderate Islamic party which was to be important because it was the creation of the man who would become Indonesia's next president, Abdurrahman Wahid.

Megawati's rising star was of little immediate relevance to the East Timor situation. She was known to share her father's anxiety to hold the nation together and also needed support from within the armed forces; hence she said little on that issue. But Golkar's setback and conceding the possibility of East Timor quitting the Republic had damaged Habibie's position. Support within Golkar for his presidential nomination began to falter and, when the Bank Bali affair came into the open a couple of months later, rumours circulated that he would not even bother to stand.

Meanwhile the military terror campaign against the people of East Timor went on escalating. Thousands of families fled or were driven from the towns into the hills amidst undisguised threats that a vote for independence on 30 August would lead to the destruction of the province. The fiction that the campaign of intimidation was not being sanctioned at a high political and military level was exploded when a British-made Hawk air-to-ground attack aircraft of the Indonesian air force was sighted making a warning pass over an urban area in contravention of the conditions of sale. In Jakarta the State Secretary, Muladi, made the extraordinary suggestion that United Nations personnel in East Timor – unarmed and constantly harassed by the army-run militias – were guilty of bias and intimidation against supporters of the autonomy option. There were still at least 23,000 uniformed Indonesian troops, not to mention the thousands of mercenary militiamen, in East Timor on referendum day.

Nevertheless, the East Timorese turned out in joyful force. Of 438,000 registered voters (in a total population of about 850,000) 432,300 voted – a 98.6 per cent turn-out. Five days later the world learned that seventy-eight percent had opted for independence, a tribute to their courage and to the determination of the multinational UN team.

After casting their votes, tens of thousands went straight back into the hills, anticipating the wave of arson unleashed by the army and its paid thugs as soon as the result was known. All over the territory towns were emptied, looted and set alight by KOPASSUS units and their mercenaries.

Thanks to modern technology, what was happening in the once secret fiefdom was known instantaneously around the world. Australian meteorological satellites recorded dozens of heat spots where towns and villages were burning. And although the telephone system was among the first targets of the rampaging army and militiamen, media representatives were still able to report using cell and satellite telephone systems. In their attempts to conceal what they were doing the scorched earth practitioners were reduced to attacking the journalists and broadcasters themselves; several were killed.

Another mass migration began. Up to 150,000 crossed into West Timor, only to find they were still to be harassed by the militias there. Others were herded onto ships and taken to various other parts of Indonesia. Witnesses in Kupang at the western tip of West Timor spoke of ships leaving full of refugees and quickly returning empty, the supposition being that the human cargo had been dumped at sea. Some, more fortunate, were flown out, packed into Australian transport aircraft.

Three hundred miles away in Darwin, capital of Australia's Northern Territory, an East Timorese Support Centre had information and welfare services up and running; additional food and medical personnel and supplies were in place. On 31 August, the day after the referendum, New Zealand supported the appeals of the East Timorese independence leaders for the United Nations to send an international peace-keeping force. Canada and Portugal joined in, calling on the United Nations to make plans.

In what can now be seen as a graduated approach to international intervention, some governments appeared to hesitate. The Australian Prime Minister, John Howard, stressed that sending a military force without Indonesian consent would be tantamount to invasion. The wave of nationalist sentiment likely to be aroused throughout Indonesia would further complicate President Habibie's predicament and clear the way for military elements awaiting an opportunity to seize power. The Indonesian army's oldest friend, the White House, used off-record briefings to plead its preoccupation with the humanitarian disaster unfolding in Kosovo.

While the crime being perpetrated in East Timor aroused heated passions internationally, its political ramifications demanded cool and calculated responses. Under the terms of the Timor Accord, signed in May, the vote for independence required endorsement at the November session of the still unreformed People's Consultative Assembly (MPR). The armed forces still occupied non-elective seats, making them power-brokers. On this and on the more fundamental issue of whether he could look forward to retaining the presidency, Habibie needed the support of the modernising, more professional and less corrupt elements within the armed forces. Antagonising them would jeopardise the hope of concluding the independence issue constitutionally.

Paradoxically, therefore, the international community had to buttress the Indonesian president against the coterie of unruly generals gathered around his predecessor by steadily raising the pressure on him. Time was short. With every day that passed hundreds more went to their death. Meanwhile, in the UN Security Council, China and Russia as well as the USA were holding back on intervention.

It was left to Australia, with its compromising history on the question of East Timorese sovereignty, to make the running. The Minister for External Affairs, Alexander Downer, found a formula to circumvent the problem of governments that would not wish to contribute to an international force by speaking of a 'coalition of the willing'. Habibie, looking for a way to compel the armed forces chief, General Wiranto, to control the maverick army command in East Timor, still held back from consenting to a peace keeping force. To help him focus his thoughts heavy hints were dropped, by the USA and in a letter from the World Bank, about postponing the aid-donors' club annual subvention of US$6 billion, as well as the US$43 billion recovery package cobbled together by the IMF to lift Indonesia out of the recession caused by Suharto's mishandling of the Asian economic crisis.

Things began to fall into place on 7 September. UN Secretary-General, Kofi Annan, passed on a Security Council warning that the Indonesian government must stop the violence within forty-eight hours or face intervention. The Australian army was placed on twenty-four hour alert, recognised as the force that would take the lead in an international intervention.

President Habibie, in line with American advice, declared martial law in East Timor (lifted two weeks later once a UN force was in control). General Wiranto, his hand forced, found the courage to admit, 'We need strong action to stop the violence'. The following day the army commander in East Timor was at last replaced. Yet the violence continued. Defiantly militias attacked United Nations compounds, and plans were made and partly carried out to evacuate their staff.

Reflecting public opinion in Australia, where there were numerous anti-Indonesian demonstrations, Downer spoke of the disappointment that would be felt if the USA, always so ready to demand help for its own initiatives, did not support a peace-keeping force in East Timor. This goaded the US Secretary of State, Madeleine Albright, to warn that Indonesia should take care of the violence or allow the international community to come in. At last, President Clinton followed: 'It is now clear that the Indonesian military is aiding and abetting the militia violence. This is simply unacceptable'.

And so the corner was turned. General Wiranto, speaking from the VIP lounge at Dili airport – which he prudently did not leave during a flying visit – conceded that a UN force was an urgent option. President Habibie could now make his move. In a televised address he admitted: 'Too many people have lost their lives since the beginning of the unrest, lost their homes and security; we cannot wait any longer; we have to stop the suffering immediately'. Even as he spoke, in West Timor, East Timorese refugees were being herded into groups and shot.

Despite some jostling over terms of engagement, within days a UN force arrived under Australian commander, Major-General Peter Cosgrove, and took over from Indonesia the responsibility for security in East Timor. It came into a devastated land with virtually no infrastructure left intact. A third of its population was displaced, thousands dead; many were dying of hunger. Smoking, flattened villages and straggling lines of refugees humping sparse belongings were the indelible images left behind as the dishonorable memorial to twenty-five years of Suharto's military tyranny in East Timor.

HABIBIE STANDS DOWN

The stage thus set for the October 1999 session of the MPR could scarcely have been less favourable to Habibie's ambition to be elected for a full term as president. His own party, Golkar, was divided over whether to nominate him; a clutch of retired generals had actually left to form a political group of their own and were tending towards supporting Megawati, whose PDI-P had come out top in the July parliamentary election. General Wiranto, with a weather eye on the likely outcome of the election, was also turning his favours towards Abdurrahman Wahid and Megawati.

Habibie, whose recognition of the reality about East Timor undoubtedly saved his country from further international opprobrium, was being blamed for its loss. Young Muslim rioters in Aceh were noisily confirming fears that East Timor's successful separatism would nourish similar demands there and elsewhere in the Republic. The one really popular thing he could have done – to bring Suharto to justice for corruption and infringements of human rights – he abstained from doing. And to make it all worse, the Bank Bali affair had thrown an ugly light on his own political and financial manipulations.

He had one last chance: the accountability speech he was required to deliver to the MPR assembly. He had made too many enemies, offered too many hostages to fortune, caused too much disruption and, when all was said, still came across as Suharto's poodle. His speech was rejected and, without waiting to be told, he withdrew from the presidential race.

At first sight, Megawati was the obvious candidate. Her PDI-P was the biggest party in parliament. On the strength of its partnership with the smaller National Awakening Party (PKB, the political arm of Abdurrahman Wahid's huge NU) she should have been fairly certain of success. But DPR arithmetic was not decisive in the larger MPR where the matter would be decided. Moreover she ran into conservative Muslim opposition to having a woman in the presidency. The solution, to which she acceded, was to let the wily and much more experienced Wahid make the running. He it was who succeeded Habibie, while Megawati became vice-president – a position which, as it turned out, was to be more important in her hands than it had ever been before.

POSTMORTEM ON TYRANNY

The pitiful end of President Habibie's interregnum was perhaps the final twitch of the Suharto era. The moral, political and economic dilapidation to which the military dictator had reduced his empire lay exposed and, despite some good intentions, Habibie never threw off the stigma of being a Suharto puppet. Releasing political prisoners, freeing the media, permitting all non-Marxist parties to contest the DPR election, allowing the East Timor referendum, preparing the way for decentralization, all were valuable reforms; but still he came across as a man of the past. His image was sullied by obstructing investigation of corruption and human rights accusations against Suharto and by his own involvement in the Bank Bali affair. His management of the East Timor issue had earned him as many enemies as friends. He turned out to be an inept manipulator of the Jakarta machine and was not helped by being non-Javanese. Insinuated into the presidency by a constitutional technicality, he had to bear the opprobrium for all the evils of the Suharto years as well as the disorders of his own short spell.

Indonesia was humiliated on almost every front. Its extravagantly beribboned generals were in disgrace around the world for the unprincipled savagery they had inflicted over the years on their own countrymen in places like West Papua, Aceh and, most recently, East Timor. While their officers had become adepts at running businesses, enriching themselves and organizing gangs of hoodlums, their predilection for highfalutin' seminars and overseas training left doubts about their actual military competence. Raping women in the communities against which they directed operations had become a routine expectation, as had looting and the use of torture in the course of interrogation. How many Indonesian citizens were murdered under Suharto's sanction can never be known, but certainly hundreds of thousands over and above the supposed million dispatched in the anti-communist slaughter in the middle and late 1960s.

The myth of the economic miracle had evaporated to reveal the reality that in one of the world's most richly endowed regions over half the people were living in poverty. In Indonesia, unlike neighbouring Malaysia, the money generated by extractive and new manufacturing industries was not percolating down to the under-classes, especially in the countryside. New business and manufacturing opportunities were not widely shared but went predominantly to the president's men, the armed services and the profoundly corrupt bureaucracy.

The rest of the new middle class – itself far smaller at seven per cent of the population than pro-Suharto propaganda had made out[2] – found it hard to break into the circle of economic privilege and resented having no say in the governance of the nation. The bureaucracy itself, castigated for its inflated size under President Sukarno, had more than doubled under Suharto. Military officers held a high proportion of the more senior posts, and ex-military officers many more. Military personnel had been insinuated into the very fabric of administration right down to district and village level.

Given the proper use of its large export revenues – and if much of the money had not been diverted into foreign bank accounts – Indonesia would not have needed the massive injections of grants and loans fed to it year on year by the Western donors' club and international institutions led by the IMF. In effect that money was used to maintain the financial and foreign exchange system needed for the operations of foreign businesses and investors and to cover the economic cronyism of a corrupt military régime.

The so-called development boom had been no more than a segment of the investment bonanza enjoyed by the whole South-East Asian region and generated largely by Japanese, Western and overseas Chinese entrepreneurs. Eighty per cent of the country's realizable capital assets were reckoned to be under the control of the three per cent of the population who were ethnically Chinese: their preeminence in business matters had not changed under Suharto. Analysts began to recognise that even the annual growth figure of six or seven per cent routinely bandied about by commentators during most of the Suharto years had limited application and did not reflect the mixed nature of the régime's economic performance.

The broad sweep of the country's real economy – the actual basis of its wealth – which had been crying out for development after the departure of the Dutch, had still not been developed. Land hunger, thanks largely to rapacious officers, bureaucrats and entrepreneurs and the abuse of the legal system, was worse than ever. The land/population ratio was deteriorating. In the feverish scramble to denude the land of its exportable raw materials, hundreds of thousands of people had been robbed of their subsistence. Programmes represented as part of a development process, like transmigration, had manifestly been designed to manipulate ethnic balance and were badly executed at that.

The boast that more children went to school disguised the truth that far too many did not. Millions of Indonesians enjoyed no access to basic health and amenity supply systems. The problem was not that nothing had been attempted or done, but that a grasping oligarchy had prioritised its own self-enrichment and allocated inadequate resources to genuine national development.

As a result, Suharto and his puppet Habibie left behind them a nation destined to be dependent for many more years on aid and subventions from countries whose principal motive is access to Indonesia's raw materials and consumer market; destined therefore to be for many more years a creature of foreign influence.

The Suharto legacy which Habibie handed on to President Abdurrahman Wahid was the result of design, not accident. All the important institutions – the judiciary, the central bank, the security services, trade unions, parliament, the Security and Exchange Commission – had been perverted into tools in Suharto's hands. The presidency itself had become the nation's only effective institution.

Politically, Indonesia had gone backward under Suharto. Parliament had no power independent of the president's. The structure of guided democracy which Sukarno had intended as a means of marshalling and reconciling the nation's political energies became in Suharto's hands an instrument to subdue them. In the whole of South-East Asia only the military dictatorship in Burma was comparable with the régime Suharto had imposed on Indonesia – supported and sustained until only days before his fall by the power that raised him in the first place, the USA, obediently assisted by Great Britain.

It is proper to ask whether the Suharto era was the result its international sponsors intended when they launched it? Some who were involved in its making shrug and speak of the 'law of unforeseen consequences'. Others merely shrug.

## Notes

1   Rachbini, Didik J., 'Growth and Private Enterprise' in *Indonesia: The Challenge of Change*, ed Richard Baker et al. Singapore: Institute of South-East Asian Studies, 1999.
2   Keiji Omura in *Indonesia Entering a New Era*, Chiba, Institute of Developing Economies, IDE-JETRO, 2000, bases the figure on ownership of private cars.

# TEN

## Diversity in Unity

THE ENEMIES WITHIN

Abdurrahman Wahid (known affectionately as Gus Dur) became Indonesia's fourth president in October 1999 with the late President Sukarno's eldest daughter Megawati as vice-president. The challenge facing them was to prove that the Republic could be held together and effectively governed within the law – and that the law was independent of the ruling institutions, the presidency and the army.

The nation was in a mess. The army especially was humiliated by its own deeds in East Timor and torn to factional shreds by personal rivalries and, more importantly, by discord over its future political rôle. In all those regions prone to separatist sentiment, notably Aceh, the East Timor referendum had triggered old ambition and fresh unrest. The economy had not recovered from the sixteen per cent shrinkage of per capita GDP caused by the East Asian economic crisis and Suharto's mismanagement of it. It was still uncertain how far the IMF would go to help. The ruins of the banking system were echoing to major scandals. The rupiah was in distress, and the financiers who had transferred large capital sums to Singapore and Hong Kong displayed no urgent disposition to bring their money back. In the new climate of non-deference an angry public demanded something be done about the results of Suharto's rampant nepotism and abuse of human rights.

The familiar problem of how to distinguish between what was urgent and what was important was complicated for Wahid by the divergent perspectives of those he had to satisfy. The first imperative, however, was clear: to concoct a cabinet reflecting on the one hand the immediate realities of power and on the other the political deals and compromises he had undertaken in order to gain the presidency. Two elements had been crucial: an understanding with the military reformist bloc, led by General Wiranto; and an opportunistic – some would have said unimaginable – accommodation between the two biggest Muslim groupings in the country, Wahid's conservative Religious Scholars League (NU) and its rival, the modernising Muhammadiyah led by Amien Rais, himself a presidential hopeful. Each organization claimed a following of around thirty million. Taken together they came to be known as the Central Axis.

Consulting closely with Megawati, Wiranto, Amien Rais (Speaker of the People's Consultative Congress) and Akbar Tandjung (Speaker of the House of Representatives), Wahid assembled a 'national unity' cabinet which largely succeeded in balancing the far from united political forces on which the stability of the new government had to rely.

Even in the new climate it was necessary to propitiate the army; this he did by appointing seven military men to the thirty-five-strong cabinet. All were reformers in the sense that they knew things had to change if the army was not to lose all influence. Wiranto, who wished to be seen as their leader, was seriously compromised by the military atrocities committed in Aceh and East Timor when he was chief of the armed forces. In what looked like an attempt to remake his image he began honing his undoubted talent as a pop singer and ostentatiously dedicated the profits from his first CD to helping refugees. He was now given the important post of coordinating minister for politics and security, which made him for a brief spell the most powerful member of the cabinet apart from the president himself. Another important reformist general, Susilo Bambang Yudhoyono, was first given mines and energy and subsequently took over the coordinating ministry for social, political and security affairs from Wiranto; yet another, Surjadi Sudirdja, was given the Home Office. These appointments represented a snub to Wiranto's rivals in the 'green' army faction led by Suharto's deflated son-in-law, General Prabowo, who forthwith became one of the new president's most venomous enemies.

Less gratifying to General Wiranto was the appointment of the first ever civilian minister of defence, and of an admiral as the first ever armed forces chief not drawn from the army – though both were in fact close associates of his.

Having thus entangled the army in a web of compromises, Wahid punctiliously allotted four cabinet posts each to Megawati's party, Amien Rais's and his own. There was a seat each for the leaders of three rather smaller parties and for a broad range of functional and religious groups. The outer regions were better represented than in the past with a dozen non-Javanese members including the prominent Acehnese human rights lawyer Marzuki Darusman as attorney-general.

To make room for this multi-faceted assemblage he consigned some experienced technocrats, among them economists who had worked for

Suharto, to non-cabinet and non-ministerial positions. Rather daringly he appointed a prominent ethnic Chinese, Kwik Gian Gie, as his first coordinating minister for economic affairs. A stern opponent of corrupt practices, Kwik was also known as a critic of some of the policies that the IMF had insisted upon. He did not remain long in his post. An innovation was the absence of a minister of information, a welcomed sign that media freedom might indeed be there to stay.

The result was a new-look cabinet, younger on average than any of its predecessors, inexperienced but also untarnished.

Which of the many matters awaiting the new government's attention were to receive the highest priority? The necessary debate between foreign economic interest, symbolized by the IMF, and the domestic political requirements of the still immature Republic was about to resume. Suharto had simply suppressed it. The urgent tasks in Indonesian eyes were political rather than, as they had been during the Suharto years, principally economic: to reduce the political power of the military; to redress the scandal of nepotism and corruption within the Suharto circle; to expose and punish those responsible for the human rights offences of Suharto's military régime; to find a publicly acceptable institutional structure to hold the nation together. The humiliation of dependence on the giants of the global economy was also a significant public concern, but as a nationalistic, thus a political, not an economic, issue.

Indonesia's creditors and potential investors, hence the majority of overseas commentators, were interested in these political issues only insofar as they bore upon the economic outlook. There was an urgent short-term requirement for enhanced cash flow. Tax collection was chronically inefficient, evasion rife. Chinese investment was not returning. While exports were beginning to recover, foreign exchange revenues were not benefiting as in theory they should have done from the weakness of the rupiah; and although the price of oil rose dramatically in 2000, it now accounted for only about a quarter of export revenue. In a population of two hundred and sixteen million people, thirty-six million were out of work.

The ineluctable necessity of securing yet another IMF rescue plan forced the economy back to the top of President Wahid's agenda, further complicating his task of establishing a fresh style of government in his new civil society. His appreciation of the balance that had to be struck between domestic and external considerations came through strongly in his first major policy statement as president. Significantly he made it not in Jakarta but in Bali, an outer region.

Addressing the mood of the moment, he ruled out all thoughts of any other region winning independence in the wake of East Timor. But in the same breath he promised to deliver administrative decentralization throughout the Republic and offered autonomy to all regions. Subsequently, he exposed himself to the danger of seeming all things to all men when he appeared to concede that Aceh, like East Timor, might after all be permitted a referendum; but performed an adroit side-step by clarifying that, if so, it would be about the application of Islamic law in that province. In the Bali speech he struck another popular chord by saying he would work to reduce the power of the military.

Then, inevitably, he added the economic message: the macro-economic policies of the Habibie government – policies dictated by the IMF and World Bank – were to continue. 'Foreign investment', he stressed, 'are two very important words'. To underline the economic orientation he let it be known that his first major trip abroad would be to Japan and – by way of innovation – China. In fact he was shortly to embark on a round of foreign travel that also included western Europe and a bridge-repairing trip to a number of Muslim countries.

The new leader, soon to emerge as a master of pacing with an instinctive understanding of when to move fast and when slowly, lost no time in assuring the public that inquiries would be launched into the scandals that most offended them: massive infringements of human rights by the security forces and world-beating levels of nepotism and corruption under the disgraced Suharto. If in this way he won favour by facing reality, he was also confronted by the other reality of conflicting interests exposed by his new openness. A proper regard for human rights in regions inflamed by separatist or culture-based sentiments might well threaten the integrity of the Republic which he wanted to hold together. And *realpolitik* required him to collaborate with a military machine which he was determined to bridle.

In a confused and agitated political environment, style was an important factor. Superficially flippant, bumbling, sometimes self-contradictory, Wahid brought intellectual clarity second to none to the long-abused office of the president. An East Javanese born in 1940, he had spent nine years overseas receiving a broad tertiary education; in Egypt he studied Islam at Al-Azhar University, then went to Iraq to study philosophy before spending some years as a semi-itinerant scholar in the Netherlands and other parts of western Europe. Like Sukarno he became a polyglot and read and wrote on a wide range of social and cultural issues. In 1984 he assumed the chairmanship of the mass-membership Religious Scholars League (NU) with impregnable credentials. Not only were both his parents the offspring of famous NU leaders, his paternal grandfather was its founder. His father, along with Sukarno and others, was among the authors of the Jakarta Charter that had institutionalized the national philosophy of Pancasila; Wahid himself had never deviated from the spirit of inter-religious and inter-ethnic tolerance that it embodied.

By turns humorous, irascible, self-deprecating and mercurial – a true son of Java – Wahid showed an early talent for opportunism. After his assumption of the NU chairmanship he had demonstrated his political acumen by leading the league out of the portmanteau United Development Party (PPP) cobbled together in Suharto's time as a means of disempowering political Islam. The actual effect of that apparent abdication from politics was to empower the NU as a political force by releasing it from Suharto's restraints.

President Wahid came to office with health problems which wove their way into his leadership style and which he knew how to turn to his advantage. He had suffered a number of minor strokes, was already blind in one eye and nearly blind in the other; he had a propensity for dozing off on public occasions and in cabinet. While it contributed to the impression he sometimes gave of disconnectedness, in the larger context none of it seemed to matter, given his humanity, his vision, his tactical skills and his gift of clear thinking.

When, as was soon the case in the new climate of uninhibited politicking, the air thickened with accusations, innuendos and verbal missiles, Wahid's mood-swings and unpredictability made him a moving target that was hard to hit. Rivals were nonplussed and wrong-footed by his cheerful, innovatory acceptance of the implications of open debate. With it went a keen and analytical mind: and never more so than when he drew the distinction between the army as an institution which he respected and certain military figures who must be ready to answer for their past deeds.

When he spoke like that everyone knew his prime target was the man he described as a trusted friend, the ambitious General Wiranto, the former defence minister and head of the armed forces under whom the army's culminating atrocities had been perpetrated in East Timor. Wahid's unhesitating support of the commission set up to investigate the army's role in East Timor and his decision to withdraw the army from Aceh were seen and welcomed as acts designed to bring Wiranto and the armed forces under control. Simultaneously his attorney-general, Marzuki Darusman, instituted inquiries into accusations of embezzlement by General Suharto and his family and friends. Quite suddenly the leading figures of the old military dictatorship found themselves bathed in the harsh light of censure at the highest level.

On the human rights front the public clamour was for the redress of the whole catalogue of wrongs dating back to the anti-communist witch-hunt and slaughter of 1965, the suppression of Muslim activism symbolized by the 1984 Tanjung Priok massacre and countless other events in between. The president promised nothing less, but the case most recent in memory and the only one under active investigation was East Timor. The United Nations Commissioner for Human Rights, Mary Robinson, galvanized the matter by ordering an international commission of inquiry which presented its report at about the same time as that appointed by Indonesia's own Human Rights Commission.

The report of the Indonesian Commission to Investigate Violations in East Timor came out at the end of January 2000. Of thirty people recommended for further investigation seventeen were military and police officers, among them General Wiranto. It called on the National Human Rights Commission to look into all violations in East Timor going back to 1975 and, most importantly, urged the creation of a human rights court. In the light of this latter recommendation the UN Secretary-General, Kofi Annan, resisted pressure to ask the Security Council to set up an international tribunal to try human rights violators in East Timor, provided Indonesia set up its own court.

As on previous occasions, opinion divided over the question of international intervention. While some welcomed the prospect of impartial justice from judges immune from coercion, others felt the country should clean its own stables – none more than Wiranto, who stood to be summoned before an international tribunal.

The first step towards setting up a human rights court had been taken in some haste towards the end of the Habibie interregnum, and Wahid's government endorsed the proposal. After some months of wheeling and dealing around the issues of retrospectivity, double jeopardy and military impunity, a draft bill was sent to the House of Representatives (DPR). To deal with the problem that the accused in the few trials there had been were mainly junior officers, the bill adopted the principle of command responsibility as laid down in the 1998 Statute of the International Criminal

Court. This says that military commanders are criminally responsible for crimes committed knowingly under their command and control.

While the draft bill excluded retroactive powers in general, it proposed enabling the president to set up ad hoc courts, presided over when necessary by ad hoc judges, to try particular gross and extraordinary crimes. Here was the ultimate challenge to the impunity the military had enjoyed and used to the full in the thirty-two years of Suharto's dictatorship. With an uncharacteristic display of solidarity the armed forces fought back. At the August 2000 session of the Peoples Consultative Congress (MPR), they succeeded in securing a majority for a constitutional amendment declaring immunity from retrospective charges to be 'a basic human right not to be breached in any circumstances'.

There were, broadly speaking, two rival camps in the army. One, led by Suharto's son-in-law General Prabowo and known as the 'greens', adhered closely to Suharto and to the rapprochement he and Habibie had tried to nurture with political Islam. The other, known as the 'red-and-white' faction, was secular, nationalist, more alive to the inevitability of institutional change post-Suharto. Led by General Wiranto, the red-and-whites became the dominant faction.

It was never Wiranto's intention to reform the army by phasing it out of politics, but rather to unite it, establish its autonomy and redefine its political role in what was spoken of as the new paradigm. The rôle he had in mind was starkly revealed in a security bill he tried to steer through parliament shortly before the election which brought Wahid to power. If enacted it would, amongst a number of provisions designed to give the army powers of quasi-independent action, have authorised the president to declare a state of emergency in 'the situation where the State is endangered because of a rebel group and/or part of the country declaring its separation from the unitary State of the Republic'. Widespread public alarm forced parliament to abandon the bill's ratification, but only weeks were to pass before turbulence in some outer regions reached a level at which its provisions would have been relevant.

Many stalwarts of the old military régime, not just Wiranto, felt threatened by Wahid's accession. They turned on him almost at once. The Suharto set were anxious about the financial and economic assets they had diverted from the nation. Allied to them were the professional thugs of KOPASSUS, the military hit force once headed by Prabowo and now suffering the humiliation of exposure by an ever more confident press.

Conservatives within the armed forces were anxious to preserve their old dual function, many of them the beneficiaries of local trading arrangements and corrupt practices inherent in the system of regional territorial commands. A large part of the civilian bureaucracy also had perforce learned to profit from the military régime and was therefore either resistant to change or vulnerable to military manipulation.

United in their fear of Wahid's reformist deeds and utterances, the army factions resorted, like many before them, to their capacity to cause trouble in the outer regions. Within a matter of weeks there were eruptions of inter-ethnic violence in Lombok, Sulawesi and Maluku. In Aceh, where the inflammable mix of local Malay nationalism and Islamic zeal had never gone away, the East Timor outcome was feeding renewed violence between the army and the Free Aceh Movement (GAM).

The line in the Wiranto camp was that the army must have the prerogative of independent action if regional crises of this sort were not to pull the country apart. The situation in Aceh, they maintained, required the declaration of martial law. President Wahid not only said no, but humiliated them with multiple apologies for the atrocities committed there by the army in the past.

The army responded with open defiance. The armed forces spokesman, a Wiranto associate called Major-General Sudradjat, publicly impugned the President's right to meddle in military matters. As commander-in-chief of the armed forces under the constitution, Wahid could not afford to countenance such insubordination. He ordered Wiranto to dismiss Sudradjat, which – after an insolent delay of several weeks – he did.

Meanwhile there had been rumours of a military coup d'état brewing. To make sure President Wahid got wind of them Wiranto went to the palace and told him he was resisting it. But Wiranto himself was on perilous ground, the victim of heavy hints that, in view of his alleged complicity in the human rights outrage in East Timor, he should resign from the cabinet or at least step down pending legal process. Just as he had declined to resign from the army when given his civilian cabinet post, he now refused to resign from the cabinet until, in February 2000, the President dismissed him.

Several factors emboldened Wahid to take this step. One was his successful enlistment of support among true reformists within the army, rivals of Wiranto who, unlike him, were genuinely committed to de-politicizing the armed services. Prominent amongst the true reformers was

Lieutenant-General Agus Wirahadikusumah, whom Wahid later tried to install as army chief of staff; his failure against army opposition to pull that off was a significant setback.

More important, however, was the intervention in mid-January by Richard Holbrooke, the American Ambassador to the United Nations. Speaking at the height of the coup rumours and with inter-religious violence raging in Maluku, he said: 'What we are watching is a great drama, a struggle between the forces of democracy and reform and the forces of backward-looking corruption and militarism'. Attempts by the generals to challenge President Wahid's authority would do Indonesia 'immense, perhaps irreparable, damage'. A coup would be disastrous and turn Indonesia into a pariah state. 'It's not what any rational or progressive Indonesian would want. No-one in the world would want it except the few people who are trying to protect their own skin'.

The warning to the Indonesian armed forces and the implied support for President Wahid could not have been stated more clearly. The possibility of this egregious intervention in Indonesian affairs producing a nationalistic backlash was obvious; for Wahid, a patriot known for his resentment of the American influence that had installed and sustained Suharto in power, it must have been a bitter-sweet moment.

At about the same time as Holbrooke's *démarche*, President Wahid was asked in an interview by British Independent Television News to comment on violence that had flared in a number of outer regions. It was, he said, due to 'dark forces', and he spelt out what he meant: former generals who were trying to undermine the government and so-called fundamentalist Muslims. He did not explicitly link the two, but it was now becoming clear that they were indeed linked.

Ethnic and sectarian tensions are endemic in many of Indonesia's regions. During Suharto's military dictatorship they had been suppressed. In the middle of the Habibie interregnum, the pace and rhythm of unrest abruptly increased. There was further escalation in the weeks after Wahid came to power and it went on growing in step with mounting political confusion in Jakarta. By August 2000, Indonesians were killing one another and burning their homes and places of worship in eight of the country's twenty-seven provinces. Violence flared in places as widely separated as Bintan in the Riau Archipelago (an important centre of trade with nearby Singapore) and West Papua. But the epicentres were Aceh and Maluku (the Moluccas), each a special but different case.

Across the years, the idyllic and largely deceptive tapestry of Muslim-Christian tolerance in the islands of Maluku had been been crumbling under a combination of pressures: rising and shifting population, the influx of transmigrants from Flores and Java, the evolving economic status of the two communities as Muslim numbers grew and Christian dominance was attenuated.

Sensitive or even oppressive management could keep Maluku under control. Equally, however, it was a powder-keg all too easy to ignite. Here, as in many other parts of eastern Indonesia, the Suharto years had fostered no profound sense of Indonesian-ness. Incidents were readily provoked and exploited in a populace quick to anger. Within months the two religious communities were virtually at war. Security forces stood by as militia gangs armed with standard issue military weapons launched organized attacks on towns and villages, or even joined in – the police often siding with the Christians, army units with the Muslims.

Public opinion throughout the Republic tended to divide along confessional lines. In January, organizers had no difficulty attracting an estimated hundred thousand Muslims to a highly charged rally in Jakarta. With an expedition suggestive of military-style organization a new para-military group called Laskar Jihad (Fighters on God's Path) was mustered in Java. Meant to provide succour to its afflicted Muslim brethren in Maluku, it was soon receiving adequate funds and supplies to manufacture bombs, acquire standard issue ammunition and pay volunteers. Much of the money, it was said, came from a trust (*yayasan*) run by KOSTRAD. A military-style training camp went into operation near Bogor until the government sent police in to close it down. The first two thousand recruits arrived in Ambon in May and further shiploads followed until the government put a stop to them. Laskar Jihad became the frontline element in the Muslim confrontation with equally well-armed Christians. Thousands on both sides lost their lives, and before the end of the year well over a quarter of a million people were homeless and displaced.

Halmahera, the biggest island, and Ambon experienced the worst and most publicised confrontations, but many other Malukan islands were affected as well. At an early stage of the campaign – for that is what it was – similar troubles erupted in Sulawesi and Lombok, surprisingly in the latter because it had a longstanding reputation for good communal relations; now, spurred by outside provocateurs, the Muslim islanders turned on the traditional scapegoats, their ethnic Chinese Christian neighbours.

It came to the point in May where senior military commanders and politicians, including the vice-president, felt they could not travel safely in Halmahera and Ambon. It was precisely the sort of situation in which in earlier times the military would have demanded and got a declaration of martial law, citing the inadequacy of the civilian administration. This time their wishes were resisted.

Here in the homeland of shadow theatre no-one needed telling who was organizing the campaign. Their ability to get away with it unchallenged and unnamed was a measure of their weight in the balance of forces, and there had to be a turning point. It came towards the end of May. Minister of Defence Juwono Sudarsono said explicitly and publicly that the people financing Laskar Jihad and fomenting the violence in various parts of the country were supporters of the old military dictator, Suharto. As the minister spoke, General Suharto was savouring his first day under house arrest while investigations went ahead into allegations of corruption and embezzlement.

With every week that passed it became more obvious that the rhythm of the communal violence was in synchrony with the frantic efforts of the Suharto gang to disrupt investigations into their past activities. In one case in the middle of July, a fresh outbreak of fighting in and around Ambon coincided very conspicuously with questioning of Suharto by the attorney-general's office. In Jakarta the former ruling pseudo-party, Golkar, busied itself deriding Wahid's erratic and seemingly inconsequential behaviour in a relentless attempt to discredit him.

The president, on the other hand, displayed remarkable nonchalance; in mid-June he visited the USA evidentially confident that there was no danger of his absence being exploited to undermine his position. In Washington he asked President Clinton, perhaps relishing the irony of the request, to authorize the US-based Center for the Study of Corruption to help the Indonesian authorites in their pursuit of assets misappropriated by Suharto and his cohort. As Attorney-General Marzuki Darusman remarked at the time, since corruption had become an international issue it was appropriate that there should be international cooperation to combat it. It was a previously unremarked aspect of globalization.

Soon after the president's return home, instead of the martial law desired by some, he declared a state of civil emergency in Maluku, with the full support of the army chief of staff, General Tyasno Sudarto. The military and security forces engaged there thus remained answerable to the civil authority, and the provincial governor immediately ordered a curfew and restrictions of movement and assembly. Days later the President announced the separation of the police from the rest of the armed forces, reversing the merger Suharto had ordered in 1967.

The turbulence in Maluku and neighbouring Sulawesi had been getting worse for more than eighteen months. It was not by accident that the government's more determined stance towards the trouble-makers came just as international concern was becoming vocal. In Washington, in the wake of Wahid's visit, a State Department spokesman referred to what he described as the 'civil war' in Maluku. Pointing to the indisposition of the security forces to master the situation, he said: 'We are extremely concerned about the escalating violence and sectarian revenge going on in that community'.

The international pressure grew. The European Union added its voice. Then, doubtless encouraged by the USA (which in previous years and situations would have spurned the United Nations), the UN Secretary-General, Kofi Annan, called Wahid to ask what measures were being taken and to offer humanitarian help.

Reactions to UN intervention in any form were mixed. Smarting from the humiliation in East Timor, many – especially the military old guard – were against it; their fear was a strong card in Wahid's hand. The chairman of an inspection committee appointed to carry out a mediation exercise, Bambang Suharto, was totally opposed. 'I am confident that the declaration of a civil emergency is the correct political decision', he said. Inviting the United Nations could be dangerous and cause a lot of embarrassment for Indonesia.

With support from both the Indonesian Legal Aid and Human Rights Association and the National Human Rights Commission the government was more ambivalent. Even the armed forces chief, Admiral Widodo, acknowledging that some troops had taken sides in the Maluku conflict, recognised that a Security Council resolution to send peace-keepers in could become inevitable.

Part of the problem was that much of the clamour for UN intervention, in Maluku and abroad, was issuing from Christian lips. For this reason it was widely coupled with the East Timor affair as further evidence that Western powers were bent on tearing the country apart. Among measures to defuse such thinking the military commander in Maluku, a Christian, was replaced by a Hindu from Bali, Brigadier-General I Made Yasa. Some troops who had compromised themselves by partisanship were posted out of Maluku. Some sixteen thousand fresh troops were ferried in.

In the event, Kofi Annan's offer of a UN contribution to humanitarian aid was accepted and 'Resource Offices' were set up in the city of Ambon and on Ternate island. The spectre of foreign intervention had moved a step closer but was still at a certain distance.

Meanwhile, there was continued agitation from within the armed forces to declare martial law, with the suggestion that the civil emergency might be upgraded if tension did not ease, which obviously it would not so long as important military forces went on increasing it. When it came to the point that even the army chief of staff appeared to be supporting a progression from civil to military emergency, the home affairs minister had to make a very explicit public statement. Martial law, he pointed out, would be a relevant option only if the turmoil in Maluku amounted to a separatist movement. But the situation held; the turbulence in Sulawesi was not a separatist movement and agitators were not seeking to overthrow the government.

In this respect the situations being exploited in Maluku and Sulawesi were different from those in Aceh and West Papua. There, independence movements did want separation from the Republic and the 'dark forces' causing President Wahid so much trouble were able to use less devious – though equally disruptive – tactics to suppress them.

GENERALS ON TRIAL

Virtually the only thing Aceh and West Papua – at the western and eastern extremities respectively of Indonesia – have in common is the huge contribution they both make to government revenues, Aceh with its natural gas, West Papua with timber, copper and gold. Their loss would be a serious blow to the national economy. Aceh has long presented central government with its most intractable outer regions problem. It wants its independence and with its economic assets and strong ties across the Malacca Strait with mainland Malaysia could probably sustain it. And that is why the army has consistently and uncompromisingly resisted the guerrilla army of the Free Aceh Movement (GAM). For the last nine years of the Suharto régime the province was a designated military operations area. By dint of torture, intimidation, abduction, rape, perversion of the judicial system and thousands murdered the security forces managed to dampen but not extinguish the GAM campaign.

Under President Habibie, the military operations area status was revoked and an independent commission was set up to collect evidence about thousands of atrocities committed during the nine years it had been in force. On the strength of its report, the House of Representatives ordered three retired generals (Benny Murdani, Try Sutrisno and Feisal Tanjung) to submit to a three-hour televised cross-examination about brutalities carried out under their command. It was an event without precedent. General Wiranto, who was then commander-in-chief of the armed forces, felt obliged to go to the capital Banda Aceh and apologise for the atrocities perpetrated under his authority. However, it was not long before he was declaring that there should be no further investigations into military human rights offences in Aceh because they would open the floodgates for many other grievances stemming from Suharto's rule.

GAM re-emerged and began a campaign of revenge, triggering a new round of army repression. With hopes refreshed by Habibie's promises of reform, the Acehnese took their political demands onto the streets, organized a province-wide strike and in November, just after President Wahid's election, staged a million-strong rally in Banda Aceh, the provincial capital, demanding a referendum.

President Wahid tried almost immediately to improve the security climate in Aceh and find a political way forward. A senior civil servant was sent to talk to the field commander of GAM forces, Abdullah Syafi'ie, and was reportedly outraged by what he saw of the army's heavy-handed stance. Wahid, keen to bring security operations under civilian control, ordered the withdrawal of military forces. It was not done, but at the beginning of June 2000 a three-month 'humanitarian pause' was agreed between the Indonesian government on one side and GAM and the Aceh Liberation Movement on the other. Far short of a cease-fire – which would have been unattainable – the pause was brought about by a Swiss conflict resolution organization, the Henry Dunant Centre. Under its auspices proximity talks got under way in Geneva involving representatives of GAM's exiled leader, Tunku Hasan di Tiro, who had been living for years in Sweden.

It began to look as if there was common ground between the two parties. A key figure on the government side was Susilo Bambang Yudhoyono, the retired general to whom Wahid had by then entrusted the ministry of security and socio-political affairs and who was playing the role in cabinet that Wiranto had hoped to play. Notwithstanding a ferocious upsurge of fighting between the army and GAM which seemed set to impede progress at the political level, Yudhoyono offered further hope at the expiry of the initial three-month humanitarian pause by announcing its extension into 2001.

Both sides had to contend with inner divisions. While Wahid and Yudhoyono were repeatedly compromised by the continuing brutality of unruly army units in Aceh – the President spoke openly and censoriously of their human rights infringements – they were able to exploit different shades of opinion amongst the Acehnese. By entering, albeit guardedly, into proximity talks in Switzerland, the Free Aceh Movement (GAM) itself laid bare differences between those who were willing to contemplate compromise based on some kind of autonomy and those holding out for independence at any price. This helped to explain a mounting resort to violent intimidation by hardline GAM guerrilla elements as a means of keeping their own people in line; countless Acehnese were thus subjected to terror tactics from both sides.

Wahid, unlike the military régime he wanted to consign to history, offered a reasoned, non-violent exit from that predicament – meaningful autonomy within the Republic. With his deep background as a religious teacher, he was well-placed to open up the distinction between Islamic sentiment and Acehnese nationalism, while seeking to propitiate both tendencies. In the wake of another huge pro-referendum rally held in Banda Aceh in November 2000 (despite lethal army measures to prevent it) he genuflected to the nationalist tendency. It was up to the Acehnese people themselves, he said, to decide whether or not to hold a referendum; they had a representative regional assembly, and if it called for a referendum, then it should go ahead. Always the proviso was that Aceh must stay within Indonesia. Apart from that, as Yudhoyono made clear, the government was willing to accommodate the wishes of all parties, including the local application of Islamic law.

By now there was a sharp line between the Wahid–Yudhoyono approach and the military. The difference concerned not only policy but Wahid's determination to break the deeply ingrained habit of resorting automatically to extreme and mindless violence. Although in theory the police were now responsible for internal security, calling for army support at their discretion, the army had in fact intensified its activities to an unprecedented level; hundreds were being killed every month. The military were pressing for the declaration of an emergency similar to that in Maluku, but this was resisted in the hope that the talks in Geneva might progress during the increasingly fictitious humanitarian pause. GAM, however, responded to the heightened violence by cooling towards the Geneva process. The conflict in Aceh had become another factor in Jakarta politics, one more issue with which to embarrass the President.

The new more conciliatory approach, coupled with firmness on the independence issue, was also adopted in West Papua. It came only just in time, because there, as in Maluku and Aceh, the example of United Nations action in East Timor led to calls for similar intervention. The independence movement was beginning to get itself organized.

Not as well armed as GAM in Aceh, its activists often wielded nothing more advanced than bows and arrows and machetes. But they developed two highly symbolic forms of action. One was to terrorise settlers who had arrived over the years as sponsored transmigrants from Bali and Java, and more recently as refugees fleeing from trouble spots in Maluku and Sulawesi. The settler population, many of them government employees, had grown to some 700,000, compared with about a million indigenous people. Clashes in the capital Jayapura and the hill town of Wamena resulted in dozens of deaths and many more seriously injured. Frightened immigrants sought refuge in military and police barracks. Others chose to quit West Papua in sufficient numbers to keep two transports of the Indonesian air force busy for several months.

The trade-mark of the separatist agitation in West Papua, however, was the long-running joust between the activists and the Indonesian authorities over the Morning Star flag of the independence movement. Serious clashes erupted around the hoisting and tearing down of this flag, and were not prevented by Wahid's various attempts to handle the issue sensitively. No matter what the authorities suggested, such as allowing the Morning Star to fly next to the Indonesian flag or tolerating it as a cultural symbol in politically insignificant places, it was never enough for the Papuans.

Although Bambang Yudhoyono spoke liberally of avoiding violence and giving the Papuans broader scope politically, economically, socially, culturally, legally and in the area of government administration, and the police adopted what they called a 'compassionate approach', security forces remained proactive in fighting the independence movement. They went on shooting to kill in situations where more restrained measures would have served their purposes.

In September 2000, Jayapura experienced a week of clashes between the police and KOPASSUS special forces. At one stage, after police had confiscated military-issue hand grenades and explosives from the pro-independence Papua Task Force, the Indonesian army commander in Jayapura warned that the only way to prevent the territory becoming 'a second Ambon' was to prevent provocateurs from infiltrating pro-independence groups. It may have been part of a ploy to split the Papuans, but some saw it as a justified warning against the intrigues of the old Suharto gang in Jakarta.

The provocateurs' motivation could only have been to discredit Wahid's demilitarising régime, since the government was no less resolute in its determination to prevent a Papuan breakaway than they were – a fact driven home by the announcement in November that the air force was to develop a big new base on Biak island off the north coast of West Papua. Supporting radar installations were planned in West Timor and the Papuan towns of Sorong, Jayapura and Merauke. Biak had been an important American air base during the Second World War and would doubtless be of interest to the USA in the twenty-first century.

DECENTRALIZATION, GLOBALIZATION

It is possible to interpret the wave of regional unrest unleashed by East Timor's secession from the Indonesian Republic as the legacy of repression under Suharto. The fundamental difficulties of governing such a diverse and fragmented nation had, however, been recognised by the Dutch and by President Sukarno long before Suharto added to them with his misrule. Presidents Habibie and Wahid both understood that cosmetic expedients and more emollient government conduct – necessary though those were – would not overcome fundamental problems. Fundamental solutions were required, both at state level and at the level of the 'state within the state' – the army.

Wahid's government inherited a body of thinking and devolutionary legislation that had grown largely out of research done by the Association of Indonesian Muslim Intellectuals (ICMI) convened under Habibie's chairmanship in 1990. In 1993 Habibie had induced Suharto to charge him with the day-to-day running of a new development council for Eastern Indonesia, thereby gaining a powerful new constituency. It reflected the truth that Java and Sumatra to the west were economically privileged in comparison with the rest of the country; eastern (including northern) Indonesia won itself the nickname Iramasuka (an acronym composed from the initials of Irian, Maluku, Sulawesi and Kalimantan). With Suharto's indulgence Habibie was allowed to conduct a number of experiments in the devolution of provincial powers and the allocation of additional funds to selected districts and towns. In the climate generated by Habibie's programme the voice of eastern Indonesia began to be heard rather more often in Jakarta. Decentralization was back on the agenda.

It became a certainty in the middle of Habibie's troubled presidency with the enactment in April 1999 of two epoch-making laws: one on the administration of regional government and the other, its necessary corollary, on the balancing of budgets between the central and regional governments. President Wahid's government adopted them and, in spite of serious problems arising from the haste with which they had been put together, accepted that they should come into operation in April 2001.

The problems were of two kinds, practical and theoretical. Time was short. The merest suggestion of delay in making ready for implementation incurred strident criticism. Yet more than a hundred consequential laws and regulations were required, and it had to be doubted whether appropriate human resources would be available to handle the new administrative and financial responsibilities of the devolved system. Anxious to push through the reforming legislation in time to impact on the 1999 presidential election Habibie and his Golkar administration had imposed their own thinking without consulting wider opinion as to where the devolutionary process should lead. For instance, was federalism the ultimate aim? And if so, federalism soon or in the longer term?

Whichever, a significant change in the balance of power was on its way. In the pre-existing system there were two streams of regional government, somewhat analogous to those in France. One consisted of a hierarchy of local councils, each accountable to the one above via the province and so to the central government. The other, similar to the French prefectural network, consisted of a descending hierarchy of local agents of central government departments. Under the old dispensation this second stream, which penetrated into the grassroots, was the more powerful.

The new law reduced the status of the prefectural stream and limited its remit to provincial level. The other stream, comprising a variety of *daerahs* down to village level, was freed of the hierarchical restraints that had subjected it to central government. Heads of regional governments (unlike provincial governors) were now to be responsible only to elected regional assemblies. No longer was the province to be the key administrative unit in regional government. Power was being devolved downward; thenceforth the *daerah* would be able to communicate directly with central government and, crucially, control the funds directed to it via the centre.

Set beside the dismantling of the army's territorial command structure, assuming that could be achieved, decentralization spelt basic change and – in disempowered quarters – major misgivings.

The success of decentralization depends on the erosion of the army's territorial command structure which is in effect the local government system with which General Suharto ruled the country for three decades. Wahid was determined to do away with it. That was what lay behind his unsuccessful attempt in October 2000 to have Lt-Gen Agus Wirahadikusumah, a radical reformer opposed to military meddling in national politics, made army chief-of-staff. Not just a setback for Wahid, his failure gave strength to army conservatives who, far from accepting reform of the territorial system, took steps after the East Timor fiasco to reinforce it.

The territorial command structure was the institutional foundation of the army's wealth and of many personal fortunes accumulated by military individuals. Were it to survive unchanged into the age of decentralization there would be a great danger of the reformed administrative system being either frustrated or appropriated by the military all over again.

Timing is therefore of the essence, concerting the many factors that bear on the decentralization project. Especially in the outer regions many want to hurry on; others to advance by slow stages. 'We cannot change overnight the practice, the mindset, the belief and behaviour of the military for almost thirtyfive years,' Bambang Yudhoyono warned, the minister charged with straddling the military–civilian divide in the cabinet. 'If decentralization goes unchecked, it may create political and administrative chaos. In the wake of reform many people have a say; they want to regulate themselves and not necessarily respect and obey the rules set up by the central government.'[1]

Measured next to the profundity, scope and delicacy of the reform being attempted, the politicking which filled the Jakarta air in the first eighteen months of Wahid's presidency achieved depths of triviality comparable with the party squabbling that led to President Sukarno stifling Western-style parliamentary democracy in 1959. A people educated by Suharto to expect nothing of their make-believe institutions were unaccustomed to the nuances and possibilities of participatory political discourse. To the young, to sections of the press, to the troublemakers of Suharto's Cendana gang, to many active politicians it seemed natural to resort without preliminaries to the blunt instruments of street protest and the invocation of extreme measures. Tempers were inflamed by the continuing aftermath of the Asian economic crisis. There was impatience over the apparent ease with which the Suharto circle and many military figures were impeding the processes that would bring them to justice. The president and the attorney-general both did their best to move things on.

In this new world of accountability and supposed transparency Wahid himself made mistakes. Two affairs in particular served him ill: the Bulog scandal and his unexplained dismissal of two cabinet ministers.

Bulog is the nation's food-logistics agency, handling huge sums of money. It was alleged that a friend of Wahid's who happened also to be his masseur tried to induce a senior Bulog official to embezzle the equivalent of four million US dollars from the pension fund; in return, it was said, the president would appoint the official as chairman of Bulog. In fact someone else got the job. Wahid did later confirm that he had considered going to Bulog for money which he wanted for relief and charitable purposes in Aceh and some other places. He had not done so, he explained, because the Sultan of Brunei had made him a personal gift of two million US dollars instead. That money had been distributed, according to a person described as Wahid's financial adviser, but there was difficulty identifying anyone who had received it. Parliamentarians flexed their freshly primed muscles and called for explanation.

They wanted him likewise to explain why in April he suddenly and unaccountably dismissed two members of his cabinet. Beyond saying that his decision had been political (thus quashing speculation about corruption), he initially refused. One of them, Laksamana Sukardi, who had been minister for state enterprise, was one of Vice-President Megawati's closest advisers; inevitably his removal sparked rumours of manoeuvring between her and the President. Perhaps more relevantly, he was an open exponent of current American thinking; he was more inclined than Wahid to follow where the IMF led, favoured an American-style inland revenue system and federal reserve and preached the American sermon on institutional reform. Shortly after his dismissal the USA, in the person of Secretary of State Madeleine Albright, conveyed its displeasure by informing Foreign Minister Alwi Shihab of American concern about the palace scandals.

Subsequently, the USA's barely concealed involvement in Jakarta politics would turn into a major embarrassment; but Wahid's prior worries were with the parliamentary bodies which he wanted to function, but also tried to elude.

There was an argument between the lower house (DPR) and the President about their respective powers. Opinion divided along party lines: the old Islamic National Development Party (PPP) and the new-look Golkar led the assault on the President, confronting Megawati's PDI-P and the pro-Wahid National Awakening Party (PKB).

In July Wahid bent a little by consenting to address the DPR. He used the occasion not to answer the questions of the moment but to deliver an ill-received polemic on the new constitutionality. The great need, he stressed, was an atmosphere of mutual respect between the various institutions. As he departed, one member uttered the only half-conciliatory warning that if he wished to remain president all he had to do was apologize. And he did apologize. In answer to questions he agreed to explain in closed session why he had sacked the two ministers and acknowledged the DPR's right to enquire. It was a significant procedural point.

The pressure on the president went on growing, however, with a suggestion that the annual assembly of the MPR in August should be turned into a special session with authority to impeach him. There were signs of public unrest; the Islamic movements led by Amien Rais and Wahid both organized mass rallies. Then, a week before the MPR assembly was to convene, in a move redolent of the political chaos of the 1960s Java's premier establishment figure stepped in. Sultan Hamengku Buwono of Yogyakarta (son of the Sultan who had served as minister of defence in Suharto's early days) invited Wahid, Megawati, Amien Rais (the MPR Speaker) and Akbar Tandjung (the DPR Speaker) to his palace.

The salient consequence of their seventy-minute gathering was a declaration that President Wahid would not be impeached. The 'Yogyakarta Document' issued to the public promised: 'In this transitional era, in which we are moving towards a democratic society, there will be changes to community values and the social order which require holistic solutions . . . To generate a spirit of cooperation, all sections of the nation must safeguard the territorial integrity of the Unitary Republic of Indonesia and the understanding that difference is the essence of achieving progress. . . . To uphold the law, state legal instruments must be empowered to ensure that cases involving corruption, collusion and nepotism are resolved as quickly as possible'.

Even Amien Rais, Wahid's principal partner-cum-rival in the Islamic Central Axis that enabled him to win the presidency, had recognized the grave implications of the mounting political crisis. As for Vice-President Megawati, leader of the biggest party in parliament, it was noted that she left the meeting early to visit her father's grave – like him, a virtuoso of the symbolic gesture.

Relieved of the threat of impeachment, President Wahid was able to present to the August session of the People's Consultative Congress (MPR) a balanced and penetrating annual report. He spoke of a nation in transition where symptoms of disintegration stemming from the centralism of the Suharto years were being compounded by an élitist power struggle. 'The meaning of democracy has been reduced to mere demonstrations; the supremacy of law reduced to the level of people's justice.' The development of national institutions was 'just at the stage of reforming the executive, legislature and judiciary'.

Acknowledging the MPR's own committee work on constitutional reform – and clearly with the army in mind – he said: 'All mechanisms of state, whatever their function and level, should be bound to and adhere to the systems, ethics and regulations developed through democratic norms and the values of the constitution'.

He called for debate to find a meeting point between regional aspirations and the central government's duty to defend the sovereignty of the unitary Republic.

Crucially, he related Indonesia's internal political issues to its global reputation, hence to its economic outlook. Without actually using the word 'globalization', he said: 'The establishment of foreign economic relations allows us to maximize the potential that these countries have to offer to improve our knowledge of financial, management and technological matters'. Pointing out that the crisis management and economic recovery programmes undertaken by the previous government by calling in the International Monetary Fund had necessitated basic changes in the public policy process, he stressed that they would require high levels of discipline and commitment.

Wahid survived the August MPR session with both his strengths and his weaknesses more clearly displayed. He had judged it prudent early in the speech to apologize for the presumptuous fashion in which he had dismissed some questioning and criticism. And now he bowed to the limitations imposed by his parlous health and near-blindness which made it difficult for him to cope with the day-to-day tasks of his office. Henceforth he would focus more on foreign affairs and consign many elements of the daily round to Vice-President Megawati; she would arrange the government agenda, chair cabinet meetings and monitor policy implementation. He was at pains to clarify that it was a working arrangement, not a transfer of power or authority.

Simultaneously, as if to emphasize his continuing command of affairs, he carried out a substantial cabinet reshuffle seen as strengthening his own party faction and weakening Megawati's. As well as Yudhoyono in his role of coordinating minister for political, social and security affairs, Wahid appointed another to oversee economic affairs. Into that post he placed a former head of Bulog, Rizal Ramli, a previously outspoken critic of IMF policies who now set about proclaiming that he had nothing against the IMF as such.

A structure was emerging in which, even if Wahid's personal scope was more circumscribed, he held the trump-card of democratic legitimacy and was therefore the necessary kingpin. Meanwhile, notwithstanding his precautions to limit her powers, Megawati was cultivating her position. While her alignment with Yudhoyono covered her need for a reformist military affiliation, she was fostering dialogue with a Golkar that was striving to distance itself from its history and earn credentials as a genuine political party.

ENTER THE USA ...

Richard Holbrooke's implicit warning in January 2000 against anyone contemplating a coup d'état had exposed American anxiety about the potentially destabilizing events afflicting the Wahid government. A new ambassador, Robert S. Gelbard, took up his post a few weeks after Holbrooke's intervention and quickly busied himself giving public currency to the concerns of Secretary of State Madeleine Albright. The IMF's new managing director, Horst Koehler, visited Jakarta. They all spoke with one voice: the rupiah was tumbling not because of the economy, but because of political uncertainties. It was imperative that the government regain control in Maluku and restrain the troublemakers. It was insinuated that President Wahid could help by curbing his tendency to throw out impromptu and sometimes inconsistent remarks in public; popular though his informality was, the mixed signals were unsettling.

At the end of May, to the jubilation of hundreds of street demonstrators, the ex-dictator Suharto was placed under house arrest. The Suharto gang and anti-reform military circles promoted disturbances wherever they could. The security situation in all the troubled outer regions worsened. Following Wahid's survival of the August MPR session there was a rash of bomb blasts in Jakarta; targets included the Malaysian and Philippine embassies, the attorney-general's department and the Jakarta stock exchange. In Indonesian West Timor they intensified their action to undermine the infant independent state in the east, arming and organizing militia groups both to terrorise the refugee camps in West Timor and to infiltrate and subvert East Timor.

Since his appointment in February Ambassador Gelbard had earned a reputation for plain speaking about Indonesia's tribulations, remarking notably that the army had lost control in places like Aceh and Maluku. As President Wahid prepared for a visit to Washington early in September, Indonesia's easily provoked xenophobia erupted in the DPR watchdog committee on foreign affairs with a demand that the ambassador be summoned to explain his various expressions of opinion. It came to nothing but was prelude to another bad month for Wahid. In West Timor, a thousand so-called militia men attacked a post at Atambua being used by the UN High Commission for Refugees, killing three members of its international staff. Indonesia was severely humiliated. The matter came to the UN Security Council and the government found itself trying yet again to fend off a UN investigation. In Jakarta crowds demonstrated outside the UNHCR heaquarters.

Into this intricate yet, as many saw it, intelligible mosaic now stepped the American Defense Secretary, William Cohen. In the course of a visit to Jakarta he spelled out American requirements at greater length. Wahid's government must control the military and disband the militias in West Timor. Only when it was satisfied that the army was under civilian rule would the USA allow military-to-military relations. Otherwise sanctions would be applied against Indonesia and these would include an embargo on the sale of arms. Americans had uttered similar threats many times during the Sukarno and Suharto years only to relent soon after. The difference however was that they were now saying them to strengthen the president, not to coerce him.

Despite significant public annoyance over this further evidence of American meddling in Indonesia's internal affairs, Wahid acted robustly. As the Cohen visit ended he ordered the disarming of Suharto's personal armed guard and summarily replaced the National Police Chief. Several dozen people believed to have connections with the Suharto gang were arrested.

It is not difficult to activate anti-American feeling in Indonesia. The USA's role in bringing General Suharto to power and supporting him over three decades, its dominant influence in enforcing IMF prescriptions and now its open partisanship in Timor and in Jakarta politics, all could be fed to a public inclined towards hostility. Confident they had Wahid on the run, his tormentors added anti-American sentiment to their armoury.

The US Embassy reported a series of threats against Ambassador Gelbard and his staff. At the end of October 2000 the Jakarta embassy was closed and US citizens were advised of the danger of violence against them if they visited the country. Further justification for this action came from the Central Javanese city of Solo, where a group of Islamic militias similar to those involved in Maluku made a trawl of the more expensive hotels, pressing American guests to leave and instructing staff not to accept them. The Speakers of the two houses of parliament complained of American overreaction but nevertheless joined the government in issuing reassurances of their desire for good relations. Yudhoyono spoke of supply problems caused by the arms embargo. The police took further vigorous action and within a week the embassy doors reopened.

### . . . AND THE IMF

American social and political engineering in Indonesia was nothing new. Its practitioners had enjoyed open season since the late 1950s. The means were usually devious and often clandestine, but the aim was clear: to keep control of the country's immense raw material resources and dominate its markets for consumer goods, heavy industrial equipment (including armaments) and investment. Indonesia was to be held in the open global market, and its assets denied to the competing world of socialistic control economies.

The USA did not stop its political manipulation, but towards the end of the Suharto régime its activities were imbued with a revised appreciation of the political conditions that would best promote the stability upon which its economic interests depend. Unconditional insistence on fiscal discipline at any political cost began to make room for parliamentary democracy. The new look revealed itself in the attitudes of the International Monetary Fund (IMF).

Throughout the second half of the twentieth century American and IMF policies coincided on the major issue: free and open trade between market economies. In Indonesia for most of that time it was seen as an instrument of American financial dictation. Suharto's Berkeley mafiosi grabbed for IMF funding like a life-raft at times of crisis, eagerly subscribing to rigorous letters of intent and blaming it for the conseqent privations inflicted on the Indonesian public, then relapsing into routine delinquency when the pressure was off. In a nation temperamentally disposed towards state enterprise and what Sukarno called 'guided economy', nationalists at every level resented the IMF as the right hand of foreign capitalism. It was blamed for inequalities caused by the fostering of large-scale rather than small and medium enterprise and for the uncertainties caused by tidal flows of capital across national borders. 'The scapegoat of first resort', its former managing director, Michel Camdessus, called it.

In fact the IMF was not wholly to blame for its unpopular image. Camdessus's last speech as managing director revealed a philosophy deeply sympathetic with the victims of Suharto's misrule and particularly critical of excessive arms sales into sensitive regions. Speaking in Bangkok to the UN Conference on Trade and Development (UNCTAD) in February 2000, he represented the assault on poverty as the proper object of our time, acknowledging that: 'The market can have major failures . . . growth alone is not enough and can even be destructive of environment or precious social goods and cultural values. Only the pursuit of high quality growth is worth the effort'.

High quality growth he defined as growth that has the human person at its centre, is accompanied by adequate investment, particularly in education and health, to take full advantage of the tremendous leverage of human capital; growth based on a continuous effort for more equity, poverty-alleviation and empowerment of poor people. These were not aspects of IMF thinking that had come to the attention of most Indonesian people. Neither would they have realized that the man photographed standing over Suharto in 1998 had been arguing their case for them: that participating democracy can maximise the effectiveness of sound economies, that transparency, openness and accountability are basic requirements for economic success.

Camdessus's parting message after heading the IMF for thirteen years was that globalization offered a major opportunity not yet appreciated because it had not demonstrated its concern for poverty, which is the great concern of our time. Hence in his unavoidable and not altogether popular pursuit of a new IMF package President Wahid, himself inclined to economic nationalism, was presented with conditions which were broadly in line with his own thinking. The confrontational atmosphere that had clouded Suharto's last encounters with the IMF was a thing of the past.

There were other favourable factors. The price of oil went up. Ironically, the take-over of major banks by IBRA, the restructuring agency created at the IMF's behest to build a new banking sector, had in effect left Indonesia with a nationalized banking industry. Not an outcome relished in IMF circles, nevertheless it gave the government some important strategic options. For instance, there was some Islamic pressure for permanent retention of bank assets formerly controlled by ethnic Chinese. An alternative view, espoused by Vice-President Megawati's party, favoured the resourcing of cooperatives within which the previously neglected small business sector might flourish. Such policies could be influenced through IBRA.

On the darker side of the economic picture facing the government was the continuing weakness of the rupiah, attributed to the lack of confidence generated in the foreign exchange market by the political uncertainties surrounding the president. Wahid's response was to hurry his ministers on all the more vigorously in negotiating the terms of a new letter of intent.

With overseas debt in excess of US$130 billion (US$11 billion of it attributable to the Bank of Indonesia) the highest short-term priority was restructuring the banking sector. That alone was a complex task with profound implications for the corrupted legal and judicial systems left behind by Suharto. The IMF resisted pressure from some Australian and other quarters to rush through a financial aid package and delay talk about deeper reforms until later. There would be no question of another large injection of first-aid funds. It called for an overhaul of tax collection. In tune with Wahid's and Megawati's own predilections, the IMF pledged support for a new emphasis on the promotion of small businesses and agriculture. It wanted evidence that resources hitherto concentrated on the greater Jakarta area would be distributed more evenly around the outer regions, and that the regions would be empowered to interact with one another free of stifling interference from the centre.

The new letter of intent was signed in September 2000. Announcing it, the coordinating minister for the economy, Rizal Ramli, pointedly noted that 'in this new agreement the government is increasing its commitment to the development of small and medium business'. The IMF also withdrew its initial opposition to a government decision to ban the export of uncut logs – a trade based on illicit logging by local entrepreneurs. The relationship was looking healthier and more even-handed.

DECENTRALIZATION YEAR

2001 therefore dawned with a high degree of harmony between the IMF and the government, the one urging profound reforms which the other was more than ready to prosecute. There were two basic laws: one on balanced budgets between the centre and the regions which came into force in

January 2001, the other on regional administration which followed in April. Now it was time to turn and face the problems the process would undoubtedly encounter.

On the practical plane there are doubts about Indonesia's ability to man and implement the decentralized régime in its early years. Neither the education system nor the restricted middle class are yielding enough local candidates for the larger bureacracy that will have to develop at sub-provincial levels. It is likely therefore that the gap will be filled from two politically controversial sources: Jakarta's inflated central bureaucracy and the armed forces. A further injection of non-local, mainly Javanese, administrators into non-Javanese regions risks creating the opposite impression to the one intended.

So too with the army, for three decades the organization used to impose Suharto's harsh and exploitative central authority. Ex-army personnel with authoritarian attitudes and corruptive habits may for several years yet be the only plentiful source of manpower with relevant qualifications and experience. And there is the larger question of how successful Indonesia's democratically legitimized civilian government will be in breaking down the army territorial structure. If that is not accomplished, it is possible that military organization will compete with, undermine or subvert the decentralized civilian administration for a long time.

Decentralization has in any case been devised so as not to detract too radically from the authority of central government. The real devolution of powers is not from the centre to the provinces but from the provinces to lower levels. Hence, especially where the allocation of financial resources and the implementation of central policies are concerned, there will be substantially increased intercourse between Jakarta and the sub-provincial layers of government. To that extent, while decentralization is meant to allay many of the grievances that have fed separatist movements, the reorganization disempowers the provinces which might otherwise be the most viable autonomous or independent entities. The mistrust of federalism engendered in the 1940s and 1950s by Dutch and American meddling is still pervasive.

A problem that could cause trouble in the future and is already creating tension has been identified in those regions which are home to disproportionately large and nationally important industrial enterprises. Characteristic are the Freeport gold and copper mine in West Papua, the Kelian gold mine in East Kalimantan, the coal extraction plants in West Kalimantan and the Newmont gold mine in Sulawesi, not to speak of petroleum extraction wherever it occurs. Contracts with big American,

British and other international corporations are involved in virtually every case. For an older generation in Indonesia the issue strikes echoes of the early 1960s when some American corporations helped the Suharto cause by soft-pedalling their obligations towards their contractual partners in the state sector and channelling resources towards the anti-Sukarno conspirators.

Local authorities strengthened by decentralization now want more say in controlling such operations and a bigger share of the revenues they generate. Companies like Britain's Rio Tinto take their stand on the inviolability of contracts. The compromise decided upon by the Indonesian government is that the contractual and fiscal regulation of all general mining is devolved to the regions, but the extraction of strategic minerals such as petroleum and uranium remain under central control.

Another potential pitfall is that decentralization will lead to even worse warlordism and landlordism than in the past, especially in weakly or venally governed areas. Military and other entrepreneurs who developed profitable independent enterprises in their local fiefdoms under Suharto – and indeed the armed services themselves, since they need the money – must be expected to seek the business advantages of decentralization. Far from evaporating, the opportunities for corruption and cronyism may well proliferate during the probably long running-in period of the new system.

Optimists repose their hopes of limiting these abuses in improved administrative transparency and an overhaul of the law and judiciary. Both indeed began once Suharto was out of the way. Notwithstanding his irritable feuding with parliament, President Wahid showed from the beginning his readiness to respond to public demand for information about previously hidden matters. In an age of accelerating and uncontrollable access to information through electronic media, he would have been imprudent to act otherwise.

Law reform was also put quickly in hand at both statutory and constitutional levels. Abusive laws which constrained the right to peaceful political activity were repealed. Given the political will, that was easy. More complicated and likely to take years to complete are the legal changes connected with bank reconstruction and the many implications of decentralization itself.

Even more frustrating than the law during the Suharto dictatorship was the judiciary. Judges were appointed administratively which meant, in fact, by Suharto. Not only were they notoriously lacking in independence, frequently they were corrupt. A large proportion of them were ex-military. They did what they were told.

The most basic need was a constitutional amendment to establish the independence of the judiciary, but timing was an issue. If it were to be done while all the long-serving judges were still in place an independent judiciary might not produce the cleansed justice system that was wanted. Within months of Wahid's assumption of the presidency, therefore, all the chief justices and many of the junior justices in Jakarta's five district courts were replaced. The majority of the new justices – who would deal with nearly all the country's corruption cases – were under forty years of age. At the same time, the government began an overhaul of the Supreme Court, retiring the chief justice and almost half of its forty-one associate justices. A similar purge was carried out in other parts of the country. To check that courts were performing correctly an ombudsman commission was set up under the direction of a former civilian attorney-general.

No matter what safeguards and precautions are applied internally to keep localized economic activity under Indonesian fiscal regulation, the temptations of unregulated inter-island trading will remain. So the real economy of the decentralized Republic, as in the past, will inevitably be influenced to some degree by the behaviour of other countries. Malaysia and Singapore, with their strong interest in stable commercial relations with Indonesia, have been relatively cooperative; it is reasonable to suppose that will continue, though no-one can be sure what might happen if, for example, a powerful local fiefdom somewhere in Sumatra took a private initiative to trade smuggled produce with a corrupt politician on the other side of the Malacca Strait. In this context the Association of Southeast Asian Nations (ASEAN) goes on growing in importance; if the project, already under active discussion at the end of 2000, for an ASEAN free trade area came to fruition, the complexion of inter-island trading would change and with it the problem of maverick fiefdoms in a decentralized Indonesia.

RIGHTS AND RESPONSIBILITIES

As the new millennium began, everything about the decentralization project and the many other reforms inextricably linked with it struck at the interests of the old ruling establishment. This was one but not the only factor behind the continuing political harassment of President Wahid. The rearguard was not all of a piece. Part of it was made up of military and bureaucratic elements which, in addition to their threatened economic and power interests, could argue a plausible, even principled case against the government's programme; among their concerns was a not wholly unreasonable anxiety about the possible consequences of strengthening the regions and weakening the centre.

More troublesome and more malevolent was the Suharto rump, motivated primarily by greed and naked fear that the law would catch up with legal and human rights outrages committed under their aegis. Allusions to these 'dark forces' as Wahid called them became more and more explicit until the defence minister, Juwono Sudarsono, declared openly – what most people knew – that Suharto followers were behind much of the violent unrest in the capital, Maluku and other parts of the country.

But those rearguard elements were not the only source of President Wahid's ongoing tribulations. Parliamentarians and party leaders were savouring the novelty of having a material role in national life. Their commissions (the equivalent of British parliamentary and American congressional committees) started revising the constitution and shaping the way ahead. They could impeach and depose the President if they so resolved. Unresolved were the realistic parameters of everyday politics, how best to use their new authority. In the bright new light of political freedom the exercise of extreme powers which might lie dormant for years in a settled political environment was being considered within months.

President Wahid with his impulsive and sometimes unyielding pronouncements went on presenting them with opportunities. As he travelled the globe proclaiming Indonesia's virtues as an investment area and consolidating brotherhood with other Muslim countries, at home the Brunei–Bulog affair was kept alive and there was discontent about the measured pace of legal action against General Suharto and his family.

The former dictator was brought to trial in September 2000, charged with embezzling more than US$500 million from charities (*yayasan*) he controlled. Compared with the vast misuse of funds for which he is widely thought to have been responsible, it was a piffling sum. There was nationwide regret that his alleged corruption appeared to be taking precedence over the grave human rights offences held against him. Bringing the case thus far was nevertheless a considerable achievement on the part of the attorney-general Marzuki Darusman and the state prosecutors. Every conceivable ploy had been used to impede its progress. One of the most obscene was a move by lawyers to appeal to the UN Human Rights Commission on the grounds that the attorney-general had infringed Suharto's 'rights as a human being' by subjecting him to questioning when he was medically unfit!

Obstruction did not end with the opening of the trial. Independent doctors testified that, having apparently suffered three minor strokes, Suharto was not in a condition to face further questioning. A judge ruled that the trial could continue without him. The Court of Appeal then set aside an attempt to overturn that ruling. As President Wahid became increasingly impatient, the attorney-general opened a new front by suggesting that Suharto's medical care should be taken out of the hands of private doctors and entrusted to the national health service.

Meanwhile, some of the Suharto nearest and dearest were also subject to legal process. A government source leaked the information that one of his sons was in a massive money-counterfeiting racket and one of his daughters trading narcotics. His former money manager and golfing partner Bob Hasan was sent to gaol for embezzlement. His younger son Tommy was brought to trial and sentenced to eighteen months' imprisonment for a land scam that cost the state ten million dollars whereupon, despite a court order forbidding him to travel, he absconded.

Because of the tactics the Suharto gang was evidently prepared to use in order to evade justice there was a judgment to be made on how to balance just revenge against the delinquents and criminals of a bygone régime with the welfare of present-day survivors and of the state itself. One minister, Muhammad Mahfud, took advantage of his inauguration as a professor of law at the Islamic University of Indonesia to float the idea of a peace and reconciliation process like South Africa's: facts exposed, misgotten gains returned – but no-one sent for trial. Yudhoyono, the voice of army reformism in the cabinet, let it be known that Wahid had asked him to broach the possibility of a conscience payment by Suharto, but the notion was flatly dismissed by one of Suharto's army of lawyers.

The president's suspected willingness to temporize only compounded his public image problem. Dissatisfaction with his leadership, questions about his own integrity and the unending bickering with the DPR gnawed at the very foundations of the coalition that won him the presidency. The Central Axis of major Muslim parties began to fall asunder, and a nine-member Islamic Parties Forum urged the DPR to send a memorandum of grievances to the upper house, the MPR.

On the secular side, Vice-President Megawati found it necessary to deny working for Wahid's overthrow, though she said she had been urged to do so. Like her father four decades before, she was becoming the one everybody wanted to have on-side – the army, the reformed and wealthy

Golkar and even some Muslim leaders who, only twelve months earlier, had balked at the thought of a woman president. She warned that replacing the president mid-term would set a bad precedent unless based on very solid constitutional grounds. An emerging cross-party group in the DPR, known as the 'cowboys', thought it had found a constitutional issue with the President's alleged failure to share power with Vice-President Megawati as required by the MPR at its August session. On the basis of this and a long list of other 'violations and shortcomings', the cowboys sought to activate procedures which could lead to impeachment.

So, at the end of President Wahid's first year in office, notwithstanding the breadth and profundity of his government's reform programme and all he had done to have light thrown on the evils of the Suharto era, his position was seriously threatened. His ability to sustain a full five-year term came into question. What if it were cut short?

What would follow was more important than who. Constitutionally it is the vice-president who succeeds to the presidency in a mid-term change. Other presidential aspirants – Bambang Yudhoyono, Amien Rais, Wirahadikusumah were all being mentioned – would have to await the quinquennial presidential election. The forces likely to be let loose in such a crisis could, however, be devastating. Opportunists would re-emerge. Major power groups – Islam, the army, the old guard, Golkar – would run for the barricades. The unfinished coalescence of all these forces into the reconciled political society that Indonesia needs in a globalized environment could be set back. The chaotic politicking that once led President Sukarno to replace parliamentary democracy with guided democracy could return to dog a new generation of Indonesians.

BACK TO THE BEGINNING

Indonesia is a land of repeating patterns. Its daunting geography and the cultural infiltrations that have shaped its history and challenged it across the centuries challenge it no less today. Ethnic and religious diversity is still a problem for a temperamentally impatient people. What the late President Sukarno wanted to mould into a united society at peace with itself is still, thanks to General Suharto's autocratic ineptitude, in many respects a Javanese colonial empire.

What we see at the start of the new millennium is a nation still in the making, picking up threads dropped when Sukarno was forced out of office in

1967. It has yet to be revealed whether the political institutions currently in place can yield a consensual balance of forces, one in which those not in power at any given time feel they have a rôle other than devoting all their energies to toppling whoever is in power. Is government to be essentially a presidential or a parliamentary process? Will the enhanced scope of regional assemblies in a decentralized nation diminish the authority of the parliament in Jakarta? What in the longer term is to be the function of the speakers of the two parliamentary assemblies who up to now have shown some disposition to behave more like party leaders? And, crucial to the final outcome, will all the armed forces accept their progressive elimination from parliament and the roots of the administration, or will they turn at the last moment and go on demanding some special status, something more than the rest of society?

Without answers to such questions the Republic's present relative unity will be seriously threatened by separatism. The number of regions that could realistically hive off as separate nations has grown rather than diminished since independence: Sulawesi, Aceh, the rest of Sumatra or indeed parts of it, to name only the most obvious. There are numerous business enterprises outside Indonesia, many of them likely to enjoy open or clandestine support from other governments, ready to collaborate with local nationalist movements for the sake of economic spoils.

On the other hand Indonesia's international environment has changed for the better. The cold war pressures which levered Suharto into power and gave arms sales such a prominent and destructive part in the economy have gone. South-East Asia is no longer post-colonial. Intra-regional collaboration has reduced many problems and may in time eliminate the worst of them in the realms of illegal trading and local political enterprise. For both better and worse, South-East Asia is now a global player, and Indonesia is the biggest part of it.

Unhappily, because of financial and economic mismanagement by the Suharto régime which has only been acknowledged relatively recently, Indonesia is going to be dependent on aid givers and lenders for many years. Therefore it will go on being subject to foreign political influence. In the globalized, post-cold war context that influence is in some ways more benign than it was. Free trade, price competitivity and the uninhibited movement of funds are still the prime requirement of the global market and profit its central motive; but there is another global market-place where human rights and representative government are the principal currencies, and the two interact. There is a better appreciation of the symbiosis between economic success and the sort of stability that comes from genuine participatory democracy. The parlous state of the Indonesian currency as President Wahid began his second year in office was universally attributed to uncertainties about the political scene. While the uncertainty and the lack of confidence were regrettable, there was perhaps consolation in the money market's overdue recognition that democracy and social stability do matter.

Another aspect of the tragedy Suharto inflicted on his country is the legacy of untreated social ills that have accompanied it into the twenty-first century. The weary presumption that politicians and officials are corrupt, the expectation that people in positions of power will use them to enrich themselves, the unthinking resort to violence all had their origins in Dutch colonial rule and are endemic in other parts of South-East Asia. But in Indonesia they all got worse during the military dictatorship and became institutionalized, accepted social mechanisms. It will take years to eradicate them.

It will be interesting in that context to see whether Islam, the sometime guardian of moral values in the past half century, will tackle those social ills or divert its considerable energy into the power politics triggered by the return of functioning democracy. Although it has its radicals – and radicalism has seemed to be on the increase recently – Islam in Indonesia has often been a modernizing and moderating force in society. The broad swathe of Islam represented by the leader of the urbanised MPR, Damien Rais, and even Wahid's more conservative and largely rural Nahdlatul Ulama recognised several decades ago the implications of the expanding middle class and secured their own position in its growth.

It is to be expected that under the stimulus of economic recovery and better investment in social, rural and regional welfare Indonesia's somewhat restricted middle class will now grow more quickly and, as in neighbouring Malaysia, help to consolidate the country politically. Conservative in the sense that it will wish to conserve its prosperity, it will also wish to safeguard the necessary educational and political foundations of its well-being.

More conservative in the sense of not wanting to forego former privileges is the army. The hope must be that new generations of officers will be responsive to the age and world they live in and be satisfied with a reduced presence in the People's Consultative Congress (MPR). But some will not. Armies the world over tend to nurture vested interest and it is hard to be optimistic about the Indonesian case. The army as it stood at the turn of the century was a destabilized institution, humiliated by its disgrace in East Timor, exposed for its lack of professionalism in Aceh, despised for its role in Suharto's tyranny.

It will take time for the army to shake off its humiliation, and some within it will be tempted to do so by engaging in fresh adventures. That bodes ill for both independent East and Indonesian West Timor where at the beginning of 2001 some old-guard soldiers, prompted by pro-Suharto trouble-makers, went on entertaining hopes of recuperating lost ground; and worse still for independence activists in Aceh and West Papua, the latter with the potential for a disaster matching that in East Timor. Aceh, with its long history of tough, well-organized and well-armed resistance, presents the government with a different set of problems. Even with a political settlement including the application of Islamic law to Acehnese Muslims, the ingrained culture of political violence could smoulder for many more years.

What is certain is that no leader at this point in Indonesia's history could willingly let either of these territories go. All therefore depends on the autonomy options offered to them and, if local leaders can be found to accept them, the intelligence and sensitivity with which they are made to work. Even that disturbs some Javanese nationalists, some of whom will stigmatize special autonomies and indeed the whole decentralization programme as federalism under a different name. However, the Indonesian political class is by now sophisticated enough to recognise the difference between a federalism devised by the Dutch in order to divide and decentralization designed to hold the nation together.

The shameful episode of Suharto's US-sponsored military dictatorship is fading quickly into the past, leaving only his shadow behind. Time may spare him the justice he deserves; as this book reached its end he was an old, stricken man with little time left. His family and cronies – his shadows – can still stir reaction in the known crucibles of religious intolerance and inter-ethnic hatred, but they too will fade.

Indonesians understand the conventions of shadow play; it is one of their traditional theatrical forms. They recognise the villains and the heroes by the direction they come from. As one shadow fades another dominates the screen, the shadow of an unfinished revolution, unrealized ideals – the shadow of a lost and, for all his errors, increasingly revered leader, President Sukarno, whose daughter Vice-President Megawati Sukarnoputri brings his name and his aspirations back into the drama.

*Note*

1   *Far Eastern Economic Review*, 26 October 2000.

# Select Bibliography

Adams, Cindy, *My Friend the Dictator*, Indianapolis, Bobbs-Merrill Co Inc, 1967.

Allison, John, *Ambassador from the Prairie*, Boston, 1973.

Anderson, Benedict and Ruth McVey, 'A Preliminary Analysis of the October 1, 1965 Coup in Indonesia', Ithaca, Cornell Modern Indonesia Project, 1971.

Aspinall, Edward, *The Last Days of President Suharto*, (Ed Herb Feith and van Klinken), Monash Asian Institute, 1999.

Baker, Richard W.; Soesastro, M. Hadi; Kristiadi, J.; Ramage, Douglas E. (Eds), *Indonesia, the Challenge of Change*, Netherlands, KITLV Press, 1999.

Barnes, Philip, *Indonesia: the Political Economy of Energy*, Oxford, OUP, 1995.

Benda, H.J., *The Crescent and the Rising Sun*, Netherlands, 's-Gravenhage, 1958.

Bharadwaj, Ram Dev, *Sukarno and Indonesian Nationalism*, Delhi, Rahul Publishing House, 1997.

Blum, William, *The CIA: a Forgotten History*, London, Zed Books, 1986.

Boland, B.J., *The Struggle of Islam in Modern Indonesia*, Netherlands, 's-Gravenhage, 1971.

Brackman, Arnold C., *The Communist Collapse in Indonesia*, New York, Norton, 1969.

Budiardjo, Carmel, *Surviving Indonesia's Gulag*, London, TAPOL, 1996.

Crouch, Harold, *The Army and Politics in Indonesia*, Ithaca, (Australian National University) Cornell University Press, 1978.

East, W. G., Spate, O.H.K. and Fisher, Charles A., *The Changing Map of Asia*, London, Methuen, 1971.

Feith, Herbert, *The Decline of Constitutional Democracy in Indonesia*, Ithaca, Cornell University Press, 1962.

Forrester, Geoff (Ed), *Post-Soeharto Indonesia*, Netherlands, KITLV Press, 1999

Hall, D.G.E., *A History of South-East Asia*, London, Macmillan, 1964.

l'Harmattan, *L'Indonésie contemporaine vue par ses intellectuels*, Paris, l'Harmattan, *c*. 1994.

Harrisson, Tom, *Brunei, Background to a Revolt*, 1963.

Harrisson, Tom, *The Malays of South-West Sarawak before Malaysia*, London, Macmillan, 1970.

Hill, Hal, *The Indonesian Economy since 1966*, Cambridge, Cambridge University Press, 1996.

Heimann, Judith M., *The Most Offending Soul Alive*, University of Hawai'i, 1999.

Hoopes, Townsend, *The Devil and John Foster Dulles*, London, Deutsch, 1974.

Hughes, John, *The End of Sukarno*, Angus and Robertson, 1968.

Jenkins, David, *Suharto and his Generals*, Ithaca, Cornell Modern Indonesia Project, 1984.

Kahin, *Nationalism and Revolution in Indonesia*, Ithaca, Cornell University Press, 1952.

Legge, J.D., *Sukarno*, London, Allen Lane The Penguin Press, 1972.

Lewis, Norman, *An Empire of the East*, London, Jonathan Cape, 1993.

Lubis, Mochtar, *Indonesia: Land under the Rainbow*, Oxford, Oxford University Press, 1990.

Monbiot, George, *Poisoned Arrows*, London, Michael Joseph, 1999.

Mossman, James, *Rebels in Paradise*, London, Jonathan Cape, 1961.

Nishihara, Masashi, *The Japanese and Sukarno's Indonesia 1951–1966*, Honolulu, 1976.

Penders, C.L.M., *Life and Times of Sukarno*, London, Sidgwick & Jackson, 1974.

Prawiro, Radius, *Indonesia's Struggle for Economic Development*, Kuala Lumpur, Oxford University Press, 1998.

Schwarz, Adam, *A Nation in Waiting*, London, Allen & Unwin, 1994.

Suryadinata, Leo, *Indonesia's Foreign Policy under Suharto*, Singapore, Times Academic Press, 1996.

Taylor, John, *Indonesia's Forgotten War*, London, Zed Books, 1990.

Vatikiotis, Michael, *Indonesian Politics under Suharto*, London, Routledge, 1998.

Walker, Walter, *Fighting On*, London, New Millennium, 1997.

Wehl, David, *The Birth of Indonesia*, London, Allen & Unwin, 1948.

# Index